Microsoft®
TCP/IP
Training

Microsoft Press

PUBLISHED BY
Microsoft Press
A Division of Microsoft Corporation
One Microsoft Way
Redmond, Washington 98052-6399

Library of Congress Cataloging-in-Publication Data
Microsoft TCP/IP training / Microsoft Corporation.
     p.   cm.
   Includes index.
   ISBN 1-57231-623-3
   1. Electronic data processing personnel--Certification.
   2. Microsoft software--Study and teaching. 3. TCP/IP (Computer
network protocol) I. Microsoft Corporation.
   QA76.3.M53 1997
   004.6'2--dc21   97-20760
                                                      CIP

Printed and bound in the United States of America.

5 6 7 8 9 WCWC 2 1 0 9 8

Distributed to the book trade in Canada by Macmillan of Canada, a division of Canada Publishing Corporation.

A CIP catalogue record for this book is available from the British Library.

Microsoft Press books are available through booksellers and distributors worldwide. For further information about international editions, contact your local Microsoft Corporation office. Or contact Microsoft Press International directly at fax (425) 936-7329.

BackOffice, Microsoft, Microsoft Press, MS, MS-DOS, Win32, Windows, the Windows logo, and Windows NT are registered trademarks and MSN and NetShow are trademarks of Microsoft Corporation.

Other product and company names mentioned herein may be the trademarks of their respective owners.

For Instructional Design Solutions
Instructional Designer: Jim Semick—Instructional Design Solutions
Editor: Shari G. Smith—R & S Consulting
Desktop Publishing: Irene Barnett—Barnett Communications

For Microsoft (Original Instructor-led Course Content)
Instructional Designers: Susan Greenberg, Nikki McCormick
Subject Matter Experts: Kelli Adam, Jeff Clark, Scott Hay, Wally Mead

For Microsoft Press
Acquisitions Editor: Eric Stroo
Project Editor: Stuart J. Stuple

Contents

About This Book   **xi**

    Course Compact Disc xii

    Reference Materials. xii

    Intended Audience xii

    Finding the Best Starting Point for You xiii

    Conventions Used in This Book xiv

        Features of This Book xiv

        Procedural Conventions xiv

        Notational Conventions xiv

        Keyboard Conventions. xv

        Notes. xv

    Getting Started xvi

        Hardware and Software Requirements xvi

        Setup Instructions. xvii

    Chapter and Appendix Overview xix

    The Microsoft Certified Professional Program. xxi

        Microsoft Online Institute xxiii

        ATECs xxiii

Chapter 1   Introduction to TCP/IP   **1**

    About This Chapter 1

    Before You Begin. 1

    Lesson 1: TCP/IP Overview 2

        TCP/IP History. 2

        The Internet Standards Process 3

    Lesson 2: TCP/IP Utilities. 6

        Diagnostics Utilities. 7

    Review 8

Chapter 2   Installing and Configuring TCP/IP   **9**

    About This Chapter 9

    Before You Begin. 9

    Lesson 1: Installing and Configuring Microsoft TCP/IP 10

        Configuration Parameters 10

    Lesson 2: Testing TCP/IP with Ipconfig and PING 15

Lesson 3: Microsoft Network Monitor 18
    Analyzing Network Traffic 20
Review 22

Chapter 3   Architectural Overview of the TCP/IP Protocol Suite   **23**
    About This Chapter 23
    Before You Begin 24
    Lesson 1: The Microsoft TCP/IP Protocol Suite 25
        The Four-Layer Model 26
        Network Interface Technologies 27
    Lesson 2: ARP 29
        Resolving a Local IP Address 30
        Resolving a Remote IP Address 31
        The ARP Cache 32
    Lesson 3: ICMP and IGMP 40
        ICMP 40
        IGMP 41
    Lesson 4: IP 42
        IP on the Router 43
    Lesson 5: TCP 46
        Ports 46
        Sockets 47
        TCP Three-Way Handshake 48
        TCP Sliding Windows 49
    Lesson 6: UDP 51
    Review 53

Chapter 4   IP Addressing   **55**
    About This Chapter 55
    Before You Begin 55
    Lesson 1: The IP Address 56
        Network ID and Host ID 57
        Converting IP Addresses from Binary to Decimal 57
    Lesson 2: Address Classes 60
    Lesson 3: Addressing Guidelines 64
        Assigning Network IDs 64
        Assigning Host IDs 66
    Lesson 4: Subnet Mask and the IP Address 71
    Lesson 5: IP Addressing with IP Version 6.0 75
    Review 77

Chapter 5   Subnetting   **81**

About This Chapter 81

Before You Begin. 81

Lesson 1: Subnet Overview. 82

   Implementing Subnetting 83

   Subnet Mask Bits 84

Lesson 2: Defining a Subnet Mask 85

   Subnetting More Than One Octet 87

Lesson 3: Defining Subnet IDs 93

   Shortcut to Defining Subnet IDs 94

Lesson 4: Defining Host IDs for a Subnet 96

Lesson 5: Supernetting. 103

Review 106

Chapter 6   Implementing IP Routing   **111**

About This Chapter 111

Before You Begin. 111

Lesson 1: IP Routing Overview. 112

   Static vs. Dynamic IP Routing. 114

Lesson 2: Static IP Routing 115

   Configuring Static IP Routers 116

   Building a Routing Table. 117

Lesson 3: Dynamic IP Routing 121

   RIP 122

   Integrating Static and Dynamic Routing. 124

Lesson 4: Implementing a Windows NT Router. 126

   The TRACERT Utility. 126

Review 128

Chapter 7   The Dynamic Host Configuration Protocol   **129**

About This Chapter 129

Before You Begin. 129

Lesson 1: DHCP Overview. 130

   Manual vs. Automatic Configuration 131

   How DHCP Works 132

   IP Lease Renewal. 136

   Using the Ipconfig Utility. 138

Lesson 2: Installing and Configuring a DHCP Server 140

   Installing and Configuring a DHCP Server. 143

Lesson 3: Enabling a DHCP Relay Agent 155
Lesson 4: Managing the DHCP Database 159
    Compacting the DHCP Database. 160
Review 162

Chapter 8   NetBIOS over TCP/IP   165
About This Chapter 165
Before You Begin. 165
Lesson 1: NetBIOS Names 166
    NetBIOS Names. 167
    NetBIOS Name Registration, Discovery, and Release. 169
    Segmenting NetBIOS Names with Scopes 169
Lesson 2: NetBIOS Name Resolution. 171
    Resolving Local NetBIOS Names Using a Broadcast 172
    Resolving Names with a NetBIOS Name Server 174
    Microsoft Methods of Resolving NetBIOS Names. 175
    NetBIOS over TCP/IP Name Resolution Nodes. 176
Lesson 3: Using the LMHOSTS File 179
    Name Resolution Problems Using LMHOSTS. 181
Review 184

Chapter 9   Windows Internet Name Service (WINS)   185
About This Chapter 185
Before You Begin. 186
Lesson 1: WINS Overview 187
Lesson 2: The WINS Resolution Process 189
    Name Registration 190
    Name Renewal 192
    Name Release. 193
    Name Query and Name Response 194
Lesson 3: Implementing WINS 196
    WINS Requirements. 196
    Configuring a WINS Proxy Agent. 201
    Configuring a DHCP Server for WINS. 203
Lesson 4: Database Replication Between WINS Servers 208
    Configuring a WINS Server As a Push or Pull Partner 209
    Configuring Database Replication. 210

Lesson 5: Maintaining the WINS Server Database 214
    Configuring the WINS Server 216
    Backing Up and Restoring the WINS Database 219
    Compacting the WINS Database 220
    Review 222

Chapter 10   IP Internetwork Browsing and Domain Functions   225
    About This Chapter 225
    Before You Begin 225
    Lesson 1: Browsing Overview 226
    Browsing Collection and Distribution 227
    Servicing Client Browsing Requests 228
    Lesson 2: Browsing an IP Internetwork 230
    Browsing with WINS 231
    Browsing Using the LMHOSTS File 232
    Lesson 3: Domain Functions in an IP Internetwork 235
    Review 240

Chapter 11   Host Name Resolution   241
    About This Chapter 241
    Before You Begin 241
    Lesson 1: TCP/IP Naming Schemes 242
    Lesson 2: Host Names 243
    Host Name Resolution 243
    Lesson 3: The HOSTS File 249
    Review 252

Chapter 12   Domain Name System (DNS)   253
    About This Chapter 253
    Before You Begin 253
    Lesson 1: Domain Name System (DNS) 254
    How DNS Works 255
    Domain Name Space 257
    Zones of Authority 258
    Name Server Roles 259
    Lesson 2: Name Resolution 261
    Caching and TTL 263

Lesson 3: Configuring the DNS Files 264
    The Database File 264
    The Reverse Lookup File 266
    The Cache File 266
    The Boot File 267
Lesson 4: Planning a DNS Implementation 269
    Registering with the Parent Domain 270
Review 278

Chapter 13   Implementing DNS   281
About This Chapter 281
Before You Begin 281
Lesson 1: The Microsoft DNS Server 282
    Installing Microsoft DNS Server 282
    Troubleshooting DNS with NSLOOKUP 283
Lesson 2: Administering the DNS Server 286
    Adding DNS Domains and Zones 288
    Adding Resource Records 291
    Configuring Reverse Lookup 292
Lesson 3: Integrating DNS and WINS 296
    Enabling WINS Lookup 298
Review 301

Chapter 14   Connectivity in Heterogeneous Environments   303
About This Chapter 303
Before You Begin 303
Lesson 1: Connectivity in Heterogeneous Environments 304
    Connecting to a Remote Host with Microsoft Networking 304
    Microsoft TCP/IP Utilities 305
Lesson 2: Remote Execution Utilities 307
Lesson 3: Data Transfer Utilities 309
    RCP 309
    FTP 309
    Web Browsers 314
Lesson 4: Printing Utilities 316
    Using the TCP/IP Print Server (LPD) 317
    Using LPR and LPQ 317
    Using Windows NT As a Print Gateway 319
Review 323

Chapter 15   Implementing the Microsoft SNMP Services   **325**

About This Chapter 325

Before You Begin. 325

Lesson 1: SNMP Defined 326

Management Systems and Agents 327

The Microsoft SNMP Service 328

Lesson 2: The MIB 330

The Hierarchical Name Tree 331

Lesson 3: Installing and Configuring the SNMP Service. 333

Defining SNMP Communities. 333

How SNMP Gathers Information 334

Installing SNMP. 336

Configuring SNMP Service Security. 338

Configuring SNMP Agent Services. 339

Identifying SNMP Service Errors 341

The SNMPUTIL Utility 344

Review 346

Chapter 16   Troubleshooting Microsoft TCP/IP   **347**

About This Chapter 347

Before You Begin. 347

Lesson 1: Windows NT Diagnostic Tools and Guidelines 348

Windows NT Utilities 348

Troubleshooting Guidelines. 349

Review 353

Questions and Answers   **355**

Index   **391**

About This Book

Welcome to *Internetworking with Microsoft® TCP/IP on Microsoft Windows NT® 4.0*. This book provides systems administrators the knowledge and skills to set up, configure, use, and support Transmission Control Protocol/Internet Protocol (TCP/IP) on the Microsoft Windows NT operating system version 4.0 in a networked environment. It will also prepare you to meet the certification requirements to become a Microsoft Internet Systems Certified Professional.

Note For more information on becoming a Microsoft Certified Professional, please see the section titled "The Microsoft Certified Professional Program" later in this chapter.

Each chapter in this book is divided into lessons. Most lessons include hands-on procedures to practice or demonstrate the concept or skill presented in the lesson. At the end of each lesson is a short summary, and at the end of each chapter is a set of review questions to test your knowledge of the chapter material. If appropriate, at the end of each chapter there are references to additional information on the lesson material or related topics.

The "Getting Started" section provides important setup instructions that describe the hardware and software requirements to complete the procedures in this course. This section also provides the networking configuration for the two computers that are necessary to complete the hands-on procedures. Read through this section thoroughly before you start the lessons.

Course Compact Disc

The compact disc provided in this course contains multimedia presentations that supplement the key concepts covered in the book. You should view these presentations when suggested, and then use them as a review tool while you work through the material.

The course compact disc also contains files required to perform the hands-on procedures, and information designed to supplement the lesson material.

The multimedia presentations, additional materials, and files can all be accessed from the *Course Materials* Web page on the course compact disc. In order to view the course Web site from the compact disc, you must first install Microsoft Internet Explorer™ 3.0. See the "Getting Started" section for information on installing Internet Explorer from the course compact disc.

Reference Materials

You may find the following reference material useful:

- Documentation for Windows NT Server version 4.0
- *Microsoft Windows NT Server Resource Kit*

Intended Audience

This book is designed for network integrators, system engineers, and support professionals who implement and support TCP/IP in local and wide area network environments. This book was developed for those who plan to take the related Microsoft Certified Professional exam 70-59, Internetworking with Microsoft TCP/IP on Microsoft Windows NT 4.0.

Prerequisites

- A knowledge of the function and uses of local area network (LAN) hardware, including network cards, cabling, bridges, and routers.
- Successful completion of the following Microsoft Certified Professional exam:

  70-67, Implementing and Supporting Microsoft Windows NT Server 4.0

  –Or–
- Completion of the following course:

  #687, Supporting Microsoft Windows NT Server 4.0 Core Technologies

Finding the Best Starting Point for You

This book is designed for you to complete at your own pace, so you can skip some lessons and revisit them later. Keep in mind that you need to complete the procedures in Chapter 2, "Installing and Configuring TCP/IP," in order to perform the procedures in the other chapters. Use the following table to find the best starting point for you.

If you	Follow this learning path
Are preparing to take the Microsoft Certified Professional exam 70-59, Internetworking with Microsoft TCP/IP on Microsoft Windows NT 4.0	Read the "Getting Started" section. Next, work through Chapters 1–3. Work through the remaining chapters in any order. Before beginning a chapter, always refer to the "Before You Begin" section to determine any prerequisites.
Need to install and configure TCP/IP	Read the "Getting Started" section. Next, work through Chapter 2. Complete Chapters 1 and 3, then work through the other chapters in any order.
Need to install TCP/IP and configure multiple departments, groups, or computers	Read the "Getting Started" section. Depending on your configuration, you should read the appropriate planning chapter. For example, if your configuration requires multiple subnets, read Chapter 5, "Subnetting," for information on how to create a range of valid IP addresses. Then complete Chapter 2 and work through the other chapters in any order.
Need information on a specific topic related to TCP/IP	Refer to the table of contents or index.

Conventions Used in This Book

Before you start any of the lessons, it is important that you understand the terms and notational conventions used in this book.

Features of This Book

- Each chapter opens with a "Before You Begin" section, which describes other chapters that must be completed before continuing.

- Whenever possible, lessons contain procedures that give you an opportunity to use the skills being presented or explore the part of TCP/IP being described. All procedures are identified with the following procedural convention: ▶

- The "Review" section at the end of most lessons allows you to test what you have learned in the lesson. They are designed to familiarize you with the Microsoft Certified Professional exam.

- The "For More Information" list at the end of many chapters provides additional resource locations for information on the concepts and skills covered in the chapter. The information referred to covers product documentation, online locations, or both.

- The "Questions and Answers" section contains all of the book's questions and corresponding answers. Each question is cross-referenced by page number.

Procedural Conventions

- Hands-on procedures that you are to follow are presented in numbered lists of steps (1, 2, and so on). A triangular bullet (▶) indicates the beginning of a procedure.

- The word *select* is used for highlighting directories, file names, text boxes, menu bars, and option buttons, and for selecting options in a dialog box.

- The word *click* is used for carrying out a command from a menu or dialog box.

Notational Conventions

- Characters or commands that you type appear in **bold lowercase** type.

- *Italic* in syntax statements indicates placeholders for variable information. *Italic* is also used for important new terms, for book titles, and for emphasis in the text.

- Names of files and folders appear in Title Caps, except when you are to type them directly. Unless otherwise indicated, you can use all lowercase letters when you type a file name in a dialog box or at a command prompt.

- File name extensions appear in all lowercase.

- Names of directories appear in initial caps, except when you are to type them directly. Unless otherwise indicated, you can use all lowercase letters when you type a directory name in a dialog box or at a command prompt.

- Acronyms appear in all uppercase.
- `Monospace` type represents code samples, examples of screen text, or entries that you might type in a command line or in initialization files.
- Square brackets [ ] are used in syntax statements to enclose optional items. For example, [*filename*] in command syntax indicates that you can choose to type a file name with the command. Type only the information within the brackets, not the brackets themselves.
- Braces { } are used in syntax statements to enclose required items. Type only the information within the braces, not the braces themselves.

Keyboard Conventions

- Names of keys that you press appear in SMALL CAPITALS; for example, TAB and SHIFT.
- A plus sign (+) between two key names means that you must press those keys at the same time. For example, "Press ALT+TAB" means that you hold down ALT while you press TAB.
- A comma (,) between two or more key names means that you must press each of the keys consecutively, not together. For example, "Press ALT, F, X" means that you press and release each key in sequence. "Press ALT+W, L" means that you first press ALT and W together, and then release them and press L.
- You can choose menu commands with the keyboard. Press the ALT key to activate the menu bar, and then sequentially press the keys that correspond to the highlighted or underlined letter of the menu name and the command name. For some commands, you can also press a key combination listed in the menu.
- You can select or clear check boxes or option buttons in dialog boxes with the keyboard. Press the ALT key, and then press the key that corresponds to the underlined letter of the option name. Or you can press TAB until the option is highlighted, and then press SPACEBAR to select or clear the check box or option button.
- You can cancel the display of a dialog box by pressing the ESC key.

Notes

Notes appear throughout the lessons.

- Notes marked **Tip** contain explanations of possible results or alternative methods.
- Notes marked **Important** contain information that is essential to completing a task.
- Notes marked **Note** contain supplemental information.
- Notes marked **Caution** contain warnings about possible loss of data.

Getting Started

Hardware and Software Requirements

This self-paced training course contains hands-on procedures to help you learn about Microsoft TCP/IP on Microsoft Windows NT 4.0. To complete many of these procedures, you must have two networked computers or be connected to a larger network.

Both computers must be capable of running Microsoft Windows NT Server 4.0 and must have the following minimum configuration:

- A 486/33 or higher Intel-based processor
- 16 MB of RAM (32 MB recommended)
- A minimum of 450 MB of available hard disk space on each computer
- SVGA display adapter and monitor capable of displaying 256 colors
- Microsoft Mouse or compatible pointing device
- Network adapter card and related cables
- One 3.5-inch high-density disk drive
- CD-ROM drive
- Sound card with headphones or speakers on one computer (optional)

All hardware should be on the Microsoft Windows NT 4.0 Hardware Compatibility List (HCL).

Software

The following software is required to complete the procedures in this course:

- Windows NT Server 4.0 retail product
- Microsoft MS-DOS® 5.0 or later
- Windows NT Server 4.0 Service Pack 2 or later (Service Pack 2 is located on the course compact disc)

Setup Instructions

It is highly recommended that you have two networked computers or be part of a larger network to perform many of the procedures.

1. Set up both computers according to the manufacturer's instructions.

2. The computers need to be networked together, either cabled together using a hub so that the two computers can communicate or as part of a larger network.

3. Each computer requires 450 MB of free disk space on drive C.

4. Set up Windows NT Server on each computer. For the Evaulation Editions included with this trainingkit, the CD-ROM key is 040-0048126. Microsoft technical support does not provide assistance with Evaulation Editions.

The first computer will be configured as a primary domain controller (PDC), and will be assigned the computer account name Server1 and the domain name, Domain1. This computer will act as a domain controller, a file and print server, and an application server in Domain1.

The second computer will act as a server and workstation for most of the procedures in this course. It is a member of Domain1 and is assigned the computer account name Server2.

Caution If your computers are part of a larger network, you *must* verify with your network administrator that the computer names, domain name, and IP address information in the following table do not conflict with network operations. If they do conflict, ask your network administrator to provide alternative values and use those values throughout all of the practices in this book.

Variable	Values used in this course
Computer name for first computer (PDC)	Server1
IP address for first computer	131.107.2.200
Computer name for second computer	Server2
IP address for second computer	131.107.2.211
IP address range	131.107.2.200 — 131.107.2.211
Subnet mask	255.255.255.0
Domain name	Domain1
Default gateway	131.107.2.1

Microsoft Internet Explorer

To use the course Web site from the course compact disc, you must first install Microsoft Internet Explorer 3.0.

▶ **To install Microsoft Internet Explorer 3.0**

1. On the course compact disc, open the Ie_setup folder, and then run Msie30.exe.

   A **Microsoft Internet Explorer 3.0** dialog box appears prompting if you want to install Microsoft Internet Explorer 3.0.

2. Click **Yes** to install Microsoft Internet Explorer 3.0.

   A **Microsoft Internet Explorer 3.0** dialog box appears indicating that files are being copied to a temporary folder on your hard disk.

3. Read the End-User License Agreement for Microsoft Internet Explorer, and then click **I Agree** to accept the terms of the agreement and continue the installation.

   A **Microsoft Internet Explorer Setup** dialog box appears indicating that files are being copied and Microsoft Internet Explorer is being set up on your computer.

4. When prompted to restart your computer, click **Yes**.

Windows NT 4.0 Service Pack

If you have not already installed the Windows NT 4.0 Service Pack 2, you should do so. This procedure shows you how to install the Service Pack from the course compact disc.

▶ **To install Windows NT 4.0 Service Pack 2**

1. Log on as Administrator.

2. Insert the course compact disc into the CD-ROM drive.

   Internet Explorer starts and the Internetworking with Microsoft TCP/IP on Microsoft Windows NT 4.0 start page opens.

   –Or–

   Start Windows NT Explorer, navigate to the drive containing the course compact disc, and then double-click the Open.htm file.

3. Click the start page icon.

4. Click **Course Materials**.

5. Click **Windows NT 4.0 Service Pack 2**.

6. Click **Service Pack**.

7. Scroll and click the **Install Service Pack** hyperlink.

   An Internet Explorer dialog box appears asking if you want to open the file or save it to disk.

8. Select **Open it**, and then click **OK**.

   This launches Spsetup.bat, which begins the upgrade process.

9. At the Welcome screen, click **Next**.

10. In the **Service Pack Setup** dialog box, select **Install the Service Pack**, and then click **Next**.

11. Select whether you want to create an Uninstall directory, and then click **Next**.

12. Click **Finish** for the Service Pack setup to complete.

   Setup inspects your computer and then begins to copy the Service Pack files.

   At the end of copying files a dialog box pops up, notifying you that Windows NT 4.0 has been updated.

13. Click **OK** to restart your computer.

Chapter and Appendix Overview

This self-paced training course combines notes, hands-on procedures, multimedia presentations, and review questions to teach you Microsoft TCP/IP on Microsoft Windows NT 4.0. It is designed to be completed from beginning to end, but you can choose a customized track and complete only the sections that interest you. If you choose the customized track option, see the "Before You Begin" section in each chapter. Any hands-on procedures that require preliminary work from preceding chapters refer to the appropriate chapters.

The self-paced training book is divided into the following chapters:

- The "About This Book" section contains a self-paced training overview and introduces the components of this training. Read this section thoroughly to get the greatest educational value from this self-paced training and to plan which lessons you will complete.

- Chapter 1, "Introduction to TCP/IP," provides an overview of TCP/IP and the Internet standards process.

- Chapter 2, "Installing and Configuring TCP/IP," covers installing and manually configuring an IP address, subnet mask, and default gateway. An overview is also provided on basic configuration testing procedures using Ipconfig, PING, and Microsoft Network Monitor.

- Chapter 3, "Architectural Overview of the TCP/IP Protocol Suite," describes the four layers of the TCP/IP protocol suite and explains how protocols at each layer work internally and in association with other protocols.

- Chapter 4, "IP Addressing," introduces IP addressing, including the differences between IP address classes, IP addressing guidelines, network components that require an IP address, and common addressing problems.

- Chapter 5, "Subnetting," teaches you fundamental subnetting and supernetting concepts and procedures, including: when subnetting is necessary, how to use a default subnet mask, how to define a custom subnet mask, and how to create a range of valid IP addresses for each subnet in an intranet from one IP address.

- Chapter 6, "Implementing IP Routing," provides an overview of IP routing concepts and terminology, and detailed information on implementing IP routing in Microsoft network environments.

- Chapter 7, "The Dynamic Host Configuration Protocol," addresses how the Dynamic Host Configuration Protocol (DHCP) centralizes and manages the allocation of TCP/IP configuration information by automatically assigning IP addresses to computers configured to use DHCP.

- Chapter 8, "NetBIOS over TCP/IP," provides an overview of NetBIOS name resolution concepts and methods.

- Chapter 9, "Windows Internet Name Service (WINS)," discusses how WINS reduces broadcast traffic with NetBIOS over TCP/IP, addresses database replication between WINS servers, and provides the knowledge and skills required to support WINS in an intranet.

- Chapter 10, "IP Internetwork Browsing and Domain Functions," discusses how browsing for NetBIOS resources occurs in a TCP/IP internetwork.

- Chapter 11, "Host Name Resolution," covers host name resolution concepts and issues.

- Chapter 12, "Domain Name System (DNS)," gives you an overview of the structure and components of the Domain Name System (DNS). You will learn about DNS database files, and how to resolve TCP/IP addresses.

- Chapter 13, "Implementing DNS," addresses installing and configuring DNS, and integrating DNS and WINS.

- Chapter 14, "Connectivity in Heterogeneous Environments," covers the options for using TCP/IP to operate in a heterogeneous environment.

- Chapter 15, "Implementing the Microsoft SNMP Services," provides an overview of the Simple Network Management Protocol (SNMP), including the functions performed by an SNMP management station and the Microsoft SNMP service (SNMP agent).

- Chapter 16, "Troubleshooting Microsoft TCP/IP," combines a review of important topics with troubleshooting guidelines. Topics include common TCP/IP-related problems, symptoms, possible causes, and the Windows NT and TCP/IP utilities useful in troubleshooting problems.

The Microsoft Certified Professional Program

The Microsoft Certified Professional (MCP) program provides the best method to prove your command of current Microsoft products and technologies. Microsoft, an industry leader in certification, is on the forefront of testing methodology. Our exams and corresponding certifications are developed to validate your mastery of critical competencies as you design and develop, or implement and support, solutions with Microsoft products and technologies. Computer professionals who become Microsoft certified are recognized as experts and are sought after industry-wide.

The Microsoft Certified Professional program offers four certifications, based on specific areas of technical expertise:

- *Microsoft Certified Product Specialists.* Demonstrated in-depth knowledge of at least one Microsoft operating system. Candidates may pass additional Microsoft certification exams to further qualify their skills with Microsoft BackOffice™ products, development tools, or desktop programs.

- *Microsoft Certified Systems Engineers.* Qualified to effectively plan, implement, maintain, and support information systems with Microsoft Windows® 95, Microsoft Windows NT, and the Microsoft BackOffice integrated family of server software.

- *Microsoft Certified Solution Developers.* Qualified to design and develop custom business solutions with Microsoft development tools, technologies, and platforms, including Microsoft Office and Microsoft BackOffice.

- *Microsoft Certified Trainers.* Instructionally and technically qualified to deliver Microsoft Official Curriculum through a Microsoft Authorized Technical Education Center (ATEC).

What Are the Requirements for Becoming a Microsoft Certified Professional?

The certification requirements differ for each certification and are specific to the products and job functions addressed by the certification.

To become a Microsoft Certified Professional, you must pass rigorous certification exams that provide a valid and reliable measure of technical proficiency and expertise. These exams are designed to test your expertise and ability to perform a role or task with a product, and are developed with the input of professionals in the industry. Questions in the exams reflect how Microsoft products are used in actual organizations, giving them "real-world" relevance.

- *Microsoft Certified Product Specialists* are required to pass one operating system exam. In addition, individuals seeking to validate their expertise in a program must pass the appropriate elective exam.

- *Microsoft Certified Systems Engineers* are required to pass a series of operating system exams and elective exams.

- *Microsoft Certified Solution Developers* are required to pass two core technology exams and two elective exams.

- *Microsoft Certified Trainers* are required to meet instructional and technical requirements specific to each Microsoft Official Curriculum course they are certified to deliver. In the United States and Canada, call Microsoft at (800) 636-7544 for more information on becoming a Microsoft Certified Trainer. Outside the United States and Canada, contact your local Microsoft subsidiary.

How to Order the Microsoft Roadmap to Education and Certification

It is easy to find the road that leads to your successful future—just use the Microsoft Roadmap to Education and Certification. The Roadmap contains everything you need to take advantage of Microsoft Education and Certification, including detailed descriptions of all of the most current Microsoft Official Curriculum courses; complete information about the Microsoft Certified Professional Program; Microsoft Certified Professional Assessment exams; and the Planning wizard, an easy-to-use tool to help you quickly map out a plan designed to meet your training goals. The Roadmap can be obtained from the following sources:

- Internet: ftp://ftp.microsoft.com/services/msedcert/e&cmap.zip

- CompuServe: Go MECFORUM, Library #2, e&cmap.zip

- TechNet: Search for "Roadmap" and install from the built-in setup link.

- Microsoft: Call us at (800) 636-7544 and ask for the Roadmap.
  Outside the United States and Canada, contact your local Microsoft subsidiary.

Microsoft Online Institute

The Microsoft Online Institute is an online interactive learning and information resource available on the World Wide Web (WWW) and the Microsoft Network (MSN™). The Microsoft Online Institute provides access to learning materials, instructor expertise, product information, developer articles, user forums, and other resources for Microsoft product and technology information.

Anyone with access to the Web or to an MSN account can access the Microsoft Online Institute to attend a class, join user forums, research library materials, purchase learning materials, or investigate other Microsoft Online Institute offerings.

To access the Microsoft Online Institute on the Web, connect to http://moli.microsoft.com. For more information about classes and other offerings, contact the Microsoft Online Institute by e-mail at moli_quest@msn.com.

ATECs

Authorized Technical Education Centers (ATECs) are the best source for instructor-led training that can help you prepare to become a Microsoft Certified Professional. The Microsoft ATEC program is a worldwide network of qualified technical training organizations that provide authorized delivery of Microsoft Official Curriculum courses by Microsoft Certified Trainers to computer professionals.

For a listing of ATEC locations in the United States and Canada, call the Microsoft fax service at (800) 727-3351. Outside the United States and Canada, call the fax service at (206) 635-2233.

C H A P T E R   1

Introduction to TCP/IP

Lesson 1   TCP/IP Overview . . . 2

Lesson 2   TCP/IP Utilities . . . 6

Review . . . 8

About This Chapter

This chapter gives you an overview of TCP/IP. The lessons provide a brief history of TCP/IP, discuss the Internet standards process, and review TCP/IP utilities.

Before You Begin

To complete the lessons in this chapter, you must have the course compact disc to view the additional technical information.

Lesson 1: TCP/IP Overview

Transmission Control Protocol/Internet Protocol (TCP/IP) is an industry-standard suite of protocols designed for wide area networks (WANs). This lesson gives you an overview of TCP/IP concepts, terminology, and how the Internet Society creates Internet standards.

After this lesson, you will be able to:

- Define TCP/IP and describe its advantages on Microsoft Windows NT 4.0.
- Describe the Internet standards process.
- Explain the purpose of a Request for Comments (RFC) document.

Estimated lesson time: 15 minutes

TCP/IP History

TCP/IP originated with the packet-switching network experiments conducted by the U.S. Department of Defense Advanced Research Projects Agency (DARPA) in the late 1960s and early 1970s. There have been several important milestones during the history of TCP/IP:

1970	Advanced Research Agency Network (ARPANET) hosts started to use Network Control Protocol (NCP).
1972	The first Telnet specification, "Ad hoc Telnet Protocol," was submitted as RFC 318.
1973	RFC 454, "File Transfer Protocol," was introduced.
1974	The Transmission Control Program (TCP) was specified in detail.
1981	The IP standard was published in RFC 791.
1982	Defense Communications Agency (DCA) and ARPA established the Transmission Control Protocol (TCP) and Internet Protocol (IP) as the TCP/IP protocol suite.
1983	ARPANET switched from NCP to TCP/IP.
1984	Domain Name System (DNS) was introduced.

Microsoft TCP/IP

Microsoft TCP/IP on Windows NT 4.0 provides enterprise networking and connectivity on computers running Windows NT. Adding TCP/IP to a Windows NT configuration offers several advantages. The primary advantage of TCP/IP is its distinction as the most complete and accepted enterprise networking protocol available today. All modern operating systems offer TCP/IP support, and most large networks rely on TCP/IP for much of their network traffic. TCP/IP is also the protocol standard for the Internet.

Another advantage of using TCP/IP technology is the ability to connect dissimilar systems. Many standard connectivity utilities are available to access and transfer data between dissimilar systems. Several of these standard utilities such as File Transfer Protocol (FTP) and Telnet are included with Windows NT Server.

TCP/IP is also a scaleable client/server framework. Microsoft TCP/IP offers the Windows Sockets interface, which is a standard networking application programming interface (API) used for Windows-based applications. You can use the Windows Sockets interface to develop client/server applications that can run on Windows Sockets-compliant stacks. Windows Sockets applications can take advantage of other networking protocols such as Microsoft NWLink used in Novell NetWare networks.

The Internet Standards Process

An international group of volunteers called the Internet Society manages the TCP/IP suite of protocols. The standards for TCP/IP are published in a series of documents called Request for Comments, or RFCs. Though no organization owns the Internet or its technologies, several are responsible for its direction.

ISOC

The Internet Society (ISOC) was created in 1992 and is a global organization responsible for the internetworking technologies and applications of the Internet. Though its principal purpose is to encourage the development and availability of the Internet, it is in turn responsible for the further development of the standards and protocols that allow the Internet to function.

IAB

The Internet Architecture Board (IAB) is the technical advisory group of the Internet Society responsible for setting Internet standards, publishing RFCs, and overseeing the Internet standards process.

The IAB governs the Internet Engineering Task Force (IETF), Internet Assigned Numbers Authority (IANA), and Internet Research Task Force (IRTF). The IETF develops Internet standards and protocols, and will develop solutions to technical problems as they arise on the Internet. The IANA oversees and coordinates the assignment of every unique protocol identifier used on the Internet. The IRTF group is responsible for coordinating all TCP/IP-related research projects.

RFCs

The standards for TCP/IP are published in a series of documents called Request for Comments (RFCs). RFCs describe the internal workings of the Internet. TCP/IP standards are always published as RFCs, although not all RFCs specify standards.

TCP/IP standards are not developed by a committee, but rather by consensus. Any member of the Internet Society can submit a document for publication as an RFC. The documents are then reviewed by a technical expert, a task force, or the RFC editor, and then assigned a *classification*. The classification specifies whether a document is being considered as a standard. There are five classifications of RFCs.

Classification	Description
Required	This must be implemented on all TCP/IP-based hosts and gateways.
Recommended	It is encouraged that all TCP/IP-based hosts and gateways implement the RFC specifications. Recommended RFCs are usually implemented.
Elective	Implementation of this is optional. Its application has been agreed to, but never became widely used.
Limited use	This is not intended for general use.
Not recommended	This is not recommended for implementation.

If a document is being considered as a standard, it goes through stages of development, testing, and acceptance. Within the Internet standards process, these stages are formally labeled *maturity levels*. There are three maturity levels of Internet standards.

Maturity level	Description
Proposed Standard	A Proposed Standard specification is generally stable, has resolved known design choices, is believed to be well understood, has received significant community review, and appears to enjoy enough community interest to be considered valuable.
Draft Standard	A Draft Standard must be well understood and known to be quite stable, both in its semantics and as a basis for developing an implementation.
Internet Standard	The Internet Standard specification (which may simply be referred to as a Standard) is characterized by a high degree of technical maturity and by a generally held belief that the specified protocol or service provides significant benefit to the Internet community.

When a document is published, it is assigned an RFC number. The original RFC is never updated. If the RFC requires changes, a new RFC is published with a new number. Therefore, it is important to verify that you have the most recent RFC on a particular topic. The IAB publishes the *IAB Official Protocol Standard*, a quarterly memo that is useful in determining the current RFC for each protocol.

Note Several RFCs are referenced throughout this course. For a copy of the RFCs, see the *Course Materials* Web page on the course compact disc.

Summary

TCP/IP is an industry-standard suite of protocols designed for WANs. Adding TCP/IP to a Windows NT configuration offers several advantages. The standards for TCP/IP are published in a series of documents called Request for Comments, or RFCs.

Lesson 2: TCP/IP Utilities

Windows NT supplies a number of application utilities that build on the lower-level protocols. This lesson introduces you to these utilities. You learn more about, and use several of, these utilities throughout this course.

After this lesson, you will be able to:
- Describe the TCP/IP utilities included with Windows NT.

Estimated lesson time: 5 minutes

Microsoft TCP/IP utilities work with TCP/IP protocols to provide access to foreign hosts and the TCP/IP-based Internet. On Windows NT, all utilities are implemented as client software except for FTP, which is implemented as both client and server software.

Data Transfer Utilities

Windows NT 4.0 provides the utilities for connecting to other TCP/IP-based hosts. The most commonly used data transfer utility is FTP. FTP provides bidirectional file transfers between two TCP/IP hosts, where one is running FTP server software.

Other utilities used for transferring data include Trivial File Transfer Protocol (TFTP) and Remote Copy Protocol (RCP). TFTP, like FTP, provides bidirectional file transfers between two TCP/IP hosts where one is running TFTP server software. RCP copies files between a computer running Windows NT and a UNIX host.

Remote Execution Utilities

Windows NT also provides the utilities for connecting to and remotely operating other TCP/IP-based hosts. The most frequently used remote execution utility is Telnet, which provides terminal emulation to a TCP/IP host running Telnet server software. Other utilities include Remote Shell (RSH), which runs commands on a UNIX host, and Remote Execution (REXEC), which runs a process on a remote computer.

Printing Utilities

Two TCP/IP utilities provide the ability to print and obtain print status on a TCP/IP printer. Line Printer Remote (LPR) prints a file to a host running the Line Printing Daemon (LPD) service. Line Printer Queue (LPQ) obtains status of a print queue on a host running the LPD service.

Note   These utilities require software on both the client and server sides. Microsoft provides FTP and LPD server applications. You learn more about these utilities in Chapter 14, "Connectivity in Heterogeneous Environments."

Diagnostics Utilities

Windows NT 4.0 provides several utilities for diagnosing TCP/IP-related problems. You will use several of these utilities throughout this course.

Diagnostics utility	Function
Packet InterNet Groper (PING)	Verifies that TCP/IP is configured correctly and that another host is available.
IPCONFIG	Verifies a TCP/IP configuration, including DHCP, DNS, and WINS server addresses.
Finger	Retrieves system information from a remote computer that supports the TCP/IP Finger service.
NSLOOKUP	Examines entries in the DNS database that pertain to a particular host or domain.
HOSTNAME	Returns the local computer's host name for authentication.
NETSTAT	Displays protocol statistics and the current state of TCP/IP connections.
NBTSTAT	Checks the state of current NetBIOS over TCP/IP connections, updates the LMHOSTS cache, or determines your registered name and scope ID.
Route	Views or modifies the local routing table.
Tracert	Verifies the route used from the local host to a remote host.
Address Resolution Protocol (ARP)	Displays a cache of locally resolved IP addresses to Media Access Control (MAC) addresses.

Summary

Windows NT supplies a number of application utilities that can help you connect to other TCP/IP-based hosts or help you troubleshoot TCP/IP connection problems.

Review

The following questions are intended to reinforce key information presented in this chapter. If you are unable to answer a question, review the appropriate lesson and then try the question again.

1. What is TCP/IP?

2. Are all TCP/IP standards published as RFCs? Do all RFCs specify standards?

For More Information

- The *Course Materials* Web page on the course compact disc contains technical information on TCP/IP.
- Read the white paper titled *Microsoft Windows NT 3.5/3.51/4.0: TCP/IP Implementation Details TCP/IP Protocol Stack and Services, Version 2.0*.
- Read *Internetworking with TCP/IP Volume I*, by Douglas E. Comer.

C H A P T E R   2

Installing and Configuring TCP/IP

Lesson 1   Installing and Configuring Microsoft TCP/IP . . . 10

Lesson 2   Testing TCP/IP with Ipconfig and PING . . . 15

Lesson 3   Microsoft Network Monitor . . . 18

Review . . . 22

About This Chapter

This chapter provides the procedures for installing and manually configuring an IP address, subnet mask, and default gateway. During the lessons you install and manually configure Microsoft TCP/IP. The lessons also give you an overview of basic configuration testing procedures using Ipconfig, PING, and Microsoft Network Monitor.

Before You Begin

To complete the lessons in this chapter, you must set up your computer(s) as described in the Setup Instructions section in About This Book.

Lesson 1: Installing and Configuring Microsoft TCP/IP

This lesson describes the procedure for installing Microsoft TCP/IP. Follow this procedure if you have not previously installed the TCP/IP network protocol on the computer(s) you are using to perform the practice procedures during this course.

After this lesson, you will be able to:

- Install and configure Microsoft TCP/IP.

Estimated lesson time: 20 minutes

TCP/IP installs several system and name resolution files to your Windows NT System32\Drivers and System32\Drivers\Etc directories. TCP/IP uses the name resolution files shown in the following table. You learn more about these files later in the course.

Configuration file	Description
HOSTS	Provides name resolution for host names to IP addresses.
LMHOSTS	Provides name resolution for NetBIOS names to IP addresses.
NETWORKS	Provides name resolution for network names to IP network IDs.
PROTOCOL	Provides resolution from a protocol name to an RFC-defined protocol number. The protocol number is a field in the IP header that identifies to which upper-layer protocol (such as TCP or UDP) the IP data should be passed.
SERVICES	Provides resolution from a service name to a port number and protocol name. The port number is a field in the TCP or UDP header that identifies the TCP or UDP process.

Configuration Parameters

TCP/IP uses an IP address, subnet mask, and default gateway to communicate with hosts. TCP/IP hosts running on a WAN require all three configuration parameters. Each network adapter card in the computer that uses TCP/IP requires these parameters.

IP Address

An IP address is a logical 32-bit address that identifies a TCP/IP host. Each IP address has two parts: the network ID and the host ID. The network ID identifies all hosts that are on the same physical network. The host ID identifies a host on the network. Each computer running TCP/IP requires a unique IP address. An example of an IP address is 131.107.2.200.

Chapter 4, "IP Addressing," covers the essential details of assigning IP addresses.

Subnet Mask

A subnet mask blocks out a portion of the IP address so that TCP/IP can distinguish the network ID from the host ID. When TCP/IP hosts try to communicate, they use the subnet mask to determine whether the destination host is on a local or remote network. An example of a subnet mask is 255.255.255.0. Chapter 5, "Subnetting," teaches you how to assign a valid subnet mask.

Default Gateway

To communicate with a host on another network, you must configure an IP address for the default gateway. TCP/IP sends packets that are destined for remote networks to the default gateway, but only if no other route is configured on the local host to the destination network. If you have not configured a default gateway, communication may be limited to the local network. A sample default gateway is 131.107.2.1.

Practice

You install and configure TCP/IP through the Network program in Control Panel. In this procedure, you first view the network protocols currently installed on your machine. If TCP/IP is not present, you continue with the installation.

Note If you have two networked computers available to you, perform this procedure on both computers.

▶ **To view the network protocols on your machine**

1. Log on as Administrator.
2. Click the **Start** button, point to **Settings**, and then click **Control Panel**.

   Control Panel appears.
3. Double-click the Network icon.

   The **Network** dialog box appears.
4. Click the **Protocols** tab.

   If the TCP/IP protocol does not appear in the list of network protocols, complete the following procedure.

▶ **To install Microsoft TCP/IP on Windows NT 4.0**

1. On the **Protocols** tab, click **Add**.

   The **Select Network Protocol** dialog box appears.

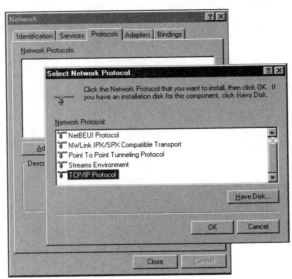

2. Select **TCP/IP Protocol**, and then click **OK**.

   The **DHCP Server** dialog box appears.

Note You manually configure TCP/IP parameters later during this procedure. Chapter 7, "The Dynamic Host Configuration Protocol," provides details about the DHCP service.

---

3. Click **No**.

   The **Windows NT Setup** dialog box appears, requesting the full path to the Windows NT distribution files.

4. Type the complete path to the Windows NT Server source files.
5. Click **Continue**.

   Setup installs the files from the path you provide.
6. Click **Close**.

   The **Microsoft TCP/IP Properties** dialog box appears.
7. If a DHCP server is not available, you can specify an IP address, a subnet mask, and a default gateway to manually configure TCP/IP. If you need to connect to hosts beyond the local network, assign a default gateway. Type your TCP/IP configuration parameters as described in the following table.

Caution If your computer(s) are part of a larger network, you *must* verify with your network administrator that the following computer names, domain name, and IP address information do not conflict with network operations. If they do conflict, ask your network administrator to provide alternative values and use those values throughout all of the practices in this course.

Parameter	Description
IP address	An IP address is required. If you are configuring two networked computers for the procedures, the IP address for Server1 should be 131.107.2.200, and the IP address for Server2 should be 131.107.2.211.
Subnet mask	A subnet mask is required. If configuring your computers for the procedures, the subnet mask is 255.255.255.0.
Default gateway	The default gateway is an optional parameter (unless you connect with hosts on a remote network). If you are configuring your computers for the procedures, the default gateway is 131.107.2.1.

Note IP communications can fail if multiple devices use the same IP address.

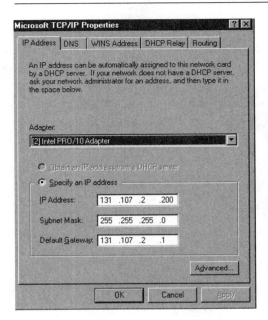

8. Click **OK**.

   A **Network Settings Change** dialog box appears, prompting you to restart your computer.

9. Click **Yes**.

   The computer restarts with your new IP address settings.

Summary

During the TCP/IP installation, several system and name resolution files are copied to your Windows NT directories. If you configure TCP/IP manually, you must assign an IP address and a subnet mask.

Lesson 2: Testing TCP/IP with Ipconfig and PING

After you install TCP/IP, it is a good idea to verify and test the configuration and any connections to other TCP/IP hosts and networks. This lesson explains basic TCP/IP configuration testing procedures using Ipconfig and PING utilities.

After this lesson, you will be able to:
- Verify TCP/IP configuration parameters with the Ipconfig utility.
- Test a TCP/IP configuration and IP connection with the PING utility.

Estimated lesson time: 10 minutes

The Ipconfig Utility

You can use the Ipconfig utility to verify the TCP/IP configuration parameters on a host, including the IP address, subnet mask, and default gateway. This is useful in determining whether the configuration is initialized or if a duplicate IP address is configured. The command syntax is:

ipconfig

If a configuration has initialized, the configured IP address, subnet mask, and default gateway appear. If a duplicate address is configured, the IP address appears as configured, but the subnet mask appears as 0.0.0.0.

Note   The WINIPCFG utility, included in Microsoft Windows 95, also verifies the TCP/IP configuration.

The PING Utility

After you verify the configuration with the Ipconfig utility, you can use the Packet InterNet Groper (PING) utility to test connectivity. The PING utility is a diagnostic tool that tests TCP/IP configurations and diagnoses connection failures. PING uses the Internet Control Message Protocol (ICMP) *echo request* and *echo reply* messages to determine whether a particular TCP/IP host is available and functional. The command syntax is:

ping *IP_address*

If PING is successful, a message similar to the following appears:

```
Pinging IP_address with 32 bytes of data:
Reply from IP_address: bytes= x time<10ms TTL= x
Reply from IP_address: bytes= x time<10ms TTL= x
Reply from IP_address: bytes= x time<10ms TTL= x
Reply from IP_address: bytes= x time<10ms TTL= x
```

Practice

In this procedure, you use the Ipconfig utility to view an IP configuration and the PING utility to test your workstation configuration and connections to another TCP/IP host.

Note You must have a second networked computer to perform part of this procedure. Review the Setup Instructions section of About This Book before you begin. Perform this procedure from the computer you designated as Server1.

▶ **To verify a computer's configuration and for test router connections**

1. Use the Ipconfig utility to verify that your TCP/IP configuration has initialized. At a command prompt, type:

   ipconfig

   If the configuration is correctly initialized, the IP address, subnet mask, and default gateway (if configured) values display.

2. Ping the loopback address to verify that TCP/IP is installed and loaded correctly. At a command prompt, type:

   ping 127.0.0.1

   and then press ENTER.

   Note The loopback address (127.0.0.1) uses loopback drivers to reroute outgoing packets back to the source computer. These loopback drivers bypass the network adapter card completely. If you are using the procedures on a stand-alone computer, you can use the loopback address to perform many of the TCP/IP procedures contained in this course.

3. Ping the IP address of your computer to verify that you added it correctly. Type:

   ping 131.107.2.200

4. Ping the IP address of your second computer to verify that you can communicate with a host on the local network. Type:

   ping 131.107.2.211

5. If a remote host is available on your configuration, ping the IP address of the remote host to verify that you can communicate through a router. Type:

   ping *IP_address_of_remote_host*

Tips If Ipconfig verifies that TCP/IP is properly installed and using the correct IP address, you may not need to perform steps 2 and 3.

If you start with step 5 and can ping successfully, then steps 2 through 4 are successful by default.

If the address is incorrect, or you have not properly configured TCP/IP, PING times out.

Summary

The Ipconfig and the PING utilities can help you verify and test your configuration after you install TCP/IP. Ipconfig verifies the IP address, subnet mask, and default gateway. The PING utility tests connectivity and can help you diagnose connection failures.

Lesson 3: Microsoft Network Monitor

Microsoft Network Monitor is a tool that simplifies the task of troubleshooting complex network problems. This lesson gives you an overview of Network Monitor. You use Network Monitor to view packets in Chapter 3, "Architectural Overview of the TCP/IP Protocol Suite."

After this lesson, you will be able to:

- Install and configure Microsoft Network Monitor.

Estimated lesson time: 15 minutes

Microsoft Network Monitor troubleshoots network problems by monitoring and capturing network traffic for analysis. Network Monitor works by configuring the network adapter card to capture all incoming and outgoing packets.

You can define capture filters so that you save only specific frames for analysis. You can define filters based on source and destination Media Access Control addresses, source and destination protocol addresses, and pattern matches. Once Network Monitor captures a packet, you can use display filtering to further analyze a problem. Once Network Monitor captures and filters a packet, it interprets trace data and presents a real-time report.

Note The version of Network Monitor included with Windows NT is limited to only capturing data for the local computer. The full version of Network Monitor is available with Microsoft Systems Management Server, a centralized management for distributed systems.

Practice

In this procedure you will install Network Monitor from the Services tab. This will prepare your computer(s) for viewing packets in Chapter 3, "Architectural Overview of the TCP/IP Protocol Suite."

▶ **To install Network Monitor**

1. Log on as Administrator.
2. Double-click the Network icon in Control Panel, and then click the **Services** tab.

3. Click **Add**.

The **Select Network Service** dialog box appears.

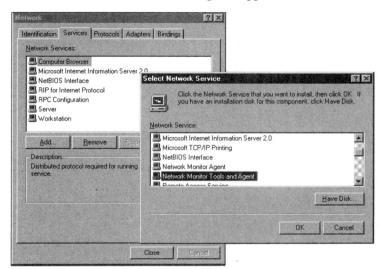

4. Click **Network Monitor Tools and Agent** in the **Network Service** list, and then click **OK**.

   Windows NT Setup displays a dialog box that asks for the full path to the Windows NT distribution files.

5. Type the path to the source files, and then click **Continue**.

6. In the **Network** dialog box, click **Close**.

7. Click **Yes** when prompted to restart your computer.

Analyzing Network Traffic

To analyze network traffic with Network Monitor, you need to start the capture process, generate the network traffic you are observing, then stop the capture and view the data. To use Network Monitor, click the **Start** button, point to **Programs**, point to **Administrative Tools**, and then click **Network Monitor**.

Starting a Capture

Network Monitor uses many windows for displaying different data. One of the primary windows is the Capture window. When this window has the focus, the toolbar shows you options to start, pause, stop, or stop and view captured data. On the **Capture** menu, click **Start** to start a capture. While the capture process is running, Network Monitor displays statistical information in the Capture window.

Stopping a Capture

After you have generated the network traffic you are analyzing, on the **Capture** menu, click **Stop** to stop the capture. You can then create another capture or display the current capture data. Then, on the **Capture** menu, click **Stop and View** to stop a capture and immediately open it for viewing.

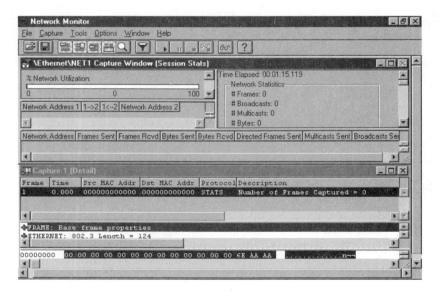

Viewing the Data

When opening a capture to view, a Summary window appears, showing each frame capture. The Summary window contains a frame number, time of frame reception, and source and destination addresses. It also contains the highest-layer protocol used in the frame and a description of the frame.

For more detailed information on a specific frame, on the **Window** menu, click **Zoom**. In the zoom view you get two additional windows, the **Detail** frame and **Hexadecimal** frame. The **Detail** frame shows the protocol information in detail. The **Hexadecimal** frame shows the raw bytes in the frame.

Note   You use Network Monitor to view packets in Chapter 3, "Architectural Overview of the TCP/IP Protocol Suite."

Summary

Network Monitor can help you troubleshoot difficult network problems. The three steps to using Network Monitor are starting the capture process, generating network traffic, and then stopping the capture to review the data.

Review

The following questions are intended to reinforce key information presented in this chapter. If you are unable to answer a question, review the appropriate lesson and then try the question again.

1. What TCP/IP utilities are used to verify and test a TCP/IP configuration?

   _____

2. What parameters are required on a Windows NT-based computer running TCP/IP on a WAN?

   _____

   _____

For More Information

- Read the Microsoft Network Monitor product documentation.

C H A P T E R   3

Architectural Overview of the TCP/IP Protocol Suite

Lesson 1 **The Microsoft TCP/IP Protocol Suite . . . 25**

Lesson 2 **ARP . . . 29**

Lesson 3 **ICMP and IGMP . . . 40**

Lesson 4 **IP . . . 42**

Lesson 5 **TCP . . . 46**

Lesson 6 **UDP . . . 51**

Review . . . 53

About This Chapter

This chapter describes the four layers of the TCP/IP protocol suite and explains in detail how protocols at each layer work with other protocols. This chapter contains two multimedia presentations that acquaint you with TCP/IP. During the lessons you view and modify the Address Resolution Protocol (ARP) cache, and view packets with Network Monitor.

Before You Begin

To complete the lessons in this chapter, you must have:

- Installed Microsoft Windows NT Server 4.0 with the TCP/IP network protocol.
- Installed the Network Monitor Tools and Agent Network service (covered in Chapter 2, "Installing TCP/IP").
- The course compact disc to view the multimedia presentations.
- A sound card with headphones or speakers (optional).

Lesson 1: The Microsoft TCP/IP Protocol Suite

This lesson describes the four layers of the TCP/IP protocol suite and explains how protocols at each layer work internally and in association with other protocols. At the beginning of the lesson, you view a multimedia presentation covering the essentials of TCP/IP.

After this lesson, you will be able to:

- Describe how the TCP/IP protocol suite maps to a four-layer model.
- Describe the network interface layer protocols that Internet Protocol (IP) supports.

Estimated lesson time: 30 minutes

Multimedia Presentation: Overview of the TCP/IP Protocol Suite

This 15-minute multimedia presentation provides an overview of the TCP/IP protocol suite and explains how the protocols in the suite work internally and with other protocols. It describes how the TCP/IP protocol suite maps to a four-layer model. The information in this presentation applies to Microsoft TCP/IP and most other implementations of TCP/IP.

▶ **To start the Overview of the TCP/IP Protocol Suite multimedia presentation**

1. Insert the course compact disc into the CD-ROM drive.

   Microsoft Internet Explorer starts and The Internetworking with Microsoft TCP/IP on Microsoft Windows NT 4.0 start page opens.

   –Or–

   Start Windows NT Explorer, navigate to the drive containing the course compact disc, and then double-click the Open.htm file.

2. Click the start page icon.
3. Click **Course Materials**.
4. Click **Multimedia Presentations**.
5. Click **Overview of the TCP/IP Protocol Suite**.

   An Internet Explorer dialog box appears asking if you want to open the file or save it to disk.

6. Select **Open it**, and then click **OK**.
7. Click **Yes** if a security box appears.

   The multimedia presentation begins. Click the **Text On** button if you do not have a sound card and speakers.

The Four-Layer Model

TCP/IP protocols follow a four-layer conceptual model: Application, Transport, Internet, and Network Interface. The Microsoft TCP/IP core protocols provide a set of standards for how computers communicate and how networks are interconnected.

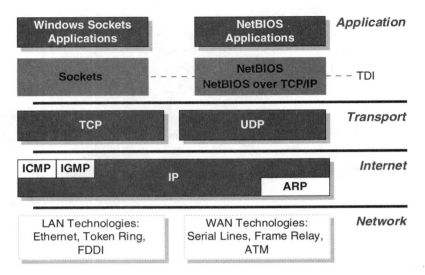

Network Interface Layer

At the base of the model is the Network Interface layer. This layer is responsible for sending and receiving frames, which are packets of information transmitted on a network as a single unit. The Network Interface layer puts frames on the network, and pulls frames off the network.

Internet Layer

Internet protocols encapsulate packets into Internet datagrams and run all of the necessary routing algorithms. The four Internet protocols are Internet Protocol (IP), Address Resolution Protocol (ARP), Internet Control Message Protocol (ICMP), and Internet Group Management Protocol (IGMP).

- IP is primarily responsible for addressing and routing packets between hosts and networks.
- ARP obtains hardware addresses of hosts located on the same physical network.
- ICMP sends messages and reports errors regarding the delivery of a packet.
- IGMP is used by IP hosts to report host group memberships to local multicast routers.

Transport Layer

Transport protocols provide communication sessions between computers. The two Transport protocols are Transmission Control Protocol and User Datagram Protocol (UDP). The transport protocol used depends upon the preferred method of data delivery.

TCP provides connection-oriented, reliable communications for applications that typically transfer large amounts of data at one time. It is also used for applications that require an acknowledgment for data received.

UDP provides connectionless communications and does not guarantee to deliver packets. Applications that use UDP typically transfer small amounts of data at one time. Reliable delivery of data is the responsibility of the application.

Application Layer

At the top of the TCP/IP model is the Application layer. This layer is where applications gain access to the network. There are many standard TCP/IP utilities and services at the Application layer such as FTP, Telnet, SNMP, and DNS.

Microsoft TCP/IP provides two interfaces for network applications to use the services of the TCP/IP protocol stack. The first, called Windows Sockets, provides a standard application programming interface (API) under Microsoft Windows for transport protocols such as TCP/IP and IPX.

The second interface for network applications is NetBIOS. This interface provides a standard interface to protocols that support the NetBIOS naming and messaging services, such as TCP/IP and NetBEUI.

Network Interface Technologies

IP uses the network device interface specification (NDIS) to submit frames to the network interface layer. IP supports LAN and WAN interface technologies.

LAN technologies supported by TCP/IP include Ethernet (Ethernet II and 802.3), Token Ring, ArcNet and Metropolitan Area Network (MAN) technologies such as fiber distributed data interface (FDDI).

Using TCP/IP in a WAN environment may require the Windows NT Remote Access Service (RAS) or additional hardware. There are two major categories of WAN technologies supported by TCP/IP: serial lines and packet-switched networks. Serial lines include dial-up analog, digital lines, and leased lines. Packet-switched networks include X.25, frame relay, and asynchronous transfer mode (ATM).

Serial Line Protocols

TCP/IP is typically transported across a serial line using either the Serial Line Internet Protocol (SLIP) or the Point-to-Point Protocol (PPP).

SLIP is an industry standard developed in the early 1980s to support TCP/IP networking over low-speed serial interfaces. With the Windows NT RAS, computers running Windows NT can use TCP/IP and SLIP to communicate with remote hosts.

Note Windows NT supports only SLIP client functionality, not SLIP server functionality. Windows NT RAS servers do not accept SLIP client connections.

The Point-to-Point Protocol (PPP) was designed as an enhancement to the original SLIP specification. PPP is a data-link protocol that provides a standard method of sending network packets over a point-to-point link. Because PPP provides greater security, configuration handling, and error detection than SLIP, it is the recommended protocol for serial line communication.

Note The transmission of IP over serial lines is described in RFC 1055. The Point-to-Point Protocol is defined in RFCs 1547 and 1661. For copies of these RFCs, see the *Course Materials* Web page on the course compact disc.

Summary

TCP/IP protocols use a four-layer conceptual model: Application, Transport, Internet, and Network Interface. IP supports both LAN and WAN interface technologies.

Lesson 2: ARP

Hosts must know the hardware address of other hosts to communicate on a network. Address resolution is the process of mapping a host's IP address to its hardware address. The Address Resolution Protocol (ARP), part of the TCP/IP Internet layer, obtains hardware addresses of hosts located on the same physical network.

After this lesson, you will be able to:
- Explain how ARP resolves an IP address to a hardware address.
- Explain how ARP adds and deletes entries to cache.
- View and modify the ARP cache.

Estimated lesson time: 45 minutes

ARP is responsible for obtaining hardware addresses of TCP/IP hosts on broadcast-based networks. ARP uses a local broadcast of the destination IP address to acquire the hardware address of the destination host or gateway.

Once ARP obtains the hardware address, both the IP address and hardware address are stored as one entry in the ARP cache. ARP always checks the ARP cache for an IP address and hardware address mapping before initiating an ARP request broadcast.

Reverse address resolution is the process of mapping a host's hardware address to its IP address. Microsoft TCP/IP does not support reverse address resolution.

Note ARP is defined in RFC 826. For a copy of this RFC, see the *Course Materials* Web page on the course compact disc.

Resolving a Local IP Address

Before communication between two hosts can occur, the IP address of each host must be resolved to the host's hardware address. The address resolution process includes an ARP request and an ARP reply, as the following example illustrates:

1. An ARP request initiates any time a host tries to communicate with another host. When IP determines that the IP address is for the local network, the source host checks its own ARP cache for the hardware address of the destination host.

2. If it finds no mapping, ARP builds a request with the question "Who is this IP address, and what is your hardware address?" The source host's IP address and hardware address are included in the request. The ARP request is sent as a broadcast so that all local hosts can receive and process it.

3. Each host on the local network receives the broadcast and checks for a match to its own IP address. If a host does not find a match, it ignores the request.

4. The destination host determines that the IP address in the request matches its own IP address and sends an ARP reply directly to the source host with its hardware address. It then updates its ARP cache with the IP address/hardware address mapping of the source host. Communication is established when the source host receives the reply.

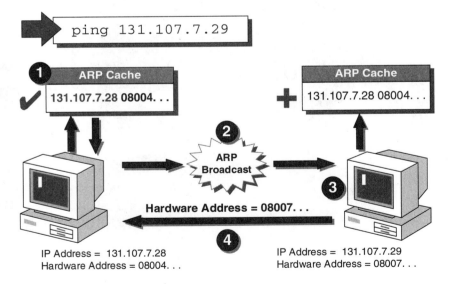

Resolving a Remote IP Address

ARP also allows two hosts on different networks to communicate. In this situation, the ARP broadcast is for the default gateway of the source host and not the IP address of the destination host.

If the destination IP address belongs to a host on a remote network, the ARP broadcast is for a router that can forward datagrams to the destination host's network, as the following example illustrates:

1. When a request for communications initiates, the destination IP address is identified as a remote address.

    The source host checks the local routing table for a route to the destination host or network. If it finds no mapping, the source host determines the IP address of the default gateway. The source host then checks the ARP cache for the IP address/hardware address mapping of the specified gateway.

2. If it finds no mapping for the specified gateway, an ARP request is broadcast for the gateway's address rather than the address of the destination host.

    The router responds to the source host's ARP request with its hardware address. The source host then sends the data packet to the router to deliver to the destination host's network, and ultimately the destination host.

3. At the router, IP determines whether the destination IP address is local or remote. If it is local, the router uses ARP (either cache or broadcast) to obtain its hardware address. If it is remote, the router checks its routing table for a specified gateway, and then uses ARP (either cache or broadcast) to obtain the gateway's hardware address. The packet is sent directly to the next destination host.

4. After the destination host receives the request, it formulates an ICMP echo reply. Because the source host is on a remote network, the local routing table is checked for a specified gateway to the source host's network. When it finds a gateway, ARP obtains its hardware address.

5. If the specified gateway's hardware address is not in the ARP cache, an ARP broadcast obtains it. Once it obtains the hardware address, the ICMP echo reply is sent to the router to be routed to the source host.

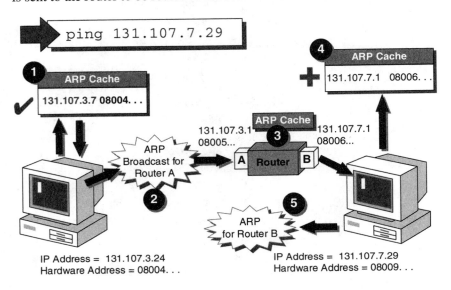

The ARP Cache

To minimize the number of broadcasts, ARP maintains address mappings in cache for future use. The ARP cache maintains both dynamic and static entries. Dynamic entries are added and deleted automatically. Static entries remain in cache until the computer is restarted.

Additionally, the ARP cache always maintains the hardware broadcast address (FFFFFFFFFFFF) for the local subnet as a permanent entry. This entry allows a host to accept ARP broadcasts. The address does not appear when you view the cache.

Each ARP cache entry has a potential lifetime of 10 minutes. As each entry is added to the ARP cache, it is timestamped. If it is not used within two minutes, the entry is deleted; otherwise, if it is used, it is deleted after 10 minutes. If the ARP cache reaches its maximum capacity before entries expire, the oldest entry is deleted so that a new entry can be added.

Note   There is a separate ARP cache for each IP address on a computer running Windows NT.

ARP Cache Aging

The default for ARP cache time-outs is two minutes on unused entries and 10 minutes on used entries. Adding the **ARPCacheLife** parameter to the registry and setting a value in seconds overrides both default values.

Note   In some TCP/IP implementations, when an entry is reused, it is given a new timestamp, adding another 10 minutes to its life. Windows NT 4.0 has not implemented this feature.

Adding Static (Permanent) Entries

Adding a static ARP entry decreases the number of ARP requests for frequently accessed hosts. Under Windows NT 4.0, if a static entry is added to the ARP cache, it is available until one of the following conditions is met:

- The computer restarts.
- The entry is deleted manually with **arp-d**.
- An ARP broadcast is received indicating a different hardware address. In this case, the entry changes from static to dynamic, and the newly received hardware address replaces the current hardware address.

Note   If you manually insert an entry into the ARP cache, the hardware address must contain hyphens.

ARP Packet Structure

Although created for IP address resolution, the ARP packet structure is adaptable to other types of address resolution. ARP has an EtherType of 0x08-06. The fields of the ARP structure are as shown in the following table.

Field	Function
Hardware Type	The type of hardware (Network Access Layer) being used.
Protocol Type	The protocol being used for the resolution process using the EtherType value. Hence, the Protocol Type for IP is 0x08–00.
Hardware Address Length	Length in bytes of the hardware address. For Ethernet and Token Ring, the length is 6 bytes.
Protocol Address Length	Length in bytes of the protocol address. For IP, the length is 4 bytes.
Operation (Opcode)	The operation field specifies the operation being performed.
Sender's Hardware Address	The hardware address of the sender (the ARP requester).
Sender's Protocol Address	The protocol address of the sender (the ARP requester).
Target's Hardware Address	The hardware address of the target (the ARP responder).
Target's Protocol Address	The protocol address of the target (the ARP responder).

Practice

You can use Network Monitor to capture and display packets. In this procedure, you capture and display ARP packets. You then examine ARP request and ARP reply details.

Note To complete this procedure, you need two networked computers as described in About This Book. Perform the procedure from the computer acting as Server1.

▶ **To start Network Monitor**

1. Log on as Administrator.

2. Click the **Start** button, point to **Programs**, point to **Administrative Tools**, and then click **Network Monitor**.

   The Network Monitor window appears.

3. Maximize the Network Monitor window.

4. Maximize the Capture window.

▶ **To capture network data**

1. On the **Capture** menu, click **Start**.

   This starts the data capture process. Network Monitor allocates buffer space for network data and begins capturing frames.

2. At a command prompt, type:

   ping 131.107.2.211

▶ **To stop the network data capture**

1. Switch back to **Network Monitor**.

2. On the **Capture** menu in **Network Monitor**, click **Stop**.

   Network Monitor stops capturing frames and displays four panes: **Graph**, **Total Stats**, **Session Stats**, and **Station Stats**.

▶ **To view captured data**

• On the **Capture** menu, click **Display Captured Data**.

   The Network Monitor Capture Summary window appears, displaying the summary record of all frames captured.

In the following procedure, you change the color of all frames that use ARP. This is useful when viewing frames for a particular protocol.

▶ **To highlight captured data**

1. On the **Display** menu, click **Colors**.

   The **Protocol Colors** dialog box appears.

2. Under **Name**, select **ARP_RARP**.

3. Under **Colors**, set **Foreground** to **Red**, and then click **OK**.

   The Network Monitor Capture Summary window appears, displaying all ARP frames in red.

▶ **To view the ARP request frame details**

1. Under **Description**, double-click the **ARP: Request**.

   Three separate windows appear. The top window displays the frame summary, the middle window displays the selected frame details, and the bottom window displays the selected frame details in hexadecimal notation.

2. In the Detail window, click **Frame** with a plus sign (**+**) preceding it.

3. Expand the **Frame** details by clicking the plus sign.

   The **Frame** details properties expand to show more detail. The contents of the packet are highlighted and displayed in hexadecimal notation in the bottom window.

   View the size of the base frame.

4. Collapse the base frame properties.

5. In the Detail window, expand **ETHERNET**.

   The **ETHERNET** frame properties are displayed.

   What is the destination address?

   _____

   Does the destination address refer to a physical address?

   _____

   What is the source address?

   _____

   What type of Ethernet frame is this?

   _____

6. Collapse the **ETHERNET** properties.

7. In the Detail window, expand **ARP_RARP**.

   What is the sender's hardware address?

   _____

   What is the target's hardware address?

   _____

   What is the target's protocol address?

   _____

▶ **To examine an ARP reply frame details**

1. Under **Description**, double-click **ARP: Reply**.

2. In the Detail window, expand **ETHERNET: ETYPE**.

   The **ETHERNET: ETYPE** frame properties are displayed.

   What is the destination address?

   _____

   Does the destination address refer to a physical address?

   _____

   What is the source address?

   _____

   What type of Ethernet frame is this?

   _____

3. Collapse the **ETHERNET** properties.

4. In the Detail window, expand **ARP_RARP**.

   What is the sender's hardware address?

   _____

If you want to save captured data for later analysis, use the following procedure.

▶ **To save the capture**

1. On the **File** menu, click **Save As**.

2. Under **File Name**, type a file name and then click **OK**.

3. On the **File** menu, click **Close**.

   The Network Monitor Capture window appears, still displaying the statistics from the last capture.

4. Exit Network Monitor.

Practice

In this procedure, you first use the ARP utility to view entries in your computer's ARP cache. You then use the ARP utility to modify entries in your computer's ARP cache.

Note In order to complete this procedure, you need two networked computers as described in About This Book. If it has been several minutes since you completed the preceding procedure, you may need to refresh the ARP cache by pinging your second computer.

▶ **To view the ARP cache**

1. At a command prompt, type **arp-g** and then press ENTER to view the ARP cache.

2. Document the entry for your default gateway (if configured)—for example: 131.107.2.1 08-00-02-6c-28-93.

_____

▶ **To ping a local host**

1. Ping the IP address of your second computer.

   This adds an entry to the cache.

2. View the new entry in the ARP cache.

   What entry was added?

_____

   What is the entry's type?

_____

Note The default gateway address is added to the ARP cache when pinging a remote host. This is because PING must use the default gateway to get to the remote host.

▶ **To add an ARP entry**

1. Type the following **arp** command to add the entry from step 1 to the cache:
   arp-s 131.107.2.1 *hardware_address*

   Note Make sure that you type the physical address using hyphens between as listed in step 1.

   ---

2. View the ARP cache to verify that the entry has been added.

   What is the entry's type?

   _____

   Why was this entry's type different from preceding entries?

   _____

   _____

IP Address Resolution Problems

You may encounter situations when ARP cannot resolve an IP address to a hardware address. If the ARP cache contains an invalid hardware address, communications with a remote host times out.

Summary

Address resolution is the process of mapping a host's IP address to its hardware address. Address resolution consists of an ARP request and an ARP reply. The ARP cache maintains both dynamic and static entries. Static entries remain in cache until you restart the computer, while dynamic entries will expire after a period of time.

Lesson 3: ICMP and IGMP

While the IP protocol is for IP internetwork routing, Internet Control Message Protocol (ICMP) reports errors and controls messages on behalf of IP. IP uses Internet Group Management Protocol (IGMP) to inform routers that hosts of a specific group are available on a network.

After this lesson, you will be able to:
- Explain how ICMP reports IP errors.
- Define IGMP and understand its packet structure.

Estimated lesson time: 10 minutes

ICMP

ICMP does not attempt to make IP a reliable protocol. It merely attempts to report errors and provide feedback on specific conditions. ICMP messages are carried as IP datagrams, and are therefore unreliable.

If a TCP/IP host is sending datagrams to another host at a rate that is saturating the routers or links between them, the router can send an *ICMP Source Quench* message. This source quench message asks the host to slow down the rate of the transmission. A Windows NT TCP/IP host honors a source quench message and slows the sending rate of datagrams. However, if a computer running Windows NT is being used as a router and is unable to forward datagrams at the rate they are arriving, it drops any datagrams that cannot be buffered. In this case, it does not send ICMP source quench messages to the senders.

ICMP Packet Structure

All ICMP packets have the same structure, as shown in the following table.

Field	Function
Type	An 8-bit Type field indicates the type of ICMP packet (Echo Request versus Echo Reply, and so on).
Code	An 8-bit Code field indicates one of possible multiple functions within a given type. If there is only one function within a type, the Code field is set to 0.
Checksum	A 16-bit checksum over the ICMP portion of the packet.
Type-Specific Data	Additional data that varies for each ICMP type.

Note ICMP is defined in RFC 792. For a copy of this RFC, see the *Course Materials* Web page on the course compact disc.

IGMP

IGMP information passes to other routers so that each router that supports multicasting is aware of which host groups are on which network. IGMP packets are carried by IP datagrams, and are therefore unreliable.

IGMP Packet Structure

The fields in the IGMP packet are as shown in the following table.

Field	Function
Version	The version of IGMP that is fixed at 0x1.
Type	The type of IGMP message. A type of 0x1 is called a Host Membership Query and is used by a multicast router to poll a network for any members of a specified multicast group. A type of 0x2 is called a Host Membership Report, and is used by hosts to either declare membership in a specific group or to respond to a router's Host Membership Query.
Unused	An unused field that is zeroed by the sender and ignored by the receiver.
Checksum	A 16-bit checksum on the 8-byte IGMP header.
Group Address	The group address is used by hosts in a Host Membership Report to store the IP multicast address. In the Host Membership Query, the group address is set to all 0's and the hardware-level multicast address is used to identify the host group.

Note IGMP is defined in RFC 1112. For a copy of this RFC, see the *Course Materials* Web page on the course compact disc.

Summary

ICMP reports errors and controls messages on behalf of IP. Routers can send an ICMP Source Quench message asking a TCP/IP host to slow down the rate of transmission if it is sending datagrams too fast.

IGMP informs routers that hosts of a specific multicast group are available on a given network.

Lesson 4: IP

IP is a connectionless protocol primarily responsible for addressing and routing packets between hosts. This lesson describes the process IP uses to route packets.

After this lesson, you will be able to:

- Explain how IP fragments and routes IP packets.
- Describe the IP packet structure.

Estimated lesson time: 15 minutes

IP is connectionless because it does not establish a session before exchanging data. IP is unreliable because it does not guarantee delivery. It always makes a "best effort" attempt to deliver a packet. Along the way, a packet might be lost, delivered out of sequence, duplicated, or delayed.

IP does not require an acknowledgment when data is received. The sender or receiver is not informed when a packet is lost or sent out of sequence. The acknowledgment of packets is the responsibility of a higher-layer transport, such as TCP.

The IP datagram fields in the following table are added to the header when a packet is passed down from the Transport layer.

Field	Function
Source IP Address	Identifies the sender of the datagram by the IP address.
Destination IP Address	Identifies the destination of the datagram by the IP address.
Protocol	Informs IP at the destination host whether to pass the packet up to TCP or UDP.
Checksum	A simple mathematical computation that is used to verify that the packet arrived intact.
Time to Live (TTL)	Designates the number of seconds a datagram is allowed to stay on the wire before it's discarded. This prevents packets from endlessly looping around an internetwork. Routers are required to decrement the TTL by the number of seconds the datagram was stuck in the router. The TTL is decremented by at least one second each time the datagram passes through a router. The default TTL in Windows NT 4.0 is 128 seconds.

Note IP is defined in RFC 791. For a copy of this RFC, see the *Course Materials* Web page on the course compact disc.

If IP identifies a destination address as a *local* address, IP transmits the packet directly to that host. If the destination IP address is identified as a *remote* address, IP checks the local routing table for a route to the remote host. If it finds a route, IP sends the packet using that route. If IP does *not* find a route, it sends the packet to the source host's default gateway, also called a router.

IP on the Router

When a router receives a packet, the packet is passed up to IP, which does the following:

1. IP decrements the TTL by at least 1 or more if the packet is stuck at the router due to congestion.

   If the TTL reaches zero, the packet is discarded.

2. IP may fragment the packet into smaller packets if the packet is too large for the underlying network.

3. If the packet is fragmented, IP creates a new header for each new packet, which includes:

   - A *Flag* to indicate that other fragments follow.

   - A *Fragment ID* to identify all fragments that belong together.

   - A *Fragment Offset* to tell the receiving host how to reassemble the packet.

4. IP calculates a new checksum.

5. IP obtains the destination hardware address of the next router.

6. IP forwards the packet.

At the next host, the packet passes up the stack to either TCP or UDP. This entire process is repeated at each router until the packet reaches its final destination. When the packets arrive at their final destination, IP assembles the pieces into the original packet.

IP Packet Structure

The fields in the IP (version 4) header are as shown in the following table.

Field	Function
Version	4 bits are used to indicate the version of IP. The current version is version 4. The next version of IP will be version 6. This next version is discussed in Chapter 4, "IP Addressing."
Header Length	4 bits are used to indicate the number of 32-bit words in the IP header. IP headers have a minimum size of 20 bytes; therefore, the smallest header length is 0x5. IP options can extend the minimum IP header size 4 bytes at a time. If an IP option does not use all 4 bytes of the IP option field, the remaining bits are padded with 0's so that the entire IP header is an integral number of 32 bits (4 bytes).
Type of Service	8 bits are used to indicate the quality of service expected by this datagram for delivery through routers across the IP internetwork. Within the 8 bits are bits for precedence, delay, throughput, and reliability characteristics.
Total Length	16 bits are used to indicate the total length of the IP datagram (IP header + IP payload); the total length does not include the Network Access Layer framing.
Identification	16 bits are used as an identifier for this specific IP packet. If the IP packet is fragmented, all of the fragments have the same original identification to be used for reassembly by the destination node.
Fragmentation Flags	3 bits are reserved as flags for the fragmentation process; however, only 2 bits are defined for current use. There is a flag to indicate whether the IP datagram may be fragmented and a flag to indicate whether more fragments are to follow.
Fragment Offset	13 bits are used as an offset counter to indicate the position of the fragment relative to the original IP payload. If unfragmented, the fragment offset is 0x0.
Time to Live	8 bits are used as an indicator of the amount of time or *hops* an IP packet can travel before being discarded. The Time to Live field (TTL) was originally used as a time count during which an IP router timed how long it took (in seconds) to forward the IP packet and decremented the TTL accordingly. Modern routers almost always forward an IP datagram in less than a second and are required by RFC 791 to decrement the TTL by at least one. Therefore, the TTL becomes a maximum hop count. A suggested default value is twice the diameter of the IP internetwork, where the diameter is the maximum number of hops between any two IP nodes.

(continued)

Field	Function
Protocol	8 bits are used as an identifier of the IP client protocol, the protocol that gave a payload for IP to send. The protocol field is used to demultiplex an IP packet to the upper-layer protocol.
Header Checksum	16 bits are used as a checksum on the IP header only. The IP payload is not included and may include its own checksum to check for errors. When an IP node receives an IP packet, it performs a checksum verification and discards the IP packet if invalid. When a router forwards a IP packet, it minimally decrements the TTL. Therefore, the checksum is recomputed at each hop in its journey from source to destination.
Source Address	32 bits are used to store the IP address of the originating host.
Destination Address	32 bits are used to store the IP address of the destination host.
Options and Padding	A multiple of 32 bits is used to store IP options. If the IP option does not use all 32 bits, it must pad the additional bits with 0's so that the IP header is an integral number of 32 bits, which can be indicated by the header length field.

Summary

IP is a connectionless protocol that addresses and routes packets between hosts. IP is unreliable because delivery is not guaranteed. If a packet is destined for a local address, it is sent directly to that host. If the destination IP address is for a remote address, IP checks the local routing table for a route.

Lesson 5: TCP

TCP is a reliable, connection-oriented delivery service. In this lesson, you learn how TCP transmits data. You also learn about related TCP ports and sockets.

After this lesson, you will be able to:
- Describe how TCP transmits data.
- Define ports and sockets.

Estimated lesson time: 25 minutes

TCP data is transmitted in segments, and a session must be established before hosts can exchange data. TCP uses byte-stream communications, which means that the data is treated as a sequence of bytes.

It achieves reliability by assigning a sequence number to each segment transmitted by TCP. If a segment is broken into smaller pieces, the receiving host knows whether all pieces have been received. An acknowledgment verifies that the other host received the data. For each segment sent, the receiving host must return an acknowledgment (ACK) within a specified period.

If the sender does not receive an ACK, then the data is retransmitted. If the segment is received damaged, the receiving host discards it. Because an ACK is not sent, the sender retransmits the segment.

Note TCP is defined in RFC 793. For a copy of this RFC, see the *Course Materials* Web page on the course compact disc.

Ports

Sockets applications identify themselves uniquely within a computer by using a *protocol port number*. For example, the FTP Server application uses a specific TCP port so that other applications can communicate with it.

Ports can use any number between 0 and 65,536. Port numbers for client-side applications are dynamically assigned by the operating system when there is a request for service. Port numbers for *well-known* server-side applications are pre-assigned by the Internet Assigned Numbers Authority (IANA) and do not change.

Tip You can examine port numbers by looking at the file *\systemroot*\System32\Drivers\Etc\Services.

Well-known port numbers range from 1 to 1024. The complete list of well-known port numbers is documented in RFC 1700. For a copy of this RFC, see the *Course Materials* Web page on the course compact disc.

Sockets

A socket is similar in concept to a file handle in that it functions as an endpoint for network communication. An application creates a socket by specifying three items: the IP address of the host, the type of service (TCP for connection-based service, UDP for connectionless), and the port the application is using.

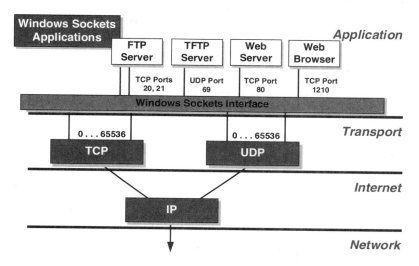

An application can create a socket and use it to send connectionless traffic to remote applications. An application can also create a socket and connect it to another application's socket. Data can then be reliably sent over this connection.

TCP Ports

A TCP port provides a specific location for delivery of messages. Port numbers below 256 are defined as commonly used ports. The following table shows a few commonly used TCP ports.

Port number	Description
21	FTP
23	Telnet
53	Domain Name System (DNS)
139	NetBIOS session service

TCP Three-Way Handshake

A TCP session is initialized through a three-way handshake. The purpose of the three-way handshake is to synchronize the sending and receiving of segments, inform the other host of the amount of data it is able to receive at once, and establish a virtual connection.

The following steps outline the three-way handshake process.

1. The initiating host requests a session by sending out a segment with the synchronization (SYN) flag set to **on**.

2. The receiving host acknowledges the request by sending back a segment with:

   ▪ The synchronization flag set to **on**.

   ▪ A sequence number to indicate the starting byte for a segment it may send.

   ▪ An acknowledgment with the byte sequence number of the next segment it expects to receive.

3. The requesting host sends back a segment with the acknowledged sequence number and acknowledgment number.

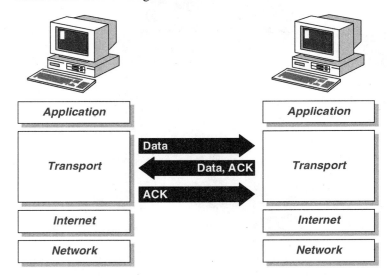

TCP uses a similar handshake process to end a connection. This guarantees that both hosts have finished transmitting and that they received all of the data.

TCP Sliding Windows

TCP buffers data for transmission between two hosts by using sliding windows. Each TCP/IP host maintains two sliding windows: one for receiving data, and the other for sending data. The size of the window indicates the amount of data that can be buffered on a computer.

Multimedia Presentation: TCP Sliding Windows

In this seven-minute presentation, you see how TCP sliding windows work and how the size of a sliding window can affect performance.

▶ **To start the TCP Sliding Windows multimedia presentation**

1. Insert the course compact disc into the CD-ROM drive.

   Internet Explorer starts and The Internetworking with Microsoft TCP/IP on Microsoft Windows NT 4.0 start page opens.

   –Or–

   Start Windows NT Explorer, navigate to the drive containing the course compact disc, and then double-click the Open.htm file.

2. Click the start page icon.

3. Click **Course Materials**.

4. Click **Multimedia Presentations**.

5. Click **TCP Sliding Windows**.

   An Internet Explorer dialog box appears asking if you want to open the file or save it to disk.

6. Select **Open it**, and then click **OK**.

7. Click **Yes** if a security box appears.

   The multimedia presentation begins. Click the **Text On** button if you do not have a sound card and speakers.

TCP Packet Structure

All TCP segments have two parts: data and header. The following table lists fields that are added to a TCP header.

Field	Function
Source Port	TCP port of sending host.
Destination Port	TCP port of destination host. This provides an endpoint for communications.
Sequence Number	The sequence of bytes transmitted in a segment. The sequence number is used to verify that all bytes have been received.
Acknowledgment Number	The sequence number of the byte the local host expects to receive next.
Data Length	Length of the TCP segment.
Reserved	Reserved for future use.
Flags	This field specifies what content is in the segment.
Window	How much space is currently available in the TCP window.
Checksum	Verifies that the header is not corrupted.
Urgent Pointer	When urgent data is being sent (as specified in the Flags field), this field points to the end of the urgent data in the segment.

Summary

TCP is a reliable, connection-oriented delivery service. Sockets applications use a unique port number. A socket functions as an endpoint for network communication. Ports and sockets consist of a related set of numbers.

A TCP session is initialized and ended through a three-way handshake. TCP uses sliding windows to buffer data for transmission between two hosts. The size of the window indicates the amount of data that can be buffered on a computer.

Lesson 6: UDP

User Datagram Protocol (UDP) provides a connectionless datagram service that offers unreliable, "best effort" delivery. This means that the arrival of datagrams or correct sequencing of delivered packets is not guaranteed.

After this lesson, you will be able to:

* Define UDP and describe the UDP packet structure.

Estimated lesson time: 5 minutes

UDP is used by applications that do not require an acknowledgment of data receipt. These applications typically transmit small amounts of data at one time. Examples of services and applications that use UDP are the NetBIOS name service, NetBIOS datagram service, and SNMP.

UDP Ports

To use UDP, the application must supply the IP address and port number of the destination application. A port provides a location for sending messages and is identified by a unique number. A port functions as a multiplexed message queue, meaning that it can receive multiple messages at a time. It is important to note that the UDP ports listed in the following table are distinct and separate from TCP ports even though some of them use the same port number.

Port	Keyword	Description
15	NETSTAT	Network status
53	DOMAIN	Domain Name Server
69	TFTP	Trivial File Transfer Protocol
137	NETBIOS-NS	NetBIOS name service
138	NETBIOS-DGM	NetBIOS datagram service
161	SNMP	SNMP network monitor

Note UDP is defined in RFC 768. For a copy of this RFC, see the *Course Materials* Web page on the course compact disc.

UDP Packet Structure

The fields in the following table are combined in the 8-byte UDP header.

Field	Function
Source Port	UDP port of sending host. The sending port value is optional. If not used, it is set to zero.
Destination Port	UDP port of destination host. This provides an endpoint for communications.
Message Length	The size of the UDP message. The minimum UDP packet contains only the header information (8 bytes).
Checksum	Verifies that the header is not corrupted.

Summary

UDP is a connectionless datagram service that does not guarantee delivery of packets. It is used by applications that do not require an acknowledgment of data receipt.

Review

The following questions are intended to reinforce key information presented in this chapter. If you are unable to answer a question, review the appropriate lesson and then try the question again.

1. What are the layers in the four-layer model used by TCP/IP?

2. What core protocols are provided in the Microsoft TCP/IP transport driver?

3. Which protocol is used to inform a client that a destination network is unreachable?

4. When an IP datagram is forwarded by a router, how is the datagram changed?

5. When is the User Datagram Protocol used?

6. When an ARP request is sent out, to what address is it sent?

_____

7. What address is requested in the ARP request packet for a local host? For a remote host?

_____

_____

For More Information

- Review all referenced RFCs on the course compact disc.

CHAPTER 4

IP Addressing

Lesson 1 The IP Address . . . 56

Lesson 2 Address Classes . . . 60

Lesson 3 Addressing Guidelines . . . 64

Lesson 4 Subnet Mask and the IP Address . . . 71

Lesson 5 IP Addressing with IP Version 6.0 . . . 75

Review . . . 77

About This Chapter

In this chapter, you review the components in an IP address, the address classes supported by Microsoft Windows NT, and addressing guidelines. The focus of this chapter is on a LAN environment. During the lessons, you identify valid and invalid IP addresses, assign IP addresses to hosts, and identify common IP addressing problems.

Before You Begin

There are no prerequisites in order to complete the lessons in this chapter.

Lesson 1: The IP Address

The IP address identifies a system's location on the network in the same way a street address identifies a house on a city block. Just as a street address must identify a unique residence, an IP address must be unique and have a uniform format.

After this lesson, you will be able to:
- Define the network ID and host ID portions of an IP address.
- Convert IP addresses from binary code to decimal format.

Estimated lesson time: 25 minutes

Each IP address has two parts—a network ID and a host ID. The network ID identifies a physical network. All hosts on the same network require the same network ID, which should be unique to the internetwork.

The host ID identifies a workstation, server, router, or other TCP/IP host within a network. The host ID must be unique to the network ID. Each TCP/IP host is identified by a logical IP address. A unique IP address is required for all hosts and network components that communicate using TCP/IP, as shown in the following illustration.

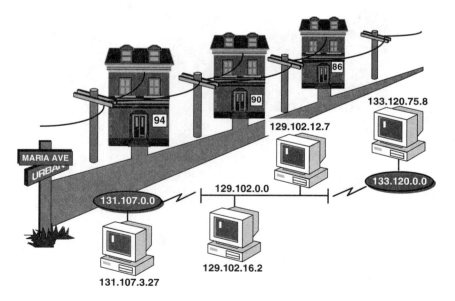

Network ID and Host ID

There are two formats for referencing an IP address—binary and dotted decimal notation. Each IP address is 32 bits long and is composed of four 8-bit fields, called octets. The octets are separated by periods and represent a decimal number in the range 0–255. The 32 bits of the IP address are allocated to the network ID and host ID.

The human-readable format of an IP address is referred to as *dotted decimal notation*. The following table contains an example of an IP address in binary and dotted decimal formats.

Binary format	Dotted decimal notation
10000011 01101011 00000011 00011000	131.107.3.24

Example: **131.107.3.24**

Converting IP Addresses from Binary to Decimal

You should be able to define the assigned bit values in an octet and convert the bits from binary code to a decimal format. In binary format, each bit in an octet has an assigned decimal value. When each bit is converted to decimal format, the highest value in the octet is 255. Each octet is converted separately.

A bit that is set to 0 always has a zero value. A bit that is set to 1 can be converted to a decimal value. The low-order bit represents a decimal value of one. The high-order bit represents a decimal value of 128. The highest decimal value of an octet is 255—that is, when all bits are set to 1.

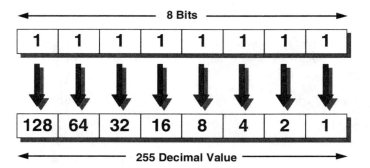

The following table shows how the bits in one octet are converted from binary code to a decimal value.

Binary code	Bit values	Decimal value
00000000	0	0
00000001	1	1
00000011	1+2	3
00000111	1+2+4	7
00001111	1+2+4+8	15
00011111	1+2+4+8+16	31
00111111	1+2+4+8+16+32	63
01111111	1+2+4+8+16+32+64	127
11111111	1+2+4+8+16+32+64+128	255

Practice

In this practice, you convert binary codes to decimal values and vice versa.

1. Convert the following binary numbers to decimal format.

   > **Tip** You can use the calculator (scientific view) in the **Accessories** group to convert decimal format to binary format, and vice versa. However, you may want to first convert some of these numbers manually until you are comfortable with the process.

Binary value	Decimal value
10001011	
10101010	
10111111 11100000 00000111 10000001	
01111111 00000000 00000000 00000001	

2. Convert the following decimal values to binary format.

Decimal value	Binary value
250	
19	
109.128.255.254	
131.107.2.89	

Summary

Each TCP/IP host is identified by a logical IP address, and a unique IP address is required for each host and network component that communicate using TCP/IP. Each IP address defines the network ID and host ID. An IP address is 32 bits long and is composed of four 8-bit fields, called octets.

Lesson 2: Address Classes

There are different classes of IP addresses. Each class defines the part of the IP address which identifies the network ID and the part which identifies the host ID. In this lesson, you learn about the A, B, and C IP address classes.

After this lesson, you will be able to:

- Identify the network ID and host ID in a class A, B, or C IP address.
- Determine the correct address class for various IP addresses.

Estimated lesson time: 15 minutes

The Internet community has defined five IP address classes to accommodate networks of varying sizes. Microsoft TCP/IP supports class A, B, and C addresses assigned to hosts. The class of address defines which bits are used for the network ID and which bits are used for the host ID. The class also defines the possible number of networks and the number of hosts per network.

You can identify the class of address by the number in the first octet. The 32-bit IP addressing scheme supports a total of 3,720,314,628 hosts. The following chart shows the network and host ID fields for class A, B, and C IP addressing.

Class	IP address	Network ID	Host ID
A	w.x.y.z	w	x.y.z
B	w.x.y.z	w.x	y.z
C	w.x.y.z	w.x.y	z

Class A

Class B

Class C

Class A

Class A addresses are assigned to networks with a very large number of hosts. The high-order bit in a class A address is always set to zero. The next 7 bits (completing the first octet) complete the network ID. The remaining 24 bits (the last three octets) represent the host ID. This allows for 126 networks and approximately 17 million hosts per network.

Class B

Class B addresses are assigned to medium-sized to large-sized networks. The two high-order bits in a class B address are always set to binary 1 0. The next 14 bits (completing the first two octets) complete the network ID. The remaining 16 bits (last two octets) represent the host ID. This allows for 16,384 networks and approximately 65,000 hosts per network.

Class C

Class C addresses are used for small LANs. The three high-order bits in a class C address are always set to binary 1 1 0. The next 21 bits (completing the first three octets) complete the network ID. The remaining 8 bits (last octet) represent the host ID. This allows for approximately 2 million networks and 254 hosts per network.

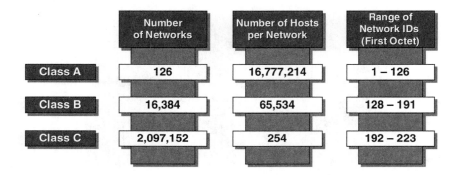

	Number of Networks	Number of Hosts per Network	Range of Network IDs (First Octet)
Class A	126	16,777,214	1 – 126
Class B	16,384	65,534	128 – 191
Class C	2,097,152	254	192 – 223

Note The network ID cannot be 127. This ID is reserved for loopback and diagnostic functions.

Class D

Class D addresses are used for multicast group usage. A multicast group can contain one or more hosts, or none at all. The four high-order bits in a class D address are always set to binary 1 1 1 0. The remaining bits designate the specific group in which the client participates. There are no network or host bits in the multicast operations. Packets are passed to a selected subset of hosts on a network. Only those hosts registered for the multicast address accept the packet. Microsoft supports class D addresses for applications to multicast data to hosts on an internetwork, including WINS and Microsoft NetShow™.

Class E

Class E is an experimental address not available for general use because it is reserved for future use. The high-order bits in a class E address are set to 1111.

Note For more information on multicasting, see the Multicasting white paper in the Additional Readings section of the *Course Materials* Web page on the course compact disc.

Practice

In this practice, you determine the correct address class for a given IP address and scenario.

1. Write the address class next to each IP address.

Address	Class
131.107.2.89	
3.3.57.0	
200.200.5.2	
191.107.2.10	

2. Which address class(es) allow you to have more than 1,000 hosts per network?

_____

3. Which address class(es) allow only 254 hosts per network?

_____

Summary

There are five address classes. Microsoft supports class A, B, and C addresses assigned to hosts. Each address class can accommodate networks of different sizes.

Lesson 3: Addressing Guidelines

Although there are no rules for how to assign IP addresses, you should follow certain guidelines to ensure that you are assigning valid network IDs and host IDs. This lesson explains how to assign IP addresses in a LAN environment.

After this lesson, you will be able to:

- Understand the guidelines for assigning valid IP addresses.
- Identify network components that require a network ID.
- Identify TCP/IP hosts that require a host ID.

Estimated lesson time: 35 minutes

There are several general guidelines you should follow when assigning network IDs and host IDs:

- The network ID cannot be 127. This ID is reserved for loopback and diagnostic functions.
- The network ID and host ID bits cannot all be 1's. If all bits are set to 1, the address is interpreted as a broadcast rather than a host ID.
- The network ID and host ID bits cannot all be 0's. If all bits are set to 0, the address is interpreted to mean "this network only."
- The host ID must be unique to the local network ID.

Assigning Network IDs

A unique network ID is required for each network and wide area connection. If you are connecting to the public Internet, you are required to obtain a network ID from the Internet Network Information Center (InterNIC). If you do not plan to connect to the public Internet, you can use any valid network ID.

The network ID identifies the TCP/IP hosts that are located on the same physical network. All hosts on the same physical network must be assigned the same network ID to communicate with each other.

If your networks are connected by routers, a unique network ID is required for each wide area connection. For example, in the following illustration:

- Networks 1 and 2 represent two routed networks.
- Network 2 represents the WAN connection between the routers.
- Network 2 requires a network ID so that the interfaces between the two routers can be assigned unique host IDs.

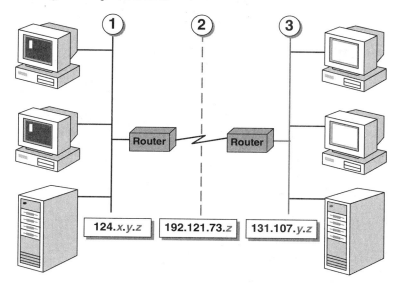

Note If you plan to connect your network to the Internet, you must obtain the network ID portion of the IP address. This will guarantee IP network ID uniqueness. For domain name registration and IP network number assignment, visit InterNIC's online registration services at http://internic.net. If you have any questions, call their registration help line at (703) 742-4777.

IP address allocation for private networks is defined in RFC 1918. For a copy of this RFC, see the *Course Materials* Web page on the course compact disc.

Assigning Host IDs

The host ID identifies a TCP/IP host within a network and must be unique to the network ID. All TCP/IP hosts, including interfaces to routers, require unique host IDs. The host ID of the router is the IP address configured as a workstation's default gateway. For example, for the host on subnet 1 with an IP address of 124.0.0.27, the IP address of the default gateway is 124.0.0.1.

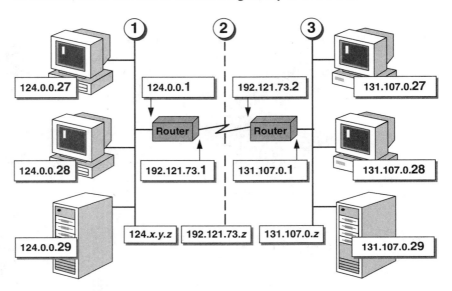

Valid Host IDs

The following table lists the valid ranges of host IDs for a private network.

Address class	Beginning range	Ending range
Class A	w.0.0.1	w.255.255.254
Class B	w.x.0.1	w.x.255.254
Class C	w.x.y.1	w.x.y.254

Suggestions for Assigning Host IDs

There are no rules for how to assign valid IP addresses. You can number all TCP/IP hosts consecutively, or you can number them so they can easily be identified—for example:

- Assign host IDs in groups based on host or server type.
- Designate routers by their IP address.

Organized numbering approaches such as these can help you prevent address conflicts from assigning duplicate IP addresses on a network.

Practice

In this practice, you identify which of the following IP addresses cannot be assigned to a host. Identify the IP addresses that would be invalid if it were assigned to a host, and then explain why it is invalid.

a. 131.107.256.80 _____

b. 222.222.255.222 _____

c. 231.200.1.1 _____

d. 126.1.0.0 _____

e. 0.127.4.100 _____

f. 190.7.2.0 _____

g. 127.1.1.1 _____

h. 198.121.254.255 _____

i. 255.255.255.255 _____

In this next practice, you decide which network components require IP addresses in a TCP/IP network environment. When a protocol is listed, assume it is the only protocol installed on the host. Review the following network components and circle the letter that corresponds to the components that do not require an IP address.

a. Microsoft Windows NT computer running TCP/IP

b. LAN Manager workstation that connects to a Windows NT computer running TCP/IP

c. Computer running Windows 95 that requires access to shared resources on a Windows NT-based computer running TCP/IP

d. UNIX host that you want to connect to using TCP/IP utilities

e. Network interface printer running TCP/IP

f. Router for connecting to a remote IP network

g. Ethernet port on local router

h. Microsoft LAN Manager workstation that is attempting to connect to a LAN Manager server running NetBEUI

i. Computer running Windows for Workgroups that requires access to shared resources on a LAN Manager server running NetBEUI

j. Serial plotter on a Windows NT-based computer running TCP/IP

k. Network printer shared off a LAN Manager server running NetBEUI

l. Communications server providing terminal access to TCP/IP host computers

m. Your default gateway

In this next practice, you decide which class of address will support the following IP network. Next, you assign a valid IP address to each type of host to easily distinguish it from other hosts (for example, UNIX, Windows NT servers, or Windows NT workstations). In this scenario, all computers are on the same subnet.

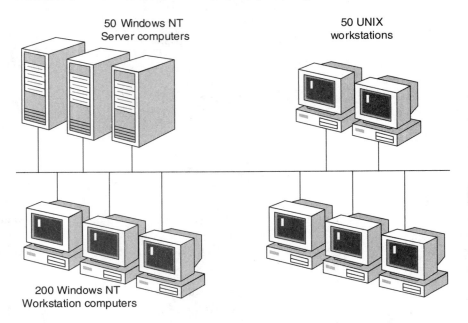

50 Windows NT
Server computers

50 UNIX
workstations

200 Windows NT
Workstation computers

Which address classes will support this network?

_____

Which of the following network addresses support this network?

a. 197.200.3.0

b. 11.0.0.0

c. 221.100.2.0

d. 131.107.0.0

Using the network ID that you chose, assign a range of host IDs to each type of host, so that you can easily distinguish the Windows NT Server computers from the Windows NT Workstation computers and the UNIX workstations.

Type of TCP/IP host	IP address range
Windows NT Server computers	
Windows NT Workstation computers	
UNIX workstations	

In this next practice, you decide how many network IDs and host IDs are required to support this network. Use the following illustration for reference.

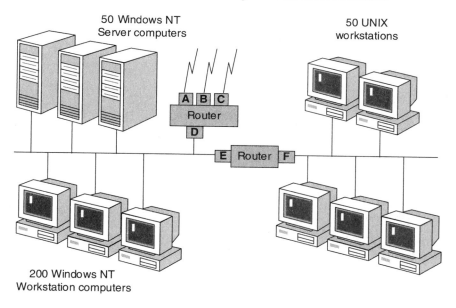

50 Windows NT Server computers

50 UNIX workstations

A B C
Router
D

E Router F

200 Windows NT Workstation computers

How many network IDs does this network environment require?

How many host IDs does this network environment require?

Which default gateway (router interface) would you assign to the Windows NT Workstation computers that communicate primarily with the UNIX workstations?

_____

Summary

There are several guidelines you should follow to make sure you assign valid IP addresses. All hosts on a given network must have the same network ID to communicate with each other. All TCP/IP hosts, including interfaces to routers, require unique host IDs.

Lesson 4: Subnet Mask and the IP Address

Each host on a TCP/IP network requires a subnet mask. This lesson describes the purpose of a subnet mask and how it is part of the process IP uses to route packets. You learn more about subnet masking in Chapter 5, "Subnetting."

After this lesson, you will be able to:

- Describe the function and purpose of a subnet mask.
- Use the ANDing process to determine an IP address destination.

Estimated lesson time: 15 minutes

A subnet mask is a 32-bit address used to block or "mask" a portion of the IP address to distinguish the network ID from the host ID. This is necessary so that TCP/IP can determine whether an IP address is located on a local or remote network.

Each host on a TCP/IP network requires a subnet mask—either a default subnet mask, which is used when a network is not divided into subnets, or a custom subnet mask, which is used when a network is divided into subnets.

Default Subnet Masks

A default subnet mask is used on TCP/IP networks that are not divided into subnets. All TCP/IP hosts require a subnet mask, even on a single-segment network. The default subnet mask you use depends on the address class.

In the subnet mask, all bits that correspond to the network ID are set to 1. The decimal value in each octet is 255. All bits that correspond to the host ID are set to 0.

Address Class	Bits Used for Subnet Mask				Dotted Decimal Notation
Class A	11111111	00000000	00000000	00000000	255.0.0.0
Class B	11111111	11111111	00000000	00000000	255.255.0.0
Class C	11111111	11111111	11111111	00000000	255.255.255.0

Class B Example

IP Address	131.107. 16.200
Subnet Mask	255.255. 0.0
Network ID	131.107. *y.z*
Host ID	*w.x.* 16.200

Determining the Destination of a Packet

ANDing is the internal process that IP uses to determine whether a packet is destined for a host on a local or remote network. Because ANDing is used internally by IP, you do not normally need to perform this task.

When TCP/IP is initialized, the host's IP address is ANDed with its subnet mask. Before a packet is sent, the destination IP address is ANDed with the same subnet mask. If the results of ANDing the source IP address and destination IP address match, IP knows that the packet belongs to a host on the local network. If the results do not match, the packet is sent to the IP address of an IP router.

To AND the IP address to a subnet mask, TCP/IP compares each bit in the IP address to the corresponding bit in the subnet mask. If both bits are 1's, the resulting bit is 1. If there is any other combination, the resulting bit is 0, as shown in the examples in the following table.

Bit combination	Result
1 AND 1	1
1 AND 0	0
0 AND 0	0
0 AND 1	0

IP Address	**10011111**	**11100000**	**00000111**	**10000001**
Subnet Mask	**11111111**	**11111111**	**00000000**	**00000000**

Result	**10011111**	**11100000**	**00000000**	**00000000**

Practice

In this practice, AND the following IP addresses to determine whether the destination IP address belongs to a host on a local network or a remote network.

Source (host) IP address	10011001 10101010 00100101 10100011
Subnet mask	11111111 11111111 00000000 00000000
Result	

Destination IP address	11011001 10101010 10101100 11101001
Subnet mask	11111111 11111111 00000000 00000000
Result	

1. Do the results match?

2. Is the destination IP address located on a local or remote network?

Summary

A default subnet mask is used on TCP/IP networks that are not divided into subnets. A custom subnet mask is used when a network is divided into subnets. ANDing is an internal IP process that determines whether a packet should be sent to a host on a local or remote network.

Lesson 5: IP Addressing with IP Version 6.0

Under the current 32-bit addressing scheme implemented in IP version 4.0 (IPv4), network IDs have become scarce. In this lesson, you learn about the future direction of IP addressing.

After this lesson, you will be able to:

- Explain how IP version 6.0 can help solve current network addressing problems.

Estimated lesson time: 5 minutes

The current IP header (known as version 4) has not been changed or upgraded since the 1970s. This is a tribute to its initial design. However, the initial design did not anticipate the growth of the Internet and the eventual exhaustion of the IP version 4.0 address space.

Therefore, a new version of IP called IPv6 has been developed. This new version, once known as IP—The Next Generation (IPng), incorporates the ideas of many different proposed methods of creating a newer version of the IP protocol.

IPv6 was created to solve the current network addressing problems and provide a long-term solution for address space depletion. IPv6 uses 16 octets. When written, it is divided into 8 octet pairs, separated by colons. The octets are represented in hexadecimal.

IPv6 is an entirely new packet structure which is incompatible with IPv4 systems, but has several benefits such as an extended address space, a simplified header format, support for time-dependent traffic, and the ability add new features.

Extended address space is one primary feature of IPv6. IPv6 has 128-bit source and destination IP addresses (four times larger than IPv4). 128 bits can express over 3×10^{38} possible combinations, thereby allowing an abundance of addresses for the foreseeable future. With IPv6, a valid IP address may appear as:

    4A3F:AE67:F240:56C4:3409:AE52:440F:1403

The IPv6 headers are designed to keep the IP header overhead to a minimum by moving nonessential fields and option fields to extension headers that are placed after the IP header. Anything not included in the base IPv6 header can be added through IP extension headers placed after the base IPv6 header.

A new field in the IPv6 header allows the preallocation of network resources along a path so that time-dependent services such as voice and video are guaranteed a requested bandwidth with a fixed delay.

One final benefit is that IPv6 can easily be extended for unforeseen features through the adding of extension headers after the IPv6 base header. Support for new hardware or application technologies is built in.

Note IPv6 is defined in RFC 1883. For a copy of this RFC, see the *Course Materials* Web page on the course compact disc.

Summary

Under the current implementation of IP, network IDs have become scarce. IPv6 is an entirely new packet structure which has several benefits such as extended address space, a simplified header format, support for time-dependent traffic, and the ability to be extended for new features.

Review

The following questions are intended to reinforce key information presented in this chapter. If you are unable to answer a question, review the appropriate lesson and then try the question again.

1. In class A, class B, and class C addresses, which octets represent the network ID and which represent the host ID?

2. Which numbers are invalid as a network ID and why? Which numbers are invalid as a host ID and why?

3. When is a unique network ID required?

4. In a TCP/IP internetwork, what components require a host ID besides computers?

Review Practice

In this review practice, you examine two examples of IP networks, identify hidden IP addressing problems, and explain the possible effects caused by the problems.

For the following illustration, list all IP addressing problems, and explain how each problem may affect communications. Are the IP addresses and default gateway addresses appropriate for each situation?

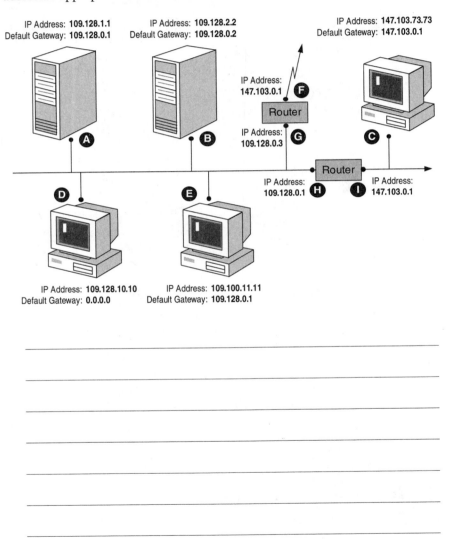

IP Address: **109.128.1.1**
Default Gateway: **109.128.0.1**

IP Address: **109.128.2.2**
Default Gateway: **109.128.0.2**

IP Address: **147.103.73.73**
Default Gateway: **147.103.0.1**

IP Address: **147.103.0.1**   **F**

Router

IP Address: **109.128.0.3**   **G**

Router

IP Address: **109.128.0.1**   **H**   **I**   IP Address: **147.103.0.1**

IP Address: **109.128.10.10**
Default Gateway: **0.0.0.0**

IP Address: **109.100.11.11**
Default Gateway: **109.128.0.1**

For the following illustration, list all IP addressing problems, and explain how each problem may affect communications. Are the IP addresses and default gateway addresses appropriate for each situation?

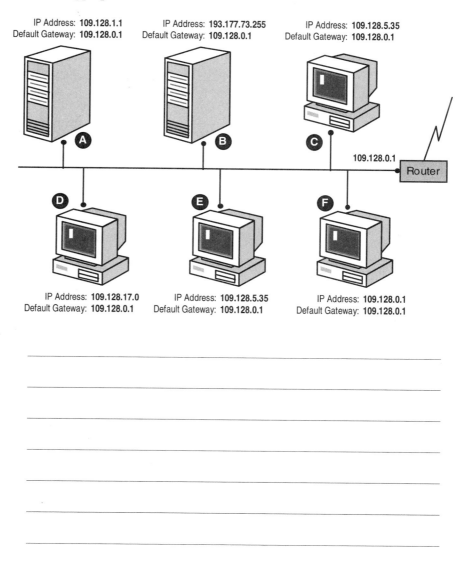

IP Address: **109.128.1.1**
Default Gateway: **109.128.0.1**

IP Address: **193.177.73.255**
Default Gateway: **109.128.0.1**

IP Address: **109.128.5.35**
Default Gateway: **109.128.0.1**

109.128.0.1

Router

IP Address: **109.128.17.0**
Default Gateway: **109.128.0.1**

IP Address: **109.128.5.35**
Default Gateway: **109.128.0.1**

IP Address: **109.128.0.1**
Default Gateway: **109.128.0.1**

For More Information

- Review all referenced RFCs on the course compact disc.

CHAPTER 5

Subnetting

Lesson 1 Subnet Overview . . . 82

Lesson 2 Defining a Subnet Mask . . . 85

Lesson 3 Defining Subnet IDs . . . 93

Lesson 4 Defining Host IDs for a Subnet . . . 96

Lesson 5 Supernetting . . . 103

Review . . . 106

About This Chapter

In this chapter, you learn how to assign IP addresses to multiple TCP/IP networks with a single network ID. The lessons provide fundamental concepts and procedures for implementing subnetting and supernetting. During the lessons, you learn when subnetting is necessary, how and when to use a default subnet mask, how to define a custom subnet mask, and how to create a range of valid IP addresses for each subnet.

Before You Begin

To complete the lessons in this chapter, you must have:

- An understanding of the ANDing and IP addressing concepts presented in Chapter 4, "IP Addressing."

- Installed Microsoft Windows NT Server 4.0 with TCP/IP.

Lesson 1: Subnet Overview

A subnet is a physical segment in a TCP/IP environment that uses IP addresses derived from a single network ID. Typically, an organization acquires one network ID from the InterNIC. In this lesson, you learn the requirements for subnetting.

After this lesson, you will be able to:

- Explain the purpose and benefits of a subnet.

Estimated lesson time: 10 minutes

Dividing the network into subnets requires that each segment use a different network ID, or subnet ID. As shown in the following example, a unique subnet ID is created for each segment by partitioning the bits in the host ID into two parts. One part is used to identify the segment as a unique network, and the other part is used to identify the hosts. This is referred to as *subnetting* or *subnetworking*. Subnetting is not necessary if your network is private.

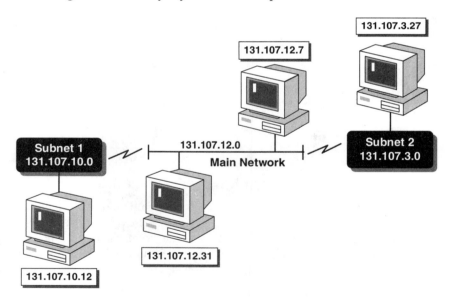

There are several benefits to subnetting. Organizations use subnetting to apply one network across multiple physical segments. With subnetting you can:

- Mix different technologies, such as Ethernet and Token Ring.
- Overcome limitations of current technologies, such as exceeding the maximum number of hosts per segment.
- Reduce network congestion by redirecting traffic and reducing broadcasts.

Note   Subnetting is defined in RFC 950. For a copy of this RFC, see the *Course Materials* Web page on the course compact disc.

Implementing Subnetting

Before you implement subnetting, you need to determine your current requirements and plan for future requirements. Follow these guidelines:

1. Determine the number of physical segments on your network.
2. Determine the number of required host addresses for each physical segment. Each TCP/IP host requires at least one IP address.
3. Based on your requirements, define:
    - One subnet mask for your entire network.
    - A unique subnet ID for each physical segment.
    - A range of host IDs for each subnet.

Subnet Mask Bits

Before you define a subnet mask, you should determine the number of segments and hosts per segment you will require in the future.

When more bits are used for the subnet mask, more subnets are available, but fewer hosts are available per subnet. For example, the following class B examples show the correlation between the number of bits and the number of subnets and hosts:

> 3 bits=6 subnets=8,000 hosts per subnet
>
> 8 bits=254 subnets=254 hosts per subnet

If you use more bits than needed, it will allow for growth in the number of subnets, but will limit the growth in the number of hosts. If you use fewer bits than needed, it will allow for growth in the number of hosts, but will limit the growth in the number of subnets.

Summary

A subnet is a physical segment in a TCP/IP environment that uses IP addresses from a single network ID. The IP addressing scheme used for subnets is referred to as *subnetting*. The number bits in the subnet mask will determine the number of subnets and hosts per subnets available to you.

Lesson 2: Defining a Subnet Mask

Defining a subnet mask is a three-step process. In this lesson, you learn the three steps and perform several practices to define subnets.

After this lesson, you will be able to:
- Explain the function of a custom subnet mask.
- Define a valid subnet mask for a variety of situations.

Estimated lesson time: 45 minutes

Defining a subnet mask is required if you are dividing your network into subnets. Follow these steps to define a subnet mask:

1. Once you have determined the number of physical segments in your network environment, convert this number to binary format.

2. Count the number of bits required to represent the number of physical segments in binary. For example, if you need six subnets, the binary value is 110. Representing six in binary requires 3 bits.

3. Convert the required number of bits to decimal format in high order (from left to right). For example, if 3 bits are required, configure the first 3 bits of the host ID as the subnet ID. The decimal value for binary 11100000 is 224. The subnet mask then is 255.255.224.0 (for a class B address).

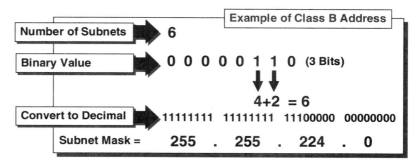

Contiguous Mask Bits

Because subnets are defined by the subnet mask, there is nothing to prevent an administrator from using low-order or unordered bits to determine the subnet ID. When subnetting was initially defined in RFC 950, it was recommended that subnet IDs be derived from high-order bits. Today, however, few router vendors support the use of low-order or non-order bits in subnet IDs. Furthermore, it is now a requirement that the subnet ID make use of contiguous, high-order bits of the local address portion of the subnet mask.

Conversion Tables

The following table lists the subnet masks already converted using one octet for class A networks.

Number of subnets	Required number of bits	Subnet mask	Number of hosts per subnet
0	1	Invalid	Invalid
2	2	255.192.0.0	4,194,302
6	3	255.224.0.0	2,097,150
14	4	255.240.0.0	1,048,574
30	5	255.248.0.0	524,286
62	6	255.252.0.0	262,142
126	7	255.254.0.0	131,070
254	8	255.255.0.0	65,534

The following table lists the subnet masks already converted using one octet for class B networks.

Number of subnets	Required number of bits	Subnet mask	Number of hosts per subnet
0	1	Invalid	Invalid
2	2	255.255.192.0	16,382
6	3	255.255.224.0	8,190
14	4	255.255.240.0	4,094
30	5	255.255.248.0	2,046
62	6	255.255.252.0	1,022
126	7	255.255.254.0	510
254	8	255.255.255.0	254

The following table lists the subnet masks already converted using one octet for class C networks.

Number of subnets	Required Number of bits	Subnet mask	Number of hosts per subnet
Invalid	1	Invalid	Invalid
1–2	2	255.255.255.192	62
3–6	3	255.255.255.224	30
7–14	4	255.255.255.240	14
15–30	5	255.255.255.248	6
31–62	6	255.255.255.252	2
Invalid	7	Invalid	Invalid
Invalid	8	Invalid	Invalid

Subnetting More Than One Octet

During this lesson, you have worked within one octet to define a subnet mask. At times, it may be advantageous to subnet using more than one octet, or more than 8 bits. This will give you greater addressing flexibility.

For example, suppose you are configuring an intranet for a large corporation. The corporation plans to internally connect its sites that are distributed across Europe, North America, and Asia. This totals approximately 30 geographical locations with almost 1,000 subnets and an average of 750 hosts per subnet.

It is possible to use several class B network IDs and further subnet them. To meet your host requirements per subnet with a class B network address, you need to use a subnet mask of 255.255.252.0. Adding our requirement of subnets, you need at least 16 class B addresses.

However, there is an easier way. Because the computers you are using are on an intranet, you can use a private network. If you choose to allocate a class A network ID of 10.0.0.0, you can plan for growth and meet your requirements at the same time. Obviously, subnetting only the second octet will not meet your requirements of one thousand subnets. However, if you subnet both the second octet and a portion of the third octet, you can meet all of your requirements with one network ID.

Network ID	Subnet mask	Subnet mask (binary)
10.0.0.0	255.255.248.0	1111111111 11111111 11111000 00000000

Using 13 bits for the subnet ID in a class A address, you have allocated 8,190 subnets, each with up to 2,046 hosts. You have met your requirements with flexibility for growth.

Practice

In this practice, you define a subnet mask for several situations. Remember that not every situation requires subnetting.

1. Class A network address on a local network.

    _____

2. Class B network address on a local network with 4,000 hosts.

    _____

3. Class C network address on a local network with 254 hosts.

    _____

4. Class A address with 6 subnets.

    _____

5. Class B address with 126 subnets.

    _____

6. Class A network address. Currently, there are 30 subnets that will grow to approximately 65 subnets within the next year. Each subnet will never have more than 50,000 hosts.

    _____

7. Using the subnet mask from the preceding scenario, how much growth will this subnet mask provide?

    _____

8. Class B network address. Currently, there are 14 subnets that may double in size within the next two years. Each subnet will have fewer than 1,500 hosts.

    _____

9. Using the subnet mask from the preceding scenario, how much growth will this subnet mask provide?

    _____

Practice

In this practice, you review two invalid subnet masks to see what would happen when you try to communicate with a host on a local network and a remote network.

Using the information below, convert your computer's IP address and the IP address of your second computer to binary format, and then AND them to the subnet mask to determine why the subnet mask is invalid.

Your IP address	131.107.2.200	1 0 0 0 0 0 1 1 0 1 1 0 1 0 1 1 0 0 0 0 0 0 1 0 1 1 0 0 1 0 0 0
Subnet mask	255.255.255.248	1 1 1 1 1 1 1 1 1 1 1 1 1 1 1 1 1 1 1 1 1 1 1 1 1 1 1 1 1 0 0 0
Result		
Destination IP address	131.107.2.211	1 0 0 0 0 0 1 1 0 1 1 0 1 0 1 1 0 0 0 0 0 0 1 0 1 1 0 1 0 0 1 1
Subnet mask	255.255.255.248	1 1 1 1 1 1 1 1 1 1 1 1 1 1 1 1 1 1 1 1 1 1 1 1 1 1 1 1 1 0 0 0
Result		

Did the result of ANDing indicate that the destination IP address and subnet mask were for a local or remote network?

_____

Why would you not be able to successfully ping your default gateway?

_____

Using the information below, convert your IP address and the IP address of a remote host to binary format, and then AND them to the subnet mask to determine why the subnet mask would be invalid.

Your IP address	131.107.2.200	1 0 0 0 0 0 1 1 0 1 1 0 1 0 1 1 0 0 0 0 0 0 1 0 1 1 0 0 1 0 0 0
Subnet mask	255.255.0.0	1 1 1 1 1 1 1 1 1 1 1 1 1 1 1 1 0 0 0 0 0 0 0 0 0 0 0 0 0 0 0 0
Result		
Destination IP address	131.107.2.211	1 0 0 0 0 0 1 1 0 1 1 0 1 0 1 1 0 0 0 0 0 0 1 0 1 1 0 1 0 0 1 1
Subnet mask	255.255.0.0	1 1 1 1 1 1 1 1 1 1 1 1 1 1 1 1 0 0 0 0 0 0 0 0 0 0 0 0 0 0 0 0
Result		

Did the result of ANDing indicate that the destination IP address and subnet mask were for a local or remote network?

_____

Why would you not be able to successfully ping a remote host?

_____

Compare the two results generated using incorrect subnet masks to see how differently TCP/IP responds when the subnet mask indicates a local network versus a remote network. What did you conclude about how TCP/IP uses a subnet mask?

_____

_____

_____

_____

Practice

In this practice, you review the following two examples, identify the hidden problems, and then explain the possible effects caused by the problems.

Example 1

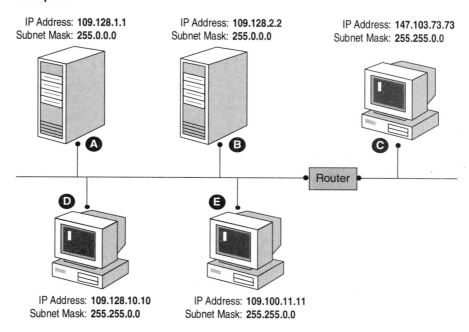

IP Address: **109.128.1.1**
Subnet Mask: **255.0.0.0**

IP Address: **109.128.2.2**
Subnet Mask: **255.0.0.0**

IP Address: **147.103.73.73**
Subnet Mask: **255.255.0.0**

IP Address: **109.128.10.10**
Subnet Mask: **255.255.0.0**

IP Address: **109.100.11.11**
Subnet Mask: **255.255.0.0**

Which hosts have an incorrect subnet mask?

_____

How will an invalid subnet mask affect these hosts?

_____

What is the correct subnet mask?

_____

Example 2

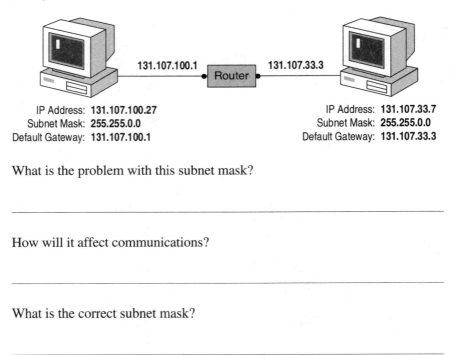

131.107.100.1   Router   131.107.33.3

IP Address: **131.107.100.27**
Subnet Mask: **255.255.0.0**
Default Gateway: **131.107.100.1**

IP Address: **131.107.33.7**
Subnet Mask: **255.255.0.0**
Default Gateway: **131.107.33.3**

What is the problem with this subnet mask?

_____

How will it affect communications?

_____

What is the correct subnet mask?

_____

Summary

If you are dividing your network into subnets, you must define a subnet mask. The steps for defining a subnet mask are converting the number of physical network segments to binary format, counting the number of required bits, and then converting the number of required bits to decimal format. You can subnet more than 8 bits to give you greater addressing flexibility.

Lesson 3: Defining Subnet IDs

Subnet IDs are defined using the same number of host bits as are used for the subnet mask. There are different ways to define a range of subnet IDs for an internetwork. In this lesson, the long and the short methods are discussed.

After this lesson, you will be able to:

- Use different methods to define a range of subnet IDs for an internetwork.

- Define a common subnet mask for a WAN that consists of multiple subnets.

Estimated lesson time: 20 minutes

You can define the subnet ID for a physical segment using the same number of host bits as used for the subnet mask. The possible bit combinations are evaluated and then converted to a decimal format. The following steps and illustration show how to define a range of subnet IDs for an internetwork:

1. Using the same number of bits as are used for the subnet mask, list all possible bit combinations.

2. Cross out values that use all 0's or 1's. All 0's and 1's are invalid IP addresses and network IDs, because all 0's indicate "this network only" and all 1's match the subnet mask.

3. Convert to decimal the subnet ID bits for each subnet. Each decimal value represents a single subnet. This value is used to define the range of host IDs for a subnet.

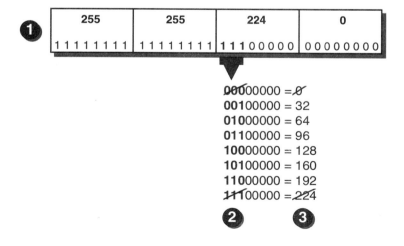

Special-Case Subnet Addresses

Subnet IDs comprised of all 0's or all 1's are called *special-case subnet addresses*. A subnet ID of all 1's indicates a subnet broadcast, and a subnet ID of all 0's indicates "this subnet." When subnetting, it is recommended not to use these subnet IDs. However, it is possible to use these special-case subnet addresses if they are supported by all routers and hardware on your network. RFC 950 discusses the limitations imposed when using special-case addresses.

Shortcut to Defining Subnet IDs

Using the preceding method to define a subnet ID is impractical when you are using more than 4 bits for your subnet mask because it requires listing and converting many bit combinations. The following steps and illustration demonstrate how to use the shortcut to define a range of subnet IDs:

1. List the number of bits in high order used for the subnet ID. For example, if 2 bits are used for the subnet mask, the binary octet is 11000000.

2. Convert the bit with the lowest value to decimal format. This is the increment value to determine each subnet. For example, if you use 2 bits, the lowest value is 64.

3. Starting with zero, increment the value for each bit combination until the next increment is 256.

Tip If you know the number of bits you need, you can raise 2 to the power of the bit, and then subtract 2 to determine the possible bit combinations.

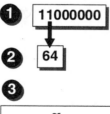

1 | 11000000 |

2 | 64 |

3

```
       0̸
    +  64
    =  64    w.x.64.1  ➡  w.x.127.254
    +  64
    = 128    w.x.128.1 ➡  w.x.191.254
    +  64
      192̸
```

Practice

In this additional practice, you determine the appropriate subnet mask for a given range of IP addresses.

1. Address range of 128.71.1.1 through 128.71.254.254.

2. Address range of 61.8.0.1 through 61.15.255.254.

3. Address range of 172.88.32.1 through 172.88.63.254.

4. Address range of 111.224.0.1 through 111.239.255.254.

5. Address range of 3.64.0.1 through 3.127.255.254.

Summary

You can define a range of subnet IDs using a long and short method. Using the long method is impractical when you are using more than 4 bits for your subnet mask.

Lesson 4: Defining Host IDs for a Subnet

You can follow a short procedure to determine the number of hosts per subnet. In fact, if you have defined your subnet IDs, then you have already defined your host IDs for each subnet. This lesson shows you how to define the host IDs for a subnet, and lets you practice the procedure in several practices.

After this lesson, you will be able to:
- Define a range of host IDs for a subnet using the subnet ID.

Estimated lesson time: 30 minutes

The result of each incremented value indicates the beginning of a range of host IDs for a subnet. If you increment the value one extra time, you can determine the end of the range (one less than the subnet mask), as shown in the following illustration.

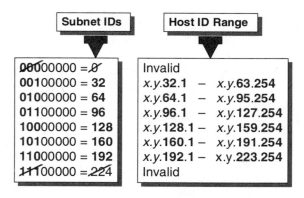

The following table shows the valid range of host IDs on a class B subnet using 3 bits for the subnet mask.

Bit values	Decimal value	Beginning range value	Ending range value
00000000	0	Invalid	Invalid
00100000	32	x.y.32.1	x.y.63.254
01000000	64	x.y.64.1	x.y.95.254
01100000	96	x.y.96.1	x.y.127.254
10000000	128	x.y.128.1	x.y.159.254
10100000	160	x.y.160.1	x.y.191.254
11000000	192	x.y.192.1	x.y.223.254
11100000	224	Invalid	Invalid

▶ **To determine the number of hosts per subnet**

1. Calculate the number of bits available for the host ID. For example, if you are given a class B address that uses 16 bits for the network ID and 2 bits for the subnet ID, you have 14 bits remaining for the host ID.

2. Convert the binary host ID bits to decimal. For example, 11111111111111 in binary is converted to 16,383 in decimal format.

3. Subtract 1.

Tip If you know the number of host ID bits you need, you can raise 2 to the power of the number of host ID bits, and then subtract 2.

Practice

In the following practices, you define a range of network IDs. Refer to the following illustration to complete the practices.

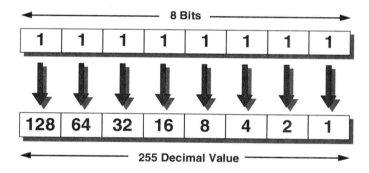

Defining a Range of Network IDs for Two Subnets

In this practice, you define a range of network IDs for an internetwork that consists of two subnets, using 2 bits from a class B subnet mask.

1. List all possible bit combinations for the following subnet mask, and then convert them to decimal format to determine the beginning value of each subnet.

255	255	192	0
1 1 1 1 1 1 1 1	1 1 1 1 1 1 1 1	**1 1** 0 0 0 0 0 0	0 0 0 0 0 0 0 0

Invalid	0 0 0 0 0 0 0 0	=	0
Subnet 1	_____	=	_____
Subnet 2	_____	=	_____
Invalid	1 1 0 0 0 0 0 0	=	192 (subnet mask)

2. List the range of host IDs for each subnet.

Subnet	Beginning value	Ending value
Subnet 1	*w.x.*_____.1	*w.x.*_____.254
Subnet 2	*w.x.*_____.1	*w.x.*_____.254

Defining a Range of Network IDs for 14 Subnets

In this practice, you define a range of network IDs for an internetwork that consists of 14 subnets, using 4 bits from a class B subnet mask.

1. List all possible bit combinations for the following subnet mask, and then convert them to decimal format to determine the beginning value of each subnet.

255	255	240	0
1 1 1 1 1 1 1 1	1 1 1 1 1 1 1 1	**1 1 1 1** 0 0 0 0	0 0 0 0 0 0 0 0

Invalid	0 0 0 0 0 0 0 0	=	0
Subnet 1	_____	=	_____
Subnet 2	_____	=	_____
Subnet 3	_____	=	_____
Subnet 4	_____	=	_____
Subnet 5	_____	=	_____
Subnet 6	_____	=	_____
Subnet 7	_____	=	_____
Subnet 8	_____	=	_____
Subnet 9	_____	=	_____
Subnet 10	_____	=	_____
Subnet 11	_____	=	_____
Subnet 12	_____	=	_____
Subnet 13	_____	=	_____
Subnet 14	_____	=	_____
Invalid	1 1 1 1 0 0 0 0	=	240 (subnet mask)

2. List the range of host IDs for each subnet.

Subnet	Beginning value	Ending value
Subnet 1	w.x._____.1	w.x._____.254
Subnet 2	w.x._____.1	w.x._____.254
Subnet 3	w.x._____.1	w.x._____.254
Subnet 4	w.x._____.1	w.x._____.254
Subnet 5	w.x._____.1	w.x._____.254
Subnet 6	w.x._____.1	w.x._____.254
Subnet 7	w.x._____.1	w.x._____.254
Subnet 8	w.x._____.1	w.x._____.254
Subnet 9	w.x._____.1	w.x._____.254
Subnet 10	w.x._____.1	w.x._____.254
Subnet 11	w.x._____.1	w.x._____.254
Subnet 12	w.x._____.1	w.x._____.254
Subnet 13	w.x._____.1	w.x._____.254
Subnet 14	w.x._____.1	w.x._____.254

Defining a Range of Network IDs Using a Shortcut

In this practice, you use a shortcut to define a range of network IDs for 14 subnets. Compare these results to the results in the preceding practice. The two should match. The first step has been done for you.

1. List the number of bits (in high order) that will be used for the subnet mask.

255	255	240	0
1 1 1 1 1 1 1 1	1 1 1 1 1 1 1 1	1 1 1 1 0 0 0 0	0 0 0 0 0 0 0 0

2. Convert the bit with the lowest value to decimal format.

_____

3. Convert the number of bits to decimal format (in low order), and then subtract 1 to determine the number of possible subnets.

_____

4. Starting with 0, increment by the value calculated in step 2 the same number of times as the possible bit combinations calculated in step 3.

_____

_____

_____

_____

_____

_____

_____

_____

_____

_____

_____

_____

_____

_____

_____

_____

Practice

In this additional practice, you define a range of host IDs for each of the following subnets.

1. Network ID of 75.0.0.0, subnet mask of 255.255.0.0, and 2 subnets.

2. Network ID of 150.17.0.0, subnet mask of 255.255.255.0, and 4 subnets.

3. Network IDs of 107.16.0.0 and 107.32.0.0, subnet mask of 255.240.0.0, and 2 subnets.

4. Network IDs of 190.1.16.0, 190.1.32.0, 190.1.48.0, and 190.1.64.0, subnet mask of 255.255.248.0, and 4 subnets.

5. Network IDs of 154.233.32.0, 154.233.96.0, and 154.233.160.0, subnet mask of 255.255.224.0, and 3 subnets.

Summary

To determine the number of hosts per subnet you use three steps. First, calculate the number of bits available for the host ID, then convert the binary host ID bits to decimal, and finally, subtract 1.

Lesson 5: Supernetting

To prevent the depletion of network IDs, the Internet authorities devised a scheme called *supernetting*. This lesson gives you an overview of supernetting.

After this lesson, you will be able to:

- Describe the concept of supernetting.

Estimated lesson time: 10 minutes

Supernetting is different than subnetting in that it borrows bits from the network ID and masks them as the host ID for more efficient routing. For example, rather than allocating a class B network ID to an organization that has 2,000 hosts, the InterNIC allocates a range of 8 class C network IDs. Each class C network ID accommodates 254 hosts for a total of 2,032 host IDs.

While this technique helps conserve class B network IDs, it creates a new problem. Using conventional routing techniques, the routers on the Internet now must have an additional seven entries in their routing tables to route IP packets to the organization. To prevent overwhelming the Internet routers, a technique called *Classless Inter-Domain Routing* (CIDR) is used to collapse the eight entries used in the following illustration to a single entry corresponding to all of the class C network IDs used by that organization.

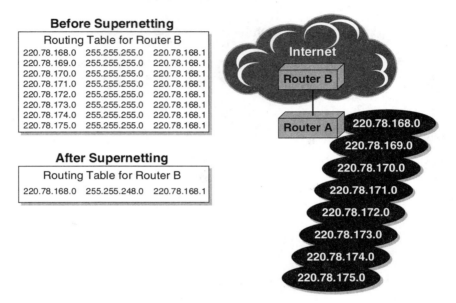

To express the situation in which eight class C network IDs are allocated starting with the network ID 220.78.168.0 and ending with network ID 220.78.175.0, the entry in the routing table becomes:

Network ID	Subnet mask	Subnet mask (binary)
220.78.168.0	255.255.248.0	11111111 11111111 11111000 00000000

In supernetting, the destination of a packet is determined by ANDing the destination IP address and the subnet mask of the routing entry. If a match is found to the network ID, the route is used. This is the same process defined in the preceding lesson.

Note *Classless Inter-Domain Routing* (CIDR) is defined in RFCs 1518 and 1519. For copies of these RFCs, see the *Course Materials* Web page on the course compact disc.

Summary

Supernetting borrows bits from the network ID and masks them as the host ID for more efficient routing.

Review

The following questions are intended to reinforce key information presented in this chapter. If you are unable to answer a question, review the appropriate lesson and then try the question again. The scenario-based review practices will help you use key information in real-world situations.

1. What is the purpose of a subnet mask?

   _____

   _____

2. What requires a subnet mask?

   _____

   _____

3. When is a default subnet mask used?

   _____

   _____

4. When is it necessary to define a custom subnet mask?

   _____

   _____

Review Practice

In the following review practices, you define a subnetting scheme for several scenarios. For each scenario, define the following:

- A subnet mask.
- A range of valid network IDs.
- A default gateway for hosts on each subnet.

After you have defined this information for each scenario, answer the questions that follow.

Scenario 1

You have been assigned one class B address of 131.107.0.0 by the InterNIC. Your intranet currently has 5 subnets. Each subnet has approximately 300 hosts. Within the next year the number of subnets will triple. The number of hosts on three of the subnets could increase to as many as 1,000.

1. How many bits did you use for the subnet mask?

   _____

   _____

2. How much growth did you allow for additional subnets?

   _____

   _____

3. How much growth did you allow for additional hosts?

   _____

   _____

Scenario 2

You have been assigned one class A address of 124.0.0.0 by the InterNIC. Your private internet currently has 5 subnets. Each subnet has approximately 500,000 hosts. In the near future, you would like to divide the 5 subnets into 25 smaller, more manageable subnets. The number of hosts on the 25 new subnets could eventually increase to 300,000.

1. How many bits did you use for the subnet mask?

   _____

   _____

2. How much growth did you allow for additional subnets?

   _____

   _____

3. How much growth did you allow for additional hosts?

_____

_____

Scenario 3

You have 5 subnets with approximately 300 hosts on each subnet. Within the next 6 months, the number of subnets could increase to more than 100. The number of hosts on each subnet will probably never be more than 2,000. You do not have any plans to connect to the worldwide public Internet.

1. Which class of address did you use?

_____

_____

2. How many bits did you use for the subnet mask?

_____

_____

3. How much growth did you allow for additional subnets?

_____

_____

4. How much growth did you allow for additional hosts?

_____

_____

Scenario 4

An Internet service provider has just been assigned the block of 2,048 class C network numbers beginning with 192.24.0.0 and ending with 192.31.255.0.

1. What IP address would begin a "supernetted" route to this block of numbers?

_____

2. What net mask would be used to supernet this block of numbers?

_____

Customers of this Internet service provider have the following requirements:

-   Customer 1 will not have more than 2,023 hosts.
-   Customer 2 will not have more than 4,047 hosts.
-   Customer 3 will not have more than 1,011 hosts.
-   Customer 4 will not have more than 500 hosts.

Assign the missing IP and subnet mask values for each customer.

1. Customer 1
    Beginning IP address   192.24.0.1
    Ending IP address   192.24.7.8
    Subnet mask   _____

2. Customer 2
    Beginning IP address   _____
    Ending IP address   192.24.31.254
    Subnet mask   255.255.240.0

3. Customer 3
    Beginning IP address   192.24.8.1
    Ending IP address   _____
    Subnet mask   255.255.252.0

4. Customer 4
    Beginning IP address   192.24.14.1
    Ending IP address   192.24.15.254
    Subnet mask   _____

For More Information

-   Review all referenced RFCs on the course compact disc.

C H A P T E R   6

Implementing IP Routing

Lesson 1   IP Routing Overview . . . 112

Lesson 2   Static IP Routing . . . 115

Lesson 3   Dynamic IP Routing . . . 121

Lesson 4   Implementing a Windows NT Router . . . 126

Review . . . 128

About This Chapter

In this chapter, you review IP routing concepts and describe how to implement IP routing on a computer running Microsoft Windows NT 4.0. The lessons explain how to build a static routing table, configure a Windows NT computer to function as an IP router, detect default gateway failure, and use the Route utility to add static routes to the route table.

Before You Begin

To complete the lessons in this chapter, you must have installed Windows NT Server 4.0 with TCP/IP.

Lesson 1: IP Routing Overview

Routing is the process of choosing a path over which to send packets. Routing occurs at a TCP/IP host when it sends IP packets, and occurs again at an IP router. A *router* is a device that forwards the packets from one physical network to another. Routers are commonly referred to as *gateways*. This lesson explains basic IP routing concepts.

After this lesson, you will be able to:

- Understand basic IP routing concepts.

- Explain the difference between static and dynamic IP routing.

Estimated lesson time: 10 minutes

For both the sending host and router, a decision has to be made as to where the packet is to be forwarded. To make routing decisions, the IP layer consults a routing table that is stored in memory as shown in the following illustration. A routing table contains entries with the IP addresses of router interfaces to other networks that it can communicate with. By default, a router can send packets only to networks to which it has a configured interface.

1. When a host attempts communication with another host, IP first determines whether the destination host is local or on a remote network.

2. If the destination host is remote, IP then checks the routing table for a route to the remote host or remote network.

3. If no explicit route is found, IP uses its default gateway address to deliver the packet to a router.

4. At the router, the routing table is again consulted for a path to the remote host or network. If a path is not found, the packet is sent to the router's default gateway address.

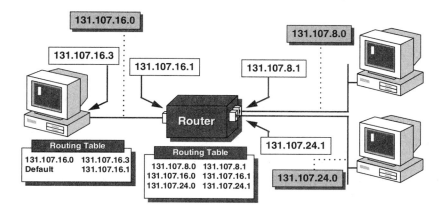

As each route is found, the packet is sent to the next router, called a "hop," and finally delivered to the destination host. If a route is not found, an error message is sent to the source host.

Dead Gateway Detection

TCP can detect the failure of the default gateway and make the necessary adjustments to the IP routing table to use another default gateway. TCP will attempt to send a packet to the default gateway configured on a computer until it receives an acknowledgment. However, if one-half of the *TcpMaxDataRetransmissions* value is exceeded and multiple gateways are configured on the computer, TCP requests that IP switch to the next default gateway in the list.

When you configure a computer running Windows NT with the IP addresses of multiple gateways, by default, dead gateway detection is set to **on**.

Note The Microsoft implementation of dead gateway detection uses TCP retries and the triggered reselection method described in RFC 816. For a copy of this RFC, see the *Course Materials* Web page on the course compact disc.

Static vs. Dynamic IP Routing

How routers obtain routing information depends on whether the router performs static or dynamic IP routing. Static routing is a function of IP. Static routers require that routing tables are built and updated manually. If a route changes, static routers do not inform each other of the change, nor do static routers exchange routes with dynamic routers.

Dynamic routing is a function of routing protocols, such as the Routing Information Protocol (RIP) and Open Shortest Path First (OSPF). Routing protocols periodically exchange routes to known networks among dynamic routers. If a route changes, other routers are automatically informed of the change.

Windows NT Server version 4.0 can function as an IP router using both static and dynamic routing. A computer running Windows NT can be configured with multiple network adapters and route between them. This type of system, which is ideal for small intranets, is referred to as a *multihomed computer*.

Windows NT Server 4.0 provides the ability to function as an RIP router that supports dynamic management of IP routing tables. RIP eliminates the need to establish static IP routing tables.

Note Microsoft provides support for inter-routing protocols on Windows NT 4.0. RIP is defined in RFC 1723. For copy of this RFC, see the *Course Materials* Web page on the course compact disc.

Summary

Routers forward packets from one physical network to another. The IP layer consults a routing table that is stored in memory. A routing table contains entries with the IP addresses of router interfaces to other networks. Static routers require that routing tables are built and updated manually. With dynamic routing, if a route changes, other routers are automatically informed of the change.

Lesson 2: Static IP Routing

A static router can communicate only with networks to which it has a configured interface. This lesson explains how to configure a static router and modify a routing table.

After this lesson, you will be able to:
- Explain the requirements for communicating with a static IP router.
- Build a static routing table.

Estimated lesson time: 25 minutes

To route IP packets to other networks, each static router must be configured. You should add either an entry in each router's routing table for each network in the internetwork, or a default gateway address of another router's local interface. As shown in the following illustration:

- Computer A has only local connections to networks 1 and 2. As a result, hosts on network 1 can communicate with hosts on network 2, but cannot communicate with hosts on network 3.

- Computer B has only local connections to networks 2 and 3. Hosts on network 3 can communicate with hosts on network 2, but cannot communicate with hosts on network 1.

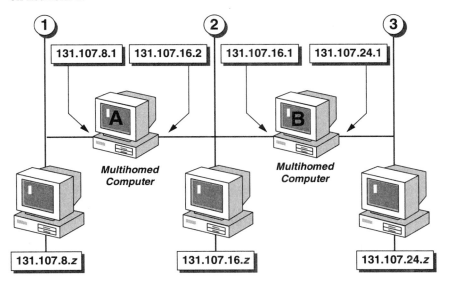

Configuring Static IP Routers

In an internetwork with at least one static router, you will need to configure static routing table entries at each router to all known networks. As shown in the following illustration:

- A static routing table entry is created on computer A. The entry contains the network ID of network 3 and the IP address (131.107.16.1) of the interface computer A can access directly to route packets from network 1 to network 3.

- A static routing table entry is created on computer B. The entry contains the network ID of network 1. The entry also contains the IP address (131.107.16.2) of the interface that computer B can access directly in order to route packets from network 3 to network 1.

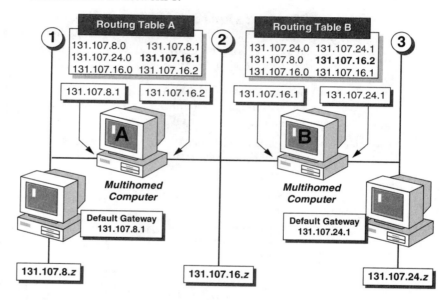

If your internetwork has more than two routers, and at least one of them is a static router, you need to configure a static routing table at each multihomed computer.

For a host to communicate with other hosts on the internetwork, its default gateway address must be configured to match the IP address of the router's local interface.

Using the Default Gateway Address

One method of configuring a static route without manually adding routes to a routing table is to configure each multihomed computer's default gateway address as the local interface to the other multihomed computer on the common network. This method only works effectively with two static routers.

Building a Routing Table

You add information to the routing table using the **route** command. The **route print** command is used to view the default entries in a routing table. A static entry should be added to the static router's routing table for all networks to which it has no configured interface. A static entry includes the following:

- *Network address.* The network ID or network name of the destination network. If a network name is used for the destination, it is looked up in the Networks file.

- *Netmask.* The subnet mask for the network address.

- *Gateway address.* The IP address or host name of the interface to the destination network. If a host name is used for the gateway, it is looked up in the Hosts file.

If you reference a network name or a host name in the routing table, the name must be configured in the appropriate file. Both files are located in the *systemroot*\System32\Drivers\Etc directory.

Default Routing Table Entries

The routing table on Windows NT 4.0 maintains the default entries shown in the following table.

Address	Description
0.0.0.0	The address used as a default route for any network not specified in the route table.
Subnet broadcast	The address used for broadcasting on the local subnet.
Network broadcast	The address used for broadcasting throughout the internetwork.
Local loopback	The address used for testing IP configurations and connections.
Local network	The address used to direct packets to hosts on the local network.
Local host	The address of the local computer. This address references the local loopback address.

Adding Static Entries

You use the **route** command to add static entries to the routing table.

To add or modify a static route	Function
route add [*network*] **mask** [*netmask*] [*gateway*]	Adds a route
route -p add [*network*] **mask** [*netmask*] [*gateway*]	Adds a persistent route
route delete [*network*] [*gateway*]	Deletes a route
route change [*network*] [*gateway*]	Modifies a route
route print	Displays the routing table
route -f	Clears all routes

For example, to add a route to enable communications with network 131.107.24.0 from a host on network 131.107.16.0, you would use the following command:

route add 131.107.24.0 **mask** 255.255.255.0 131.107.16.2

Note Static routes are stored in memory unless the **-p** parameter is used. Persistent routes are stored in the registry. If you restart a computer running Windows NT, you need to recreate all non-persistent routes.

Practice

In this procedure, you use the Route utility to view entries in your local routing table.

▶ **To view the routing table**

- At a command prompt, type **route -p print** and then press ENTER.

What address, other than your IP address and the loopback address, is listed under **Gateway Address**? If you are working with a stand-alone machine, the gateway address will not appear.

In this procedure, you remove the address for the default gateway. This prevents any packets being sent to the default gateway for routing, and requires all routing to be done from existing route entries.

▶ **To remove the default gateway address**

1. Double-click the Network icon in Control Panel, and then click the **Protocols** tab.

2. Click **TCP/IP Protocol**, and then click **Properties**.

   The **Microsoft TCP/IP Properties** dialog box appears.

3. Delete the **Default Gateway** address.

4. Click **OK** twice.

▶ **To view the routing table**

- At a command prompt, use the **route print** command.

   Is the default gateway address listed under **Gateway Address**?

   _____

In this procedure, you attempt to communicate with both local and remote hosts.

Note In order to complete this procedure, you must have two networked computers.

▶ **To attempt network communication**

- Ping the IP address of a your second computer or a computer on your local network.

   Was the ping successful?

   _____

   Without a gateway address in the routing table, would you be able to ping the IP address of a remote host?

   _____

In this procedure, you add a static routing table entry for the router.

▶ **To add a route entry**

1. Type the following command:

   route add 131.107.2.0 mask 255.255.255.0 131.107.2.1

2. View the entries in the route table, and verify that the route is listed.

3. If you were to ping a host on another network, would the ping be successful? Why or why not?

_____

In the following procedure, you restore the address for the default gateway. This allows packets to be sent to the default gateway when no route entry exists for the destination network.

▶ **To restore the default gateway address**

1. Switch to the **Microsoft TCP/IP Properties** dialog box.

2. In the **Default Gateway** box, type your default gateway address.

3. Click **OK** twice.

Summary

Static IP routing is a function of IP. This means that routers do not automatically exchange route information. A static route can be configured as either a default gateway address or an entry in a routing table.

Lesson 3: Dynamic IP Routing

With dynamic routing, routers automatically exchange path to known networks with each other. If a path changes, routing protocols automatically update a router's routing table and inform other routers on the internetwork of the change. In large internetworks, dynamic routing plays an important role in network communications.

After this lesson, you will be able to:
- Explain the concept of dynamic IP routing.
- Explain the host configuration requirements for dynamic routing.
- Integrate static and dynamic routing.

Estimated lesson time: 15 minutes

Dynamic routing is typically implemented on large internetworks because minimal configuration is required by a network administrator. Dynamic routing requires a routing protocol such as RIP or OSPF.

The Host Configuration

For a host to communicate with other hosts on the internetwork, its default gateway address must be configured to match the IP address of the local router's interface. No other configuration is required.

As shown in the following illustration, computer A requires a default gateway address configured as 131.107.8.1 (the local interface of the router). Computer B's default gateway address is configured as 131.107.24.1. A host on network 2 can use either 131.107.16.2 or 131.107.16.1 as its default gateway address.

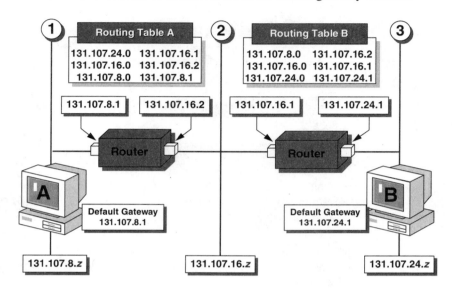

RIP

The Routing Information Protocol (RIP) for IP facilitates the exchange of routing information on an IP internetwork. All RIP messages are sent over UDP port 520.

RIP-enabled routers exchange the network IDs of the networks (that the router can reach), and the distance to these networks. RIP uses a hop-count field, or metric, in its routing table to indicate the distance to a network ID. The hop count is the number of routers that must be crossed to reach the target network ID. The maximum hop count for an RIP entry is 15. Network IDs that require 16 or more hops are considered unreachable. Hop counts can be adjusted to indicate slow or congested links. If multiple entries for a network ID are listed in the routing table, an RIP router will choose the route with the lowest number of hops.

Note An RIP router that receives RIP broadcasts but does not send out any RIP messages is known as a *Silent RIP router*.

The following illustration shows three subnets connected by two computers running Windows NT Server software with RIP routing enabled. Each router is configured with the default update interval; therefore, every 30 seconds each router broadcasts its routing table. Router A sends a limited broadcast to network 2 and all RIP-enabled routers on network 2 informing them about network 1. Router B then adds the new routes to its routing table. If router B has an existing entry in its routing table for a route broadcast by router A, router B will check to see if the new route has a smaller metric. If it is a better route, router B will update its routing table.

Router B also sends a limited broadcast to network 2 and all RIP-enabled routers on network 2 informing them of network 3. Router B then evaluates the new entries and updates its routing table, if necessary.

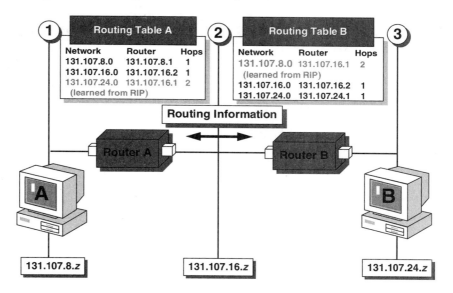

Problems with RIP

While simple and well-supported in the industry, RIP for IP suffers from some problems inherent to its original LAN-based design. These problems make RIP a good solution only in small IP internetworks with a low number of routers.

With RIP, each router's routing table has a complete list of all of the network IDs and all of the possible ways to reach each network ID. This routing table can have hundreds or even thousands of entries in a large IP internetwork with multiple paths. Because the maximum size of a single RIP packet is 512 bytes, large routing tables must be sent as multiple RIP packets.

RIP routers advertise the contents of their routing tables through a Media Access Control-level broadcast on all attached networks every 30 seconds. Large IP internetworks carry the broadcast RIP overhead of large routing tables. This can be especially problematic on WAN links where significant portions of the bandwidth of the WAN link are devoted to the passing of RIP traffic. As a result, RIP-based routing does not scale well to large internetworks or WAN implementations.

Each routing table entry learned through RIP is given a time-out value of 3 minutes past the last time it was last received in an RIP advertisement. When a router goes down, it can take several minutes for the changes to be propagated throughout the internetwork. This is known as the *slow convergence problem*.

Integrating Static and Dynamic Routing

A static router does not trade routing information with dynamic routers. To route from a static router through a dynamic router (such as an RIP-enabled, or OSPF-enabled IP router), you need to add a static route to the routing tables on both the static and dynamic routers. As shown in the following illustration:

- Computer A requires a route added to its routing table. The route must include the IP address (131.107.16.1) of the interface that can access the dedicated IP router to the Internet to route packets from network 1 to the Internet.

- To route packets from networks 2 and 3 to the Internet, a static entry must be added to computer B's routing table that includes the IP address (131.107.24.2) of the interface on the dedicated IP router to the Internet.

- To enable computers on the Internet to communicate with hosts on networks 1 and 2, it is necessary to statically configure the dynamic IP router with the IP address of the interface to computer B. Computer B then acts as a gateway to the other subnets.

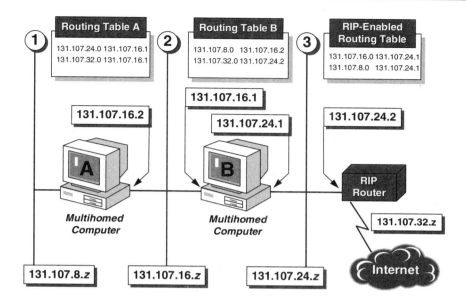

Note Some implementations of RIP do not propagate static routing tables. In this case, it is necessary to statically configure the remote routers in the internetwork. Configuring a static route on an RIP router varies with each router. Refer to the router vendor's documentation for more information.

Summary

Dynamic routing is an important component for large networks. The default gateway address for a host must be configured to match the IP address of the local router's interface. RIP for IP facilitates the exchange of routing information on an IP internetwork; however, RIP is a good solution only in small IP networks.

A static router does not trade routing information with dynamic routers. To route from a static router through a dynamic router, you need to add a static route to the routing tables on both the static and dynamic routers.

Lesson 4: Implementing a Windows NT Router

Static routing can work well for small networks and remote sites, but for large internetworks, the overhead of manually maintaining routing tables is significant. This lesson helps you understand what is required to implement a Windows NT router.

After this lesson, you will be able to:

- Understand how to implement a Windows NT router.
- Understand how the Tracert utility can verify a packet route.

Estimated lesson time: 10 minutes

By enabling the RIP for IP routing protocol, Windows NT Server 4.0 can be a dynamic IP router. Windows NT 4.0 RIP for IP eliminates the manual configuration of routing tables. RIP for IP is suitable for medium-size internetworks, but is not suitable for large IP internetworks because of the significant amount of broadcast traffic it generates.

▶ **To implement a Windows NT router**

1. Install multiple adapter cards and appropriate drivers, or configure multiple IP addresses on a single adapter card.
2. Configure the adapter card(s) with a valid IP address and subnet mask.
3. On the **Routing** tab of the **Microsoft TCP/IP Properties** dialog box, select the **Enable IP Forwarding** check box.
4. Depending on which version of Windows NT you are running:
   - On the **Services** tab of the Control Panel Network program, add the RIP for Internet Protocol service.

     –Or–

   - Add static routes to the static router's routing table for all networks to which the computer has no configured interface.

The TRACERT Utility

The TRACERT utility verifies the route a packet takes to reach its destination. This is useful for determining if a router has failed. If the command is unsuccessful, you can determine where routing failed, possibly indicating router or WAN link problems.

TRACERT is also useful for determining a slow router. The response time is returned in the output, indicating the effectiveness of a router or WAN link. This information can be compared with another route to the same destination.

For example, the following command displays the path taken from the local host to the destination host www.microsoft.com (207.68.137.36):

tracert www.microsoft.com

The output from the preceding command verifies that the router address was used as the route from the local host to the destination host.

```
Tracing route to www.microsoft.com [207.68.137.36]
over a maximum of 30 hops:
1   <10 ms   <10 ms   <10 ms   206.213.84.57
2    30 ms    40 ms    30 ms   fast1.accessone.com [206.213.95.11]
3    30 ms    80 ms    30 ms   198.68.188.1
4    30 ms    40 ms    30 ms   Fddi1-0.GW1.SEA1.ALTER.NET [137.39.63.65]
5    40 ms    40 ms    40 ms   Dist1-Sea.MOSWEST.MSN.NET [137.39.176.22]
6    40 ms    40 ms    40 ms   msft1-f0.moswest.msn.net [207.68.145.46]
7   231 ms   170 ms   170 ms   www.microsoft.com [207.68.137.36]

Trace complete.
```

Summary

Windows NT Server 4.0 can be made a dynamic IP router by enabling the RIP for IP routing protocol. This eliminates the manual configuration of routing tables. The TRACERT utility is useful for determining if a router has failed or if there is a slow router.

Review

The following questions are intended to reinforce key information presented in this chapter. If you are unable to answer a question, review the appropriate lesson and then try the question again.

1. How is IP routing enabled?

   _____

   _____

2. Is a routing table required on a multihomed computer connecting a two-subnet internet? Why or why not?

   _____

   _____

3. When is it necessary to build a static routing table?

   _____

   _____

4. What information is required in a routing table?

   _____

   _____

   _____

5. Why is RIP typically not used in a large internetwork?

   _____

   _____

For More Information

- Review all referenced RFCs on the course compact disc.

CHAPTER 7

The Dynamic Host Configuration Protocol

Lesson 1 DHCP Overview . . . 130

Lesson 2 Installing and Configuring a DHCP Server . . . 140

Lesson 3 Enabling a DHCP Relay Agent . . . 155

Lesson 4 Managing the DHCP Database . . . 159

Review . . . 162

About This Chapter

In this chapter, you learn how to use the Dynamic Host Configuration Protocol (DHCP) to automatically configure TCP/IP and eliminate some common configuration problems. During the lessons, you install and configure a DHCP server, test the DHCP configuration, install a DHCP relay agent, and then obtain an IP address from a DHCP server.

Before You Begin

To complete the lessons in this chapter, you must have installed Microsoft Windows NT Server 4.0 with TCP/IP.

Lesson 1: DHCP Overview

The Dynamic Host Configuration Protocol (DHCP) automatically assigns IP
addresses to computers. DHCP overcomes the limitations of configuring TCP/IP
manually. This lesson gives you an overview of DHCP and how it works.

After this lesson, you will be able to:

- Describe the function and benefits of DHCP.
- Explain how a DHCP client obtains IP addresses from a DHCP server.
- Understand how the Ipconfig utility can renew or release a lease.

Estimated lesson time: 35 minutes

DHCP is an extension of the BOOTP protocol. BOOTP enables diskless clients to
start up and automatically configure TCP/IP. DHCP centralizes and manages the
allocation of TCP/IP configuration information by automatically assigning IP
addresses to computers configured to use DHCP. Implementing DHCP eliminates
some of the configuration problems associated with manually configuring TCP/IP.

As shown in the illustration below, each time a DHCP client starts, it requests IP
addressing information from a DHCP server, including the IP address, the subnet
mask, and optional values. The optional values may include a default gateway
address, Domain Name Server (DNS) address, and NetBIOS name server address.

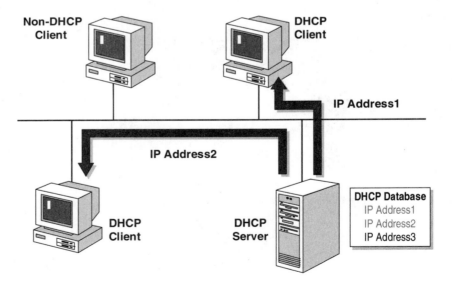

When a DHCP server receives a request, it selects IP addressing information from a pool of addresses defined in its database and offers it to the DHCP client. If the client accepts the offer, the IP addressing information is leased to the client for a specified period of time. If there is no available IP addressing information in the pool to lease to a client, the client cannot initialize TCP/IP.

Note Windows NT 4.0 Service Pack 2 enables support for BOOTP client requests.

The BOOTP protocol is defined in RFC 1532. DHCP is defined in RFCs 1533, 1534, 1541, and 1542. For copies of these RFCs, see the *Course Materials* Web page on the course compact disc.

Manual vs. Automatic Configuration

To understand why DHCP is beneficial in configuring TCP/IP on client computers, it is useful to contrast the manual method of configuring TCP/IP with the automatic method using DHCP.

Configuring TCP/IP Manually

Configuring TCP/IP manually means that users can easily pick a random IP address instead of getting a valid IP address from the network administrator. Using incorrect addresses can lead to network problems that can be very difficult to trace to the source.

In addition, typing the IP address, subnet mask, or default gateway can lead to problems ranging from trouble communicating if the default gateway or subnet mask is wrong, to problems associated with a duplicate IP address.

Another limitation of configuring TCP/IP manually is the administrative overhead on internetworks where computers are frequently moved from one subnet to another. For example, when a workstation is moved to a different subnet, the IP address and default gateway address must be changed for the workstation to communicate from its new location.

Configuring TCP/IP Using DHCP

Using DHCP to automatically configure IP addressing information means that users no longer need to acquire IP addressing information from an administrator to configure TCP/IP. The DHCP server supplies all of the necessary configuration information to all of the DHCP clients. Most of the difficult-to-trace network problems are eliminated by using DHCP.

How DHCP Works

DHCP uses a four-phase process to configure a DHCP client as shown in the following table and illustration. If a computer has multiple network adapters, the DHCP process occurs separately over each adapter. A unique IP address will be assigned to each adapter in the computer. All DHCP communication is done over UDP ports 67 and 68.

Most DHCP messages are sent by broadcast. For DHCP clients to communicate with a DHCP server on a remote network, the IP routers must support forwarding DHCP broadcasts. DHCP configuration phases are shown in the following table.

Phase	Description
IP lease request	The client initializes a limited version of TCP/IP and broadcasts a request for the location of a DHCP server and IP addressing information.
IP lease offer	All DHCP servers that have valid IP addressing information available send an offer to the client.
IP lease selection	The client selects the IP addressing information from the first offer it receives and broadcasts a message requesting to lease the IP addressing information in the offer.
IP lease acknowledgment	The DHCP server that made the offer responds to the message, and all other DHCP servers withdraw their offers. The IP addressing information is assigned to the client and an acknowledgment is sent.
	The client finishes initializing and binding the TCP/IP protocol. Once the automatic configuration process is complete, the client can use all TCP/IP services and utilities for normal network communications and connectivity to other IP hosts.

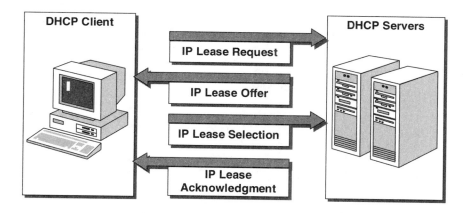

IP Lease Request and Offer

In the first two phases, the client requests a lease from a DHCP server, and a DHCP server offers an IP address to the client.

IP Lease Request

The first time a client initializes, it requests to lease an IP address by broadcasting a request to all DHCP servers. Because the client does not have an IP address or know the IP address of a DHCP server, it uses 0.0.0.0 as the source address, and 255.255.255.255 as the destination address.

The request for a lease is sent in a DHCPDISCOVER message. This message also contains the client's hardware address and computer name so that DHCP servers know which client sent the request.

The IP lease process is used when one of the following occurs:

- TCP/IP is initialized for the first time as a DHCP client.
- The client requests a specific IP address and is denied, possibly because the DHCP server dropped the lease.
- The client previously leased an IP address, but released the lease and now requires a new lease.

IP Lease Offer

All DHCP servers that receive the request and have a valid configuration for the client broadcast an offer with the following information:

- The client's hardware address
- An offered IP address
- Subnet mask
- Length of the lease
- A server identifier (the IP address of the offering DHCP server)

A broadcast is used because the client does not yet have an IP address. As shown in the following illustration, the offer is sent as a DHCPOFFER message.

The DHCP server reserves the IP address so that it will not be offered to another DHCP client. The DHCP client selects the IP address from the first offer it receives.

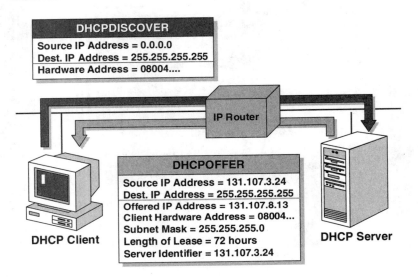

When No DHCP Servers Are Online

The DHCP client waits one second for an offer. If an offer is not received, the client will not be able to initialize and it will rebroadcast the request three times (at 9-, 13-, and 16-second intervals, plus a random length of time between 0 and 1,000 milliseconds). If an offer is not received after four requests, the client will retry every five minutes.

IP Lease Selection and Acknowledgment

In the last two phases, the client selects an offer and the DHCP server acknowledges the lease.

IP Lease Selection

After the client receives an offer from at least one DHCP server, it broadcasts to all DHCP servers that it has made a selection by accepting an offer.

The broadcast is sent in a DHCPREQUEST message and includes the server identifier (IP address) of the server whose offer was accepted. All other DHCP servers then retract their offers so that their IP addresses are available for the next IP lease request.

IP Lease Acknowledgment (Successful)

The DHCP server with the accepted offer broadcasts a successful acknowledgment to the client in the form of a DHCPACK message. This message contains a valid lease for an IP address and possibly other configuration information.

When the DHCP client receives the acknowledgment, TCP/IP is completely initialized and is considered a bound DHCP client. Once bound, the client can use TCP/IP to communicate on the internetwork.

The client stores the IP address, subnet mask, and other IP addressing information locally in the registry under the following key:

HKEY_LOCAL_MACHINE\SYSTEM\CurrentControlSet\Services \adapter\Parameters\Tcpip

IP Lease Acknowledgment (Unsuccessful)

An unsuccessful acknowledgment (DHCPNACK) is broadcast if the client is trying to lease its previous IP address and the IP address is no longer available. It is also broadcast if the IP address is invalid because the client has been physically moved to a different subnet.

As shown in the following illustration, when the client receives an unsuccessful acknowledgment, it returns to the process of requesting an IP lease.

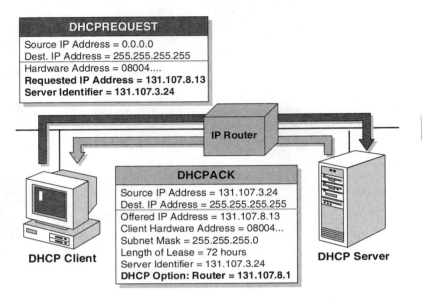

IP Lease Renewal

Initial Renewal Attempt

All DHCP clients attempt to renew their lease when 50 percent of the lease time has expired. To renew its lease, a DHCP client sends a DHCPREQUEST message directly to the DHCP server from which it obtained the lease.

If the DHCP server is available, it renews the lease and sends the client a successful acknowledgment (DHCPACK) with the new lease time and any updated configuration parameters.

When the client receives the acknowledgment, it updates its configuration. If a client attempts to renew its lease, but is unable to contact the original DHCP server, the client receives a message indicating that the lease was not renewed. The client can still use the address because 50 percent of the lease life is available.

When a DHCP client restarts, it attempts to lease the same IP address from the original DHCP server. It does this by broadcasting a DHCPREQUEST specifying the last IP address it leased. If it is unsuccessful, and there is still lease time available, the DHCP client continues to use the same IP address for the remainder of the lease.

Subsequent Renewal Attempts

If a lease could not be renewed by the original DHCP server at the 50 percent interval, the client will attempt to contact any available DHCP server when 87.5 percent of the lease time has expired. As shown in the following illustration, the client will broadcast a DHCPREQUEST message. Any DHCP server can respond with a DHCPACK message (renewing the lease) or a DHCPNACK message (forcing the DHCP client to re-initialize and obtain a lease for a different IP address).

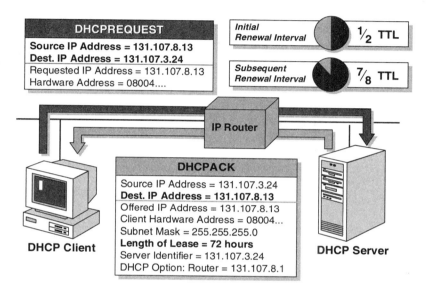

If the lease expires or a DHCPNACK message is received, the DHCP client must immediately discontinue using the IP address. The DHCP client then returns to the process of leasing a new IP address.

If the client's lease expires and it cannot acquire a new lease, communication over TCP/IP stops until a new IP address can be assigned to the client. Network errors occur for any applications that attempt to communicate over the invalid TCP/IP protocol stack interface.

Using the Ipconfig Utility

In addition to its use for verifying a computer's IP configuration, the Ipconfig utility can also be used to renew options and lease time, and to relinquish a lease. At a command prompt, type the following command to verify a computer's IP address, subnet mask, and default gateway:

ipconfig

At a command prompt, type the following command to verify a computer's IP configuration for the operating system and the network adapter:

ipconfig /all

Using the **/all** switch provides the following IP configuration information:

- Host name assigned to the local computer
- IP address of any DNS servers the local computer is configured to use
- NetBIOS node type, such as broadcast, hybrid, peer-peer, and mixed
- NetBIOS scope ID
- Whether or not IP routing is enabled
- Whether or not WINS proxy is enabled
- Whether or not NetBIOS resolution uses DNS

Using the **/all** switch provides the following network adapter IP configuration information:

- Description of the adapter card, such as EtherLink II
- Physical address of the adapter card
- Whether or not DHCP is enabled
- IP address of the local computer
- Subnet mask of the local computer
- Default gateway of the local computer
- IP addresses of the primary and secondary WINS servers

Updating a Lease

The **/renew** switch causes a DHCPREQUEST message to be sent to the DHCP server to get updated options and lease time. If the DHCP server is unavailable, the client will continue using the current DHCP-supplied configuration options. At a command prompt, type:

ipconfig /renew

Releasing a Lease

The **/release** switch causes the DHCP client to send a DHCPRELEASE message to the DHCP server and give up its lease. This is useful when the client is changing to a different network and will not need the previous lease. After this command has been carried out, TCP/IP communications will stop. At a command prompt, type:

ipconfig /release

Microsoft DHCP clients do not initiate DHCPRELEASE messages when shutting down. If a client remains shut down for the length of its lease (and the lease is not renewed), it is possible for the DHCP server to assign that client's IP address to a different client after the lease expires. By not sending a DHCPRELEASE message, the client has a better chance of receiving the same IP address during initialization.

Summary

DHCP was developed to solve configuration problems by centralizing IP configuration information for allocation to clients. DHCP uses a four-phase process to configure a DHCP client. The phases are, in order,: lease request, lease offer, lease selection, and lease acknowledgment.

In addition to verifying a computer's IP configuration, you can use the Ipconfig utility to renew options and lease time, and to relinquish a lease.

Lesson 2: Installing and Configuring a DHCP Server

Before you install DHCP, you should consider several questions about your configuration. This lesson leads you through these questions, helps you understand the server and client requirements for DHCP, and then shows you how to install DHCP.

After this lesson, you will be able to:

- Understand the questions you should ask before implementing DHCP.
- Install DHCP in an internetwork.
- Configure a DHCP scope for multiple subnets.

Estimated lesson time: 75 minutes

Before you install DHCP, answer the following questions:

- Will all of the computers become DHCP clients? If not, consider that non-DHCP clients have static IP addresses, and static IP addresses must be excluded from the DHCP server configuration. If a client requires a specific address, the IP address needs to be reserved.
- Will a DHCP server supply IP addresses to multiple subnets? If so, consider that any routers connecting subnets act as DHCP relay agents. If your routers are not acting as DHCP relay agents, at least one DHCP server is required on each subnet that has DHCP clients.
- How many DHCP servers are required? Consider that a DHCP server does not share information with other DHCP servers. Therefore, it is necessary to create unique IP addresses for each server to assign to clients.
- What IP addressing options will clients obtain from a DHCP server? The IP addressing options might be:
  - Router
  - DNS server
  - NetBIOS over TCP/IP name resolution
  - WINS server
  - NetBIOS scope ID

The IP addressing options determine how to configure the DHCP server, and whether the options should be created for all of the clients in the internetwork, clients on a specific subnet, or individual clients.

Implementing Multiple DHCP Servers

If your internetwork requires multiple DHCP servers, it is necessary to create a unique scope for each subnet. A scope is a range of IP addresses that are available to be leased or assigned to clients.

To ensure that clients can lease IP addresses, it is important to have multiple scopes for each subnet distributed among the DHCP servers in the internetwork. For example:

- Each DHCP server should have a scope containing approximately 75 percent of the available IP addresses for the local subnet.

- Each DHCP server should have a scope for each remote subnet containing approximately 25 percent of the available IP addresses for a subnet.

When a client's DHCP server is unavailable, the client can still receive an address lease from another DHCP server on a different subnet, assuming the router is a DHCP relay agent.

As shown in the following illustration, Server A has a scope for the local subnet with an IP address range of 131.107.4.20 through 131.107.4.150, and Server B has a scope with an IP address range of 131.107.3.20 through 131.107.3.150. Each server can lease IP addresses to clients on its own subnet.

Additionally, each server has a scope containing a small range of IP addresses for the remote subnet. For example, Server A has a scope for Subnet 2 with the IP address range of 131.107.3.151 through 131.107.3.200. Server B has a scope for Subnet 1 with the IP address range of 131.107.4.151 through 131.107.4.200.

When a client on Subnet 1 is unable to lease an address from Server A, it can lease an address for its subnet from Server B, and vice versa.

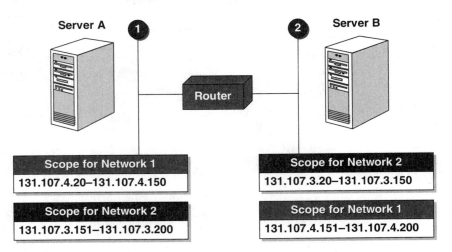

DHCP Requirements

To implement DHCP, both the server and the client require configuration. All routers connecting subnets with DHCP servers and clients must support RFC 1542 and act as BOOTP relay agents.

A DHCP server requires:

- The DHCP Server service configured on at least one computer within the TCP/IP internetwork running Windows NT Server (it does not have to be a domain controller), provided that your IP routers support RFC 1542. Otherwise, you need a DHCP server on each subnet.

- The DHCP server configured with a static IP address, subnet mask, default gateway, and other TCP/IP parameters (it cannot be a DHCP client).

- A DHCP scope created on the DHCP server. A DHCP scope consists of a range, or pool, of IP addresses that the DHCP server can assign, or lease, to DHCP clients—for example, 131.107.3.51 through 131.107.3.200.

A DHCP client requires a computer running any of the following supported operating systems with DHCP enabled:

- Windows NT Server 4.0.
- Windows NT Workstation 4.0.
- Microsoft Windows 95.

- Microsoft Windows for Workgroups 3.11 running Microsoft TCP/IP-32 (provided on the Windows NT Server 3.5 compact disc).
- Microsoft Network Client 3.0 for MS-DOS with the real-mode TCP/IP driver included on the Windows NT Server 3.5 compact disc.
- LAN Manager 2.2c, included on the Windows NT Server 3.5 compact disc. LAN Manager 2.2c for OS/2 is not supported.

Installing and Configuring a DHCP Server

The DHCP Server service must be running to communicate with DHCP clients. Once the DHCP server is installed and started, several options must be configured. The following are the general steps for installing and configuring DHCP:

- Install the Microsoft DHCP Server service.
- A scope, or pool of valid IP addresses, must be configured before a DHCP server can lease IP addresses to DHCP clients.
- Global, scope, and client scope options can be configured for a particular DHCP client.
- The DHCP server can be configured to always assign the same IP address to the same DHCP client.

Note The DHCP server cannot be a DHCP client. It must have a static IP address, subnet mask, and default gateway address.

Practice

In this procedure, you install and configure a DHCP server to automatically assign TCP/IP configuration information to DHCP clients.

Note You must have two networked computers to complete this procedure. Complete this procedure from the computer you designate as the DHCP server (Server1). In the next procedure, you work with the second computer (Server2) to configure it as a DHCP client.

Caution It is recommended that you do not perform these procedures if your computer(s) are part of larger network. Installing a DHCP server could conflict with network operations.

In this procedure, you determine the physical hardware address of your network adapter card. This address is used to create a client reservation.

▶ **To determine the network adapter card address**

- At a command prompt, type **ipconfig /all** and then press ENTER.

  Document the physical address here for reference, without the hyphens (–).

  _____

  There are at least two other ways to check the physical address of your network adapter card. What are they?

  _____

  _____

▶ **To install the DHCP Server service**

Note Complete this procedure only from the computer you designate as the DHCP server.

1. Click the **Start** button, point to **Settings**, and then click **Control Panel**.
2. Double-click the **Network** icon.

   The **Network Settings** dialog box appears.
3. Click the **Services** tab.
4. Click **Add**.

   The **Select Network Service** dialog box appears.
5. Select **Microsoft DHCP Server**, and then click **OK**.

   The **Windows NT Setup** box appears, prompting for the full path of the Windows NT distribution files.
6. Type the full path and then click **Continue**.

   The appropriate files are copied to your computer, and then a message box appears, informing you that a static IP address is now required for the network adapter card.
7. Click **OK**.

   The **Network** dialog box appears.

8. Click **Close**.

   The **Network Settings Change** dialog box appears, indicating that the computer needs to be restarted to initialize the new configuration.

9. Click **Yes**.

10. Log on as Administrator.

Configuring a DHCP Scope

Once the DHCP server is installed and started, the next step is to configure a scope of configuration information. As shown in the following illustration, every DHCP server requires at least one scope with a pool of IP addresses available for leasing to clients. You can create multiple scopes for other DHCP servers as a backup method. They are also created for assigning IP addresses specific to a subnet, such as a default gateway address.

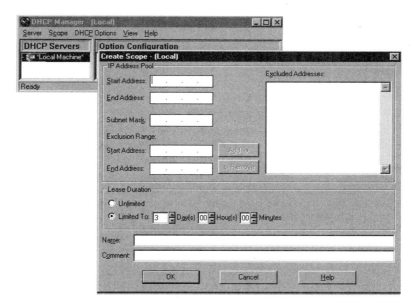

Note   Only one scope can be assigned to a specific subnet.

Because DHCP servers do not share scope information, it is important that each scope contain a unique IP address. If more than one scope contains the same IP address, it is possible for both servers to lease the same IP address to different DHCP clients, causing duplicate IP addressing problems.

Practice

In this procedure, you create a DHCP scope that consists of one IP address (your other computer's) with an assigned lease time of one day.

Note Complete this procedure only from the DHCP server.

▶ **To create a DHCP scope**

1. Click the **Start** button, point to **Settings**, and then click **Control Panel**.
2. Double-click the **Services** icon. What are the names of the DHCP services?

   _____

3. Close the **Services** dialog box.
4. Click the **Start** button, point to **Programs**, point to **Administrative Tools**, and then click **DHCP Manager**.

   The DHCP Manager window appears.
5. Under **DHCP** Servers, double-click ***Local Machine***.
6. On the **Scope** menu, click **Create**.

   The **Create Scope** dialog box appears. The available options are shown in the following table.

Option	Description
IP Address Pool Start Address	The starting IP address that can be assigned to a DHCP client.
IP Address Pool End Address	The ending IP address that can be assigned to a DHCP client.
Subnet Mask	The subnet mask to be assigned to DHCP clients.
Exclusion Range Start Address	The starting IP address to be excluded from the IP address pool of addresses. The addresses in this exclusion will not be assigned to DHCP clients. This is important if you have static IP addresses configured on non-DCHP clients.
Exclusion Range End Address	The ending IP address to be excluded from the IP address pool of addresses. The addresses in this exclusion will not be assigned to DHCP clients. This is important if you have static IP addresses configured on non-DCHP clients.
Lease Duration Unlimited	The DHCP leases assigned to clients will never expire.

(*continued*)

Option	Description
Lease Duration Limited To	The number of days, hours, and minutes that a DHCP client lease is available before it must be renewed.
Name	A name to be assigned to the DHCP scope. The name displays after the IP address in the DHCP Manager.
Comment	Optional comment for the scope.

7. Configure the scope using the information in the following table.

In this box	Type this
IP Address Pool Start Address	Your second computer's IP address
IP Address Pool End Address	Your second computer's IP address
Subnet Mask	**255.255.255.0**
Lease Duration Limited To (Days)	**1**

8. Click **OK**.

    A **DHCP Manager** message box appears, indicating that the scope was successfully created, and now needs to be activated. The scope must be activated before it is available for lease assignments.

9. To activate the scope, click **Yes**.

    Note Another way to activate the scope is to select the inactive scope in the DHCP Manager window, and then, on the **Scope** menu, click **Activate**.

    The DHCP Manager window appears with the new scope added. Notice the yellow light bulb next to the IP address, indicating an active scope. A message box informs you that no more data is available.

    Important If the internetwork has non-DHCP clients, it is important to exclude their static IP addresses from the scope, or the DHCP server could allocate the same IP address to a DHCP client, causing duplicate addressing problems.

    ---

10. Click **OK**.

Configuring DHCP Scope Options

Once you have created the DHCP scope, you can configure options for DHCP clients. You configure these options from the **DHCP Options: Scope** dialog box. There are three levels of scope options—global, scope, and client, as follows:

- *Global*. Global options are available to all DHCP clients. Global options are used when all clients on all subnets require the same configuration information. For example, you might want all clients configured to use the same WINS server. Global options are always used, unless scope or client options are configured.

- *Scope*. Scope options are available only to clients who lease an address from the scope. For example, if you have a different scope for each subnet, you can define a unique default gateway address for each subnet. Scope options override global options.

- *Client*. Client options are created for a specific client using a reserved DHCP address lease. Client options are always used before scope or global options.

Important Even though a Microsoft DHCP server can offer all of the options in the options list, Microsoft DHCP clients will accept only the options in the following table. Non–Microsoft DHCP clients can receive and use any configured option.

Option	Description
003 Router	Specifies the IP address of a router, such as the default gateway address. If the client has a locally defined default gateway, that configuration takes precedence over the DHCP option.
006 DNS Servers	Specifies the IP address of a DNS server.
046 WINS/NBT node type	Specifies the type of NetBIOS over TCP/IP name resolution to be used by the client. Options are: 1 = B-node (broadcast) 2 = P-node (peer) 4 = M-node (mixed) 8 = H-node (hybrid)
044 WINS/NBNS servers	Specifies the IP address of a WINS server available to clients. If a WINS server address is manually configured on a client, that configuration overrides the values configured for this option.
047 NetBIOS Scope ID	Specifies the local NetBIOS scope ID. NetBIOS over TCP/IP will communicate only with other NetBIOS hosts using the same scope ID.

Practice

In this procedure, you create a DHCP scope option that automatically assigns a default gateway address to DHCP clients.

Note   Complete this procedure only from the DHCP server.

▶ **To configure DHCP scope options**

1. Click the light bulb icon for the scope you just created.
2. On the **DHCP Options** menu, select **Scope**.

   The **DHCP Options: Scope** dialog box appears.

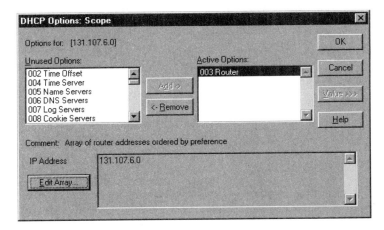

3. Under **Unused Options**, select **003 Router**, and then click **Add**.

   The **003 Router** option moves to the **Active Options** box.
4. Click **Value**.

   The **DHCP Options: Scope** dialog box expands to add the **Router IP Address** values box.

   The **Router IP Address** box contains six types of values, as shown in the following table.

Type	Description
IP Address	Designates the IP address of a server added to the options. For example: 003 Routers.
Long	Configures a 32-bit numeric value. For example: 035 ARP Cache Time-out.
String	Designates a string of characters. For example: 015 Domain Name.

(*continued*)

Type	Description
Word	Assigns a 16-bit numeric value of specific block sizes. For example: 022 Max DG Reassembly Size.
Byte	Assigns a numeric value consisting of a single byte. For example: 046 WINS/NBT Node Type.
Binary	Specifies a binary value. For example: 043 Vendor-Specific Information.

5. Click **Edit Array**.

   The **IP Address Array Editor** dialog box appears.

6. Under **New IP Address**, type your default gateway address (**131.107.2.1**), and then click **Add**.

   The new IP address appears under **IP Addresses**.

7. Click **OK** to return to the **DHCP Options: Scope** dialog box.

   The new router is listed in the IP address list.

8. Click **OK**.

   A message box informs you that no more data is available.

9. Close DHCP Manager.

Note You must exit and restart DHCP Manager to view the new options in the left pane.

Configuring a Client Reservation

You can configure DHCP so that a DHCP server always assigns the same IP address to a client. This is called a *client reservation*.

For some DHCP clients it is important that the same IP address is reassigned when its lease expires—for example, servers on a network that contain clients that are not WINS-enabled should always lease the same IP address. Clients that are not WINS-enabled must use the LMHOSTS file to resolve NetBIOS computer names of hosts on remote networks. If the IP address of the server changes because it is not reserved, name resolution using LMHOSTS will fail. Reserving an IP address for the server ensures that its IP address will remain the same.

Practice

In this procedure, you create a reservation for your second computer. This ensures that each DHCP server is able to lease an address to a unique DHCP client in an environment of multiple DHCP servers.

Note Complete this procedure only from the DHCP server.

▶ **To add a client lease reservation**

1. Ping your second computer's IP address, and then type **arp -a** to obtain the physical address of your second computer's network adapter. Document the address here for reference. (Do *not* include hyphens in the physical address.)

   _____

2. Start DHCP Manager.

3. Double-click ***Local Machine***.

   The light bulb icon and the IP address appear.

4. Click the light bulb icon.

   The Option Configuration window displays an active scope option of 003 Router.

5. On the **Scope** menu, click **Add Reservations**.

   The **Add Reserved Clients** dialog box appears.

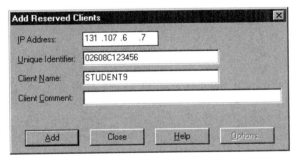

6. In the **IP Address** box, type your second computer's IP address.

7. In the **Unique Identifier** box, type the physical address of your second computer's network adapter.

Note Do not include hyphens in the physical address.

Important If the Unique Identifier is incorrectly typed, it will not match the value sent by the DHCP client. As a result, the DHCP server will assign the client any available IP address instead of the IP address reserved for the client.

8. In the **Client Name** box, type **Server2** (where **Server2** is your second computer's name) and then click **Add**.

   This name is used for identification purposes in the DHCP Manager application. The name is associated with the hardware address of the network adapter card.

   The **Add Reserved Clients** dialog box appears.

9. To return to DHCP Manager, click **Close**.

Note If there are multiple DHCP servers in the internetwork, it is important that all DHCP servers have the same client reservations. The client can receive its lease from any DHCP server and will be guaranteed the same IP address.

Practice

In this procedure, you test the DHCP server configuration by starting the DHCP client on your second computer, and determining the TCP/IP configuration information assigned to it by the DHCP server.

> **Note** Perform this procedure from your second computer. This computer will become the DHCP client, and should have the physical address and computer name that was used to create the DHCP client reservation.

▶ **To install the DHCP client**

1. In the **Microsoft TCP/IP Properties** dialog box, click the **IP Address** tab.
2. Click **Obtain an IP address from a DHCP server**.

   You are prompted to enable DHCP.
3. Click **Yes**.
4. Click **OK**.

   This installs and activates the DHCP client on your computer.
5. Click **OK** again.

▶ **To verify the DHCP-assigned TCP/IP information**

> **Note** Complete this procedure only from the DHCP client.

1. At a command prompt, type **ipconfig /all** to view the TCP/IP configuration.
2. What IP address was assigned to the DHCP client computer by the DHCP server?

   _____

3. What is the address of the default gateway?

   _____

▶ **To view DHCP-assigned addresses**

In this procedure, you view the DHCP server listing of leased addresses.

Note Complete this procedure from the DHCP server.

---

1. In the DHCP Manager window, select the local scope (designated by the light bulb icon).
2. On the **Scope** menu, click **Active Leases**.

    The **Active Leases** dialog box appears, displaying the list of IP addresses that have been leased to clients.
3. Click **Properties**.

    The **Client Properties** dialog box appears. The **Lease expires time** is listed as **infinite**.
4. Click **OK** to return to the **Active Leases** dialog box.
5. Click **OK** to return to the DHCP Manager window.

▶ **To renew a DHCP lease**

In this procedure, you renew the lease assigned to the DHCP client computer.

Note Complete this procedure only from the DHCP client.

---

1. At a command prompt, type **ipconfig /all**
2. When does the lease expire?

    _____

3. To renew the lease, type **ipconfig /renew** at a command prompt, and then press ENTER.

    The Windows IP Configuration information is displayed.
4. Type **ipconfig /all** to view the lease information.
5. When does the lease expire?

    _____

Summary

A scope is a range of IP addresses that are available to be leased or assigned to clients. Multiple scopes and separate scopes for each subnet can be created to allow DHCP clients to obtain a valid IP address from any DHCP server. To implement DHCP, software is required on both the client and the server. Every DHCP server requires at least one scope.

Lesson 3: Enabling a DHCP Relay Agent

Windows NT Server has the ability to be an RFC 1542–compliant DHCP relay agent. A relay agent, when used in conjunction with either the static or dynamic IP router, relays DHCP messages between DHCP clients and servers on different IP networks.

After this lesson, you will be able to:
- Install and configure a DHCP relay agent.

Estimated lesson time: 25 minutes

If routers separate your DHCP clients and servers, you can configure Windows NT Server to be a DHCP relay agent. A relay agent will intercept DHCP broadcasts and forward the packets to the DHCP server, crossing IP routers. You add Microsoft DHCP Relay Agent through the Control Panel Network program.

When a dynamic client computer on the subnet where the DHCP relay agent resides requests an IP address, the request is forwarded to the subnet's DHCP relay agent as shown in the following illustration. The DHCP relay agent, in turn, is configured to forward the request directly to the correct computer running the Windows NT Server DHCP service. The computer running the Windows NT Server DHCP service returns an IP address directly to the requesting client.

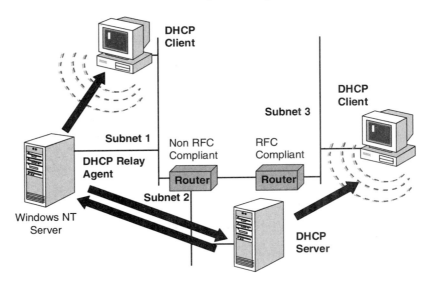

The DHCP relay agent is configured with the IP address of the computer running Windows NT Server DHCP so that the agent will know where to forward requests from clients for available IP addresses.

Practice

In this procedure, you use the Control Panel Network program to install the DHCP relay agent, and then configure the relay agent using the DHCP property sheet to specify the IP address of the DHCP server. Keep in mind that in a production environment you will be installing a DHCP relay agent to forward requests from different subnets.

Note Perform this procedure from Server2.

▶ **To install DHCP Relay Agent**

1. Click the **Start** button, point to **Settings**, and then click **Control Panel**.

2. Double-click the **Network** icon.

   The **Network** dialog box appears.

3. Click the **Services** tab.

   The **Services** tab displays the list of Network Services currently running on this computer.

4. Click **Add**.

   The **Select Network Service** dialog box displays the Network Services available.

5. Click **DHCP Relay Agent**.

   The DHCP Relay Agent is highlighted in the list box.

6. Click **OK**.

   The **Windows NT Setup** dialog box appears.

7. Type the path to the Windows NT Server files, and then click **Continue**.

   The **Network** dialog box appears.

8. Click **Close**.

   The **Unattended Setup** dialog box appears.

   You are prompted to add an IP address to the DHCP Servers list.

9. Click **Yes**.

   The **TCP/IP Properties** dialog box appears.

10. Click the **DHCP Relay** tab, and then click **Add**.

    The **DHCP Relay Agent** property sheet appears.

11. Type the IP address of the DHCP Server, and then click **Add**.

    The IP address is added to the **DHCP Servers** list.

12. Click **OK**.

    You are prompted to restart your computer.

13. Click **Yes**.

    Your computer restarts with DHCP Relay Agent enabled.

Practice

In this procedure, you set the computer to its original configuration to prepare for later procedures.

▶ **To disable the DHCP relay agent**

Note   Complete this procedure from Server2.

1. Click the **Start** button, point to **Settings**, and then click **Control Panel**.
2. Double-click the **Services** icon.

   The **Services** dialog box appears.
3. Click **DHCP Relay Agent**.
4. Click the **Startup** tab.

   The **Service** dialog box appears.
5. Click **Disabled**.
6. Click **OK**.
7. Click **Close**.
8. Shut down and restart your computer.

▶ **To use a static IP address**

Note   Complete this procedure only from the DHCP client computer.

1. Access the **Microsoft TCP/IP Properties** dialog box.
2. Click **Specify an IP address**.
3. Type the configuration information shown in the following table.

In this box	Type
IP Address	**131.107.2.211**
Subnet Mask	**255.255.255.0**
Default Gateway	**131.107.2.1**

4. Click **OK**.

   The **Network** dialog box appears.

5. Click **OK**.

6. Shut down and restart your computer.

Summary

A relay agent relays DHCP messages between DHCP clients and servers on different IP networks.

Lesson 4: Managing the DHCP Database

The DHCP database is automatically backed up every 60 minutes. If the Windows NT Server detects a corrupted database, it automatically restores a backup copy. This lesson explains when to manually back up and compact the database.

After this lesson, you will be able to:

- Back up and restore the DHCP database.
- Use the Jetpack utility to compact the DHCP database.

Estimated lesson time: 10 minutes

Backing Up the DHCP Database

By default, the DHCP database is backed up every 60 minutes. Backup copies are stored in the *systemroot*\System32\Dhcp\Backup\Jet directory.

The default backup interval can be changed by setting the **BackupInterval** value to the appropriate number of minutes and restarting the DHCP Server service. This **BackupInterval** parameter is located in the registry under the following key:

HKEY_LOCAL_MACHINE\SYSTEM\CurrentControlSet\Services \DHCPServer\Parameters\BackupInterval

A copy of this registry subkey is stored in the *systemroot*\System32\Dhcp\Backup directory as DHCPCFG.

Restoring the DHCP Database

The DHCP database can be restored either automatically or manually. The restore process is done using any of the following methods:

- Restart the DHCP Server service. If the DHCP Server service detects a corrupt database, it automatically restores a backup copy of the database.
- Set the **RestoreFlag** value to **1**, and then restart the DHCP Server service. The **RestoreFlag** parameter is located in the registry under the following key:

  HKEY_LOCAL_MACHINE\SYSTEM\CurrentControlSet\Services \DHCPServer\Parameters

  Once the database has been successfully restored, the server automatically changes the value back to the default value of 0.

- Copy the contents of the *systemroot*\System32\Dhcp\Backup\Jet directory to the *systemroot*\System32\Dhcp directory, and then restart the DHCP Server service.

The DHCP Database Files

The files listed in the following table are stored in the *systemroot*\System32\Dhcp directory. You should not tamper with or remove these files.

File	Description
Dhcp.mdb	The DHCP database file.
Dhcp.tmp	A temporary file that DHCP creates for temporary database information while the DHCP Server service is running.
Jet.log and Jet*.log	Logs of all transactions done with the database. These are used by DHCP to recover data if necessary.
System.mdb	Used by DHCP for storing information about the structure of the database.

Compacting the DHCP Database

Windows NT Server 4.0 is designed to automatically compact the DHCP database, so normally you should not need to run this procedure. However, if you are using Windows NT Server version 3.51 or earlier, after DHCP has been running for a while the database might need to be compacted to improve DHCP performance. You should compact the DHCP database whenever its size approaches 30 MB.

Practice

You can use the Jetpack utility provided with Windows NT Server to compact a DHCP database. Jetpack is a command-line utility that is run in the Windows NT Server command window.

▶ **To compact the DHCP database**

1. Stop the DHCP Server service. This can be done from **Control Panel**, **Services**, **Microsoft DHCP Server**, or at a command prompt. To stop the service at a command prompt, use the following command syntax:

    net stop dhcpserver

2. At a command prompt, go to the *systemroot*\System32\Dhcp directory, and then run the Jetpack utility using the following command syntax (assign any file name to *temporary_name*):

    jetpack dhcp.mdb *temporary_name*.**mdb**

    The contents of Dhcp.mdb are compacted in *temporary_name*, the temporary file is copied to Dhcp.mdb, and then the temporary name is deleted.

3. Restart the DHCP Server service from **Control Panel**, **Services**, **Microsoft DHCP Server**, or at a command prompt. To restart the service at a command prompt, use the following command syntax:

    net start dhcpserver

Note The *Microsoft Windows NT Server Resource Kit* includes a command-line version of DHCP Manager, and a utility that detects unauthorized DHCP servers.

Summary

The DHCP database is automatically backed up every 60 minutes. However, there are some situations when you want to manually back up the database. You can use the Jetpack utility provided with Windows NT Server to compact a DHCP database.

Review

The following questions are intended to reinforce key information presented in this chapter. If you are unable to answer a question, review the appropriate lesson and then try the question again.

1. What are the four steps in the DHCP lease process?

2. At what lease expiration points do DHCP clients attempt to renew their lease?

3. What must be configured on the DHCP server for a DHCP client to receive a lease?

4. In what situations is it necessary to have more than one DHCP server on an internetwork?

5. How are DHCP servers configured to provide backup for each other?

6. In what situations is it necessary to reserve an IP address for a client?

_____

_____

_____

_____

CHAPTER 8

NetBIOS over TCP/IP

Lesson 1   NetBIOS Names . . . 166

Lesson 2   NetBIOS Name Resolution . . . 171

Lesson 3   Using the LMHOSTS File . . . 179

Review . . . 184

About This Chapter

In a preceding chapter, you learned how an IP address is resolved to a hardware address for communicating. In this chapter, you learn NetBIOS name resolution concepts and methods. The lessons clarify how a NetBIOS name is resolved to an IP address using broadcasts, the LMHOSTS file, a NetBIOS name server, a Domain Name Server (DNS), and the HOSTS file. In the lessons in this chapter, you configure and use the LMHOSTS file.

Before You Begin

To complete the lessons in this chapter, you must have installed Microsoft Windows NT Server 4.0 with TCP/IP.

Lesson 1: NetBIOS Names

The NetBIOS name is the name assigned to your computer. This lesson explains how the NetBIOS name is used by Windows NT to communicate with other NetBIOS-based computers.

After this lesson, you will be able to:
- Define NetBIOS and NetBIOS names.
- Describe the types of services provided by NetBIOS over TCP/IP.
- Explain how NetBIOS names are registered, released, and discovered.

Estimated lesson time: 25 minutes

NetBIOS was developed for IBM in 1983 by Sytek Corporation to allow applications to communicate over a network. As shown in the following illustration, NetBIOS defines two entities: a session level *interface* and a session management/data transport *protocol*.

The NetBIOS interface is a standard API for user applications to submit network I/O and control directives to underlying network protocol software. An application program that uses the NetBIOS interface API for network communication can be run on any protocol software that supports the NetBIOS interface.

NetBIOS also defines a protocol that functions at the session/transport level. This is implemented by the underlying protocol software such as NBFP (NetBEUI) or NetBT to perform the network I/O required to accommodate the NetBIOS interface command set. NetBT, or NetBIOS over TCP/IP, is a session-layer network service.

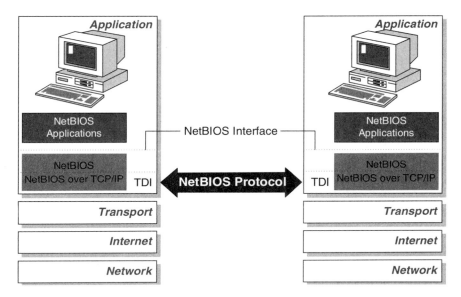

NetBIOS provides commands and support for the following services:

- Network name registration and verification
- Session establishment and termination
- Reliable connection-oriented *session* data transfer
- Unreliable connectionless *datagram* data transfer
- Support protocol (driver) and adapter monitoring and management

NetBIOS Names

A NetBIOS name is a unique 16-byte address used to identify a NetBIOS resource on the network. This name is either a unique (exclusive) or group (non-exclusive) name. Unique names are typically used to send network communication to a specific process on a computer. Group names are used to send information to multiple computers at one time.

You can use the **nbtstat -n** command to view your computer's NetBIOS name.

An example of a process using a NetBIOS name is the server service on a computer running Windows NT. When your computer starts up, the server service registers a unique NetBIOS name based on the computer name. The exact name used by the server is the 15-character computer name plus a 16th character of 20 hexadecimal. Other network services also use the computer name to build their NetBIOS names, so the 16th character is used to uniquely identify each specific service such as the Redirector, Server, or Messenger services.

When you attempt to connect to a computer running Windows NT Server with the **net use** command, the NetBIOS name for the server service is searched for with a *Name Query* request. The matching server process is found and communication is established.

All Windows NT network services register NetBIOS names. All Windows NT network commands (Windows NT Explorer, File Manager, and **net** commands) use NetBIOS names to access these services.

NetBIOS names are also used by other NetBIOS-based computers, such as Windows for Workgroups, LAN Manager, and LAN Manager for UNIX hosts.

Common NetBIOS Names

Viewing the registered names can be helpful in determining which services are running on a computer. The following table describes common NetBIOS names that you see in the Windows Internet Name Service (WINS) database. In Chapter 9, "Implementing Windows Internet Name Service (WINS)," you review WINS.

Registered name	Description
\\computer_name[00h]	The name registered for the Workstation service on the WINS client.
\\computer_name[03h]	The name registered for the Messenger service on the WINS client.
\\computer_name[20h]	The name registered for the Server service on the WINS client.
\\username[03h]	The name of the user currently logged on to the computer. The user name is registered by the Messenger service so that the user can receive **net send** commands sent to their user name. If more than one user is logged on with the same user name (such as Administrator), only the first computer from which a user logged on will register the name.
\\domain_name[1Bh]	The domain name registered by the Windows NT Server primary domain controller (PDC) that is functioning as the Domain Master Browser. This name is used for remote domain browsing. When a WINS server is queried for this name, it returns the IP address of the computer that registered this name.

NetBIOS Name Registration, Discovery, and Release

All nodes of NetBIOS over TCP/IP use name registration, name discovery, and name release for interacting with NetBIOS hosts, such as a Windows NT host.

Name Registration

When a NetBIOS over TCP/IP host initializes, it registers its NetBIOS name using a NetBIOS *name registration request.* This registration can be done using a broadcast or a directed send to a NetBIOS name server.

If another host has registered the same NetBIOS name, either the host or a NetBIOS name server responds with a *negative name registration response.* The initiating host receives an initialization error as a result.

Name Discovery

Name discovery on a local network is handled by local broadcasts or a NetBIOS name server. When Windows NT wants to communicate with another TCP/IP host, a NetBIOS *name query request* containing the destination NetBIOS name is broadcast on the local network or sent to the NetBIOS name server for resolution.

The host that owns the NetBIOS name, or a NetBIOS name server, responds by sending a *positive name query response.*

Name Release

Name release occurs whenever a NetBIOS application or service is stopped. For example, when the Workstation service on a host is stopped, the host discontinues sending a negative name registration response when someone else tries to use the name. The NetBIOS name is said to be *released* and available for use by another host.

Segmenting NetBIOS Names with Scopes

Another useful parameter is the NetBIOS scope ID. The scope ID is used to segment the NetBIOS namespace. Using a scope ID will not increase performance, but it will reduce the number of packets that are accepted and evaluated by a host.

The NetBIOS scope ID is a character string that is appended to the NetBIOS name. It is used to segment the NetBIOS 16-character flat namespace. Without scopes, a NetBIOS name must be unique across all NetBIOS resources on the network. With scopes, a NetBIOS name is unique only within the particular scope, not across the whole namespace.

NetBIOS resources within a scope are isolated from all NetBIOS resources outside the scope. The NetBIOS scope ID on two hosts must match, or the two hosts will not be able to communicate with each other using NetBIOS over TCP/IP. You configure a scope ID from the **WINS Address** tab of the **Microsoft TCP/IP Properties** dialog box.

As shown in the following illustration, two NetBIOS scopes are used—APPS and MIS.

- HOST1.APPS and HOST2.APPS will be able to communicate with SERVER.APPS but not with HOST3.MIS, HOST4.MIS, or SERVER.MIS.

- The NetBIOS scope also allows computers to use the same NetBIOS name (as long as they have a different scope ID). The NetBIOS scope becomes part of the NetBIOS name, making the name unique. In the following illustration, two servers have the same NetBIOS name but different scope IDs.

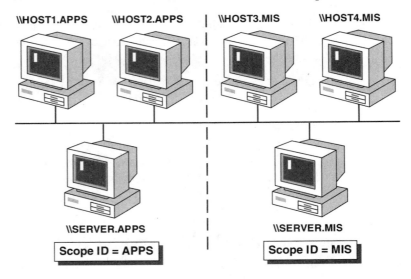

Note The NetBIOS scope ID is defined in RFC 1001. For a copy of this RFC, see the *Course Materials* Web page on the course compact disc.

Summary
NetBIOS defines a session level interface and a session management/data transport protocol. NetBIOS uses name registration, name release, and name discovery for interacting with NetBIOS hosts. The NetBIOS scope ID is used to segment the NetBIOS namespace.

Lesson 2: NetBIOS Name Resolution

Resolving a computer's NetBIOS name to an IP address is called NetBIOS name resolution. This lesson defines NetBIOS name resolution and provides an overview of the different methods used by Windows NT to resolve a NetBIOS name to an IP address. It also provides a brief overview of the NetBIOS name resolution nodes supported by Microsoft TCP/IP.

After this lesson, you will be able to:

- Explain how NetBIOS names of hosts on remote networks are resolved using the LMHOSTS file and a NetBIOS name server.
- Explain how NetBIOS names on a local network are resolved using broadcasts.
- Describe the NetBIOS over TCP/IP node types.

Estimated lesson time: 25 minutes

NetBIOS name resolution is the process of successfully mapping a computer's NetBIOS name to an IP address. Before the IP address can be resolved to a hardware address, a computer's NetBIOS computer name must be resolved to an IP address.

Microsoft TCP/IP can use several methods to resolve NetBIOS names. The type of method depends on whether a host is local or remote.

Standard methods of resolution	Description
NetBIOS name cache	The local cache containing the NetBIOS names that the local computer recently resolved.
NetBIOS Name Server (NBNS)	A server implemented under RFCs 1001 and 1002 to provide name resolution of NetBIOS computer names. The Microsoft implementation of this is WINS.
Local broadcast	A broadcast on the local network for the IP address of the destination NetBIOS name.

Microsoft methods of resolution	Description
LMHOSTS file	A local text file that maps IP addresses to the NetBIOS computer names of Windows networking computers on remote networks.
HOSTS file	A local text file in the same format as the 4.3 Berkeley Software Distribution (BSD) UNIX\Etc\Hosts file. This file maps host names to IP addresses. This file is typically used to resolve host names for TCP/IP utilities.
Domain Name System (DNS)	A server that maintains a database of IP address/computer name (host name) mappings.

Resolving Local NetBIOS Names Using a Broadcast

When the destination host is on the local network, NetBIOS resolves the names of hosts using a broadcast. The following steps and illustration show the process:

1. When a user initiates a Windows NT command, such as **net use**, the NetBIOS name cache is checked for the IP address that corresponds to the NetBIOS name of the destination host. This eliminates extraneous broadcasts on the network. If the name had been resolved recently, a mapping for the destination host would already be in the source host's NetBIOS name cache, and the broadcast would not be sent.

2. If the NetBIOS name is not resolved from the cache, the source host broadcasts a name query request on the local network with the destination NetBIOS name.

3. Each computer on the local network receives the broadcast and checks its local NetBIOS table to see if it owns the requested name.

The computer that owns the name formulates a name query response. Before the response can be sent, ARP is used (either cache or broadcast) to obtain the source host's hardware address. When the hardware address is obtained, the name query response is sent.

When the source host receives the name query response, the **net use** session is established.

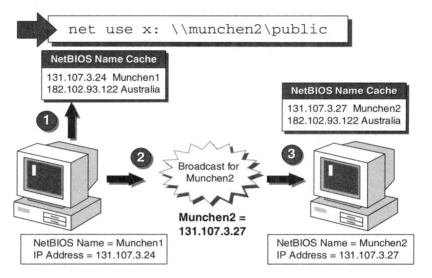

Limitations of Broadcasts

Not all routers can forward broadcasts. Those that can typically have this feature disabled because forwarding broadcasts increases internetwork traffic, which can affect network performance. As a result, broadcasts remain on the local network.

Note For a router to forward broadcasts, forwarding of broadcast frames for UDP ports 137 and 138 must be enabled on the router.

Resolving Names with a NetBIOS Name Server

A common method of resolving NetBIOS names to IP addresses is with a NetBIOS name server. The resolution process is as follows:

1. When a user initiates a Windows NT command, such as **net use**, the NetBIOS name resolution process begins. The NetBIOS name cache is checked for the NetBIOS name/IP address mapping of the destination host. If the NetBIOS name is not found in the cache, the Windows NT client will attempt to determine the IP address of the destination host using other methods.

2. If the name cannot be resolved using the NetBIOS name cache, the NetBIOS name of the destination host is sent to the NetBIOS name server that is configured for the source host. When the NetBIOS name is resolved to an IP address, it is returned to the source host.

   By default, the Windows NT client attempts to locate the primary WINS server three times. If there is no response, the Windows NT client attempts to contact the secondary WINS server. If, however, the primary WINS server notifies the client that it does not have a name/IP address mapping for the destination host, the client accepts this as the response and does not attempt to contact the secondary WINS server.

3. After the NetBIOS name is resolved, the source host uses ARP to resolve the IP address to a hardware address for communicating with the source host.

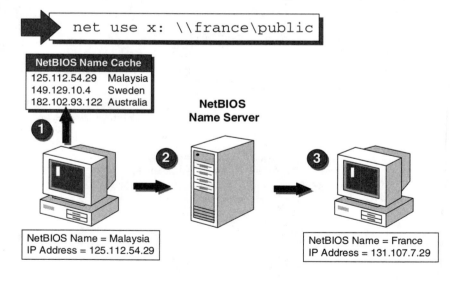

Microsoft Methods of Resolving NetBIOS Names

NetBIOS names can be resolved using a combination of Microsoft-supported methods. Windows NT 4.0 and later can be configured to resolve NetBIOS names using the LMHOSTS file, HOSTS file, and a DNS, in addition to broadcasts and the NetBIOS name server. If one of these methods fails, the other methods provide backup. The following example illustrates how the combined methods might work:

1. When a user types a Windows NT command, such as **net use**, the NetBIOS name cache is checked for the NetBIOS name/IP address mapping of the destination host. If a mapping is found, the name is resolved without generating network activity.

2. If the name is not resolved from the NetBIOS name cache, three attempts are made to contact the NetBIOS name server (if one is configured). If the name is resolved, the IP address is returned to the source host.

3. If the name is not resolved by the NetBIOS name server, the client generates three broadcasts on the local network. If the NetBIOS name is found on the local network, it is resolved to an IP address.

4. If the NetBIOS name is not resolved using broadcasts, the local LMHOSTS file is parsed. If the NetBIOS name is found in the LMHOSTS file, it is resolved to an IP address.

5. If the NetBIOS name is not resolved from the LMHOSTS file, Windows NT begins attempting to resolve the name through host name resolution techniques if the **Enable DNS for Windows Resolution** check box is enabled in the **WINS Address Property** page of the **TCP/IP** protocol dialog box. The first step in host name resolution techniques is to check for a match against the local host name.

   If the host name is found in the HOSTS file, it is resolved to an IP address. The HOSTS file must reside on the local computer.

6. If the name is not resolved from the HOSTS file, the source host sends a request to its configured DNS server. If the host name is found by a DNS server, it is resolved to an IP address.

If the DNS server does not respond to the request, additional attempts are made at intervals of 5, 10, 20, and 40 seconds.

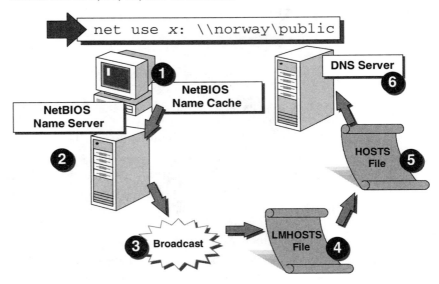

If none of these methods resolve the NetBIOS name, the Windows NT command will return an error to the user, indicating that the computer could not be found.

NetBIOS over TCP/IP Name Resolution Nodes

Windows NT 4.0 provides support for all of the NetBIOS over TCP/IP nodes defined in RFCs 1001 and 1002. Each node resolves NetBIOS names differently.

Node	Description
B-node (broadcast)	B-node uses broadcasts (UDP datagrams) for name registration and resolution. B-node has two major problems: (1) In a large internetwork, broadcasts can increase the network load, and (2) Routers typically do not forward broadcasts, so only computers on the local network can respond.
P-node (peer-peer)	P-node uses a NetBIOS name server (NBNS) such as WINS to resolve NetBIOS names. P-node does not use broadcasts; instead, it queries the name server directly. Because broadcasts are not used, computers can span routers. The most significant problems with P-node are that all computers must be configured with the IP address of the NBNS, and if the NBNS is down, computers will not be able to communicate even on the local network.

(continued)

Node	Description
M-node (mixed)	M-node is a combination of B-node and P-node. By default, an M-node functions as a B-node. If it is unable to resolve a name by broadcast, it uses the NBNS of P-node.
H-node (hybrid)	H-node is a combination of P-node and B-node. By default, an H-node functions as a P-node. If it is unable to resolve a name through the NetBIOS name server, it uses a broadcast to resolve the name.
Microsoft enhanced B-node	Microsoft uses an enhanced B-node for resolving NetBIOS computer names of remote hosts. The LMHOSTS file is a static file that maps a remote computer's NetBIOS name to its IP address. Entries in the LMHOSTS file designated with "**#PRE**" are cached when TCP/IP initializes. Before a broadcast is sent, the cache is checked for the NetBIOS name/IP address mapping. If the mapping is not found in cache, a broadcast is initiated. If the broadcast is not successful, the LMHOSTS file is parsed in an attempt to resolve the name.

Note NetBIOS over TCP/IP nodes are defined in RFCs 1001 and 1002. For a copy of these RFCs, see the *Course Materials* Web page on the course compact disc.

Configuring Node Types

You can configure which NetBIOS name resolution method NetBT will use to register and resolve names with the following registry parameter:

HKEY_LOCAL_MACHINE\SYSTEM\CurrentControlSet\Services\Netbt \Parameters

Note The system defaults to Microsoft enhanced B-node if there are no WINS servers configured. If there is at least one WINS server configured, the system defaults to H-node.

NBTSTAT Utility

The NBSTAT utility checks the state of current NetBIOS over TCP/IP connections, updates the LMHOSTS cache, and determines your registered name and scope ID. This program is also useful for troubleshooting and pre-loading the NetBIOS name cache.

Command	Description
nbtstat -n	Lists the NetBIOS names registered by the client.
nbtstat -c	Displays the NetBIOS name cache.
nbtstat -R	Manually reloads the NetBIOS name cache using entries in the LMHOSTS file with a **#PRE** parameter.

Summary

NetBIOS name resolution is the process of mapping a computer's NetBIOS name to an IP address. There are several methods available for resolving NetBIOS names, each depending on your network configuration. The methods are NetBIOS name cache, NetBIOS name server (NBNS), local broadcast, LMHOSTS file, HOSTS file, and Domain Name System.

Microsoft supports multiple methods of resolving NetBIOS names. If one method fails, another provides a backup. Windows NT 4.0 supports all of the NetBIOS over TCP/IP nodes.

Lesson 3: Using the LMHOSTS File

Now that you have seen conceptually how the different name resolutions work, you focus on the enhanced B-node implementation using the LMHOSTS file. The LMHOSTS file maps an IP address to its corresponding NetBIOS name of a remote host.

After this lesson, you will be able to:

- Configure an LMHOSTS file for resolving NetBIOS names of hosts on remote networks.

Estimated lesson time: 35 minutes

The LMHOSTS file is a static ASCII file used to resolve NetBIOS names/IP addresses of remote computers running Windows NT and other NetBIOS-based hosts. The LMHOSTS file has the following characteristics:

- It resolves NetBIOS names used in Windows NT commands.

- Entries consist of one NetBIOS name and its corresponding IP address.

- Each computer has its own file. The default directory location is in the form:

  systemroot\System32\Drivers\Etc

  A sample LMHOSTS file (Lmhosts.sam) is included in this directory.

- It is used by Windows NT utilities.

The following is an example of the LMHOSTS file:

```
#This file is used by Microsoft TCP/IP
122.107.9.10    Mexico  # Sales Server
131.107.7.29    France  # Database Server
191.131.54.73   UK  # Training Server
149.129.10.4    Sweden  #PRE    # Main Office Server
182.102.93.122  Australia   #PRE    # MIS Server
```

Predefined Keywords

A Windows NT LMHOSTS file also contains predefined keywords which are prefixed with a #. If you use this LMHOSTS file on an older NetBIOS over TCP/IP system such as LAN Manager, these directives are ignored as comments because they begin with a number sign (#). The following table lists the possible LMHOSTS keywords.

Predefined keyword	Description
#PRE	Defines which entries should be initially preloaded as permanent entries in the name cache. Preloaded entries reduce network broadcasts, because names are resolved from cache rather than from broadcast or by parsing the LMHOSTS file. Entries with a **#PRE** tag are loaded automatically at initialization or manually by typing **nbtstat –R** at a command prompt.
#DOM:[*domain_name*]	Facilitates domain activity, such as logon validation over a router, account synchronization, and browsing.
#NOFNR	Avoids using NetBIOS directed name queries for older LAN Manager UNIX systems.
#BEGIN_ALTERNATE **#END_ALTERNATE**	Defines a redundant list of alternate locations for LMHOSTS files. The recommended way to **#INCLUDE** remote files is using a UNC path, to ensure access to the file. Of course, the universal naming convention (UNC) names must exist in the LMHOSTS file with a proper IP address to NetBIOS name translation.
#INCLUDE	Loads and searches NetBIOS entries in a separate file from the default LMHOSTS file. Typically, a **#INCLUDE** file is a centrally located shared LMHOST file.
#MH	Adds multiple entries for a multihomed computer.

Note The NetBIOS name cache and file are always read sequentially. Add the most frequently accessed computers to the top of the list. Add the **#PRE** tagged entries near the bottom, because they will not be accessed again once TCP/IP initializes.

Name Resolution Problems Using LMHOSTS

The most common NetBIOS name resolution problems occur when an entry in the LMHOSTS file is incorrect.

Problem	Solution
An entry for a remote host does not exist in the LMHOSTS file.	Verify that the IP address/NetBIOS name mappings of all remote hosts that a computer needs to access are added to the LMHOSTS file.
The NetBIOS name in the LMHOSTS file is misspelled.	Verify the spelling of all names as you add them.
The IP address is invalid for the NetBIOS name.	Verify that the IP address is correct for the corresponding NetBIOS name.
There are multiple entries for the same NetBIOS name.	Verify that each entry in the LMHOSTS file is unique. If there are duplicate names, the first name listed in the file is used. If the first name has an incorrect mapping, the LMHOSTS file will not be re-read for the next entry, and possibly, the correct mapping for the same name.

Tip After you add entries to the LMHOSTS file, use a **net** command with each NetBIOS name to verify that entries were added correctly.

Practice

In this procedure, you configure the LMHOSTS file to resolve NetBIOS names to IP addresses.

Note If you have not already done so, you should remove the NWLink IPX/SPX Compatible Transport Protocol from the **Select Network Protocol** dialog box.

Perform this procedure from your primary computer (Server1).

▶ **To configure LMHOSTS for computer names**

1. Open a command prompt.
2. Using the **edit** command, change the directory and file as follows:

   systemroot\System32\Drivers\Etc\Lmhosts.sam
3. At the beginning of the LMHOSTS file, read the instructions for adding entries.
4. Go to the end of the file, and then add the following entry:

   131.107.2.211   Server2
5. Save the file as LMHOSTS.
6. Start Windows NT Explorer.

7. On the **Tools** menu, click **Map Network Drive**.

   The **Map Network Drive** dialog box appears.

8. In the **Path** box, type **\\Server2** and then click **OK**.

   What was the response?

   _____

If you receive an error message, compare the command syntax to the spelling of the LMHOSTS file entry.

Practice

In this practice, you use the following illustration to determine which entries should be added to an LMHOSTS file for each network, so that hosts on network A can communicate with hosts on network B, and vice versa.

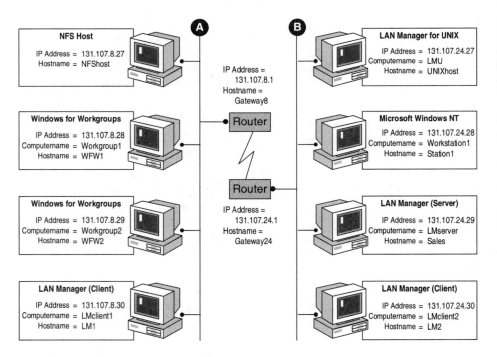

Add the appropriate entries to the following LMHOSTS files so that hosts on both networks can communicate with each other.

LMHOSTS File for Hosts on Network A

IP address   **Name**

LMHOSTS File for Hosts on Network B

IP address   **Name**

Summary

The LMHOSTS file maps an IP address to its corresponding NetBIOS name of a remote host. A Windows NT LMHOSTS file contains predefined keywords that facilitate name resolution.

Review

The following questions are intended to reinforce key information presented in this chapter. If you are unable to answer a question, review the appropriate lesson and then try the question again.

1. What methods are used to resolve NetBIOS names?

_____

_____

2. What is the function of the LMHOSTS file?

_____

_____

CHAPTER 9

Windows Internet Name Service (WINS)

Lesson 1 WINS Overview . . . 187

Lesson 2 The WINS Resolution Process . . . 189

Lesson 3 Implementing WINS . . . 196

Lesson 4 Database Replication Between WINS Servers . . . 208

Lesson 5 Maintaining the WINS Server Database . . . 214

Review . . . 222

About This Chapter

The preceding chapters reviewed the different methods of resolving NetBIOS names. In this chapter you will learn how to implement WINS, and understand how WINS reduces broadcast traffic associated with the B-node implementation of NetBIOS over TCP/IP. The lessons in this chapter contain detailed information on installing and configuring a WINS server, WINS client, and WINS proxy agent.

In this chapter, you also learn how to administer a WINS environment. The lessons discuss database replication between WINS servers and maintaining the WINS server database. During the lessons, you configure a push and pull partner, and back up the WINS database.

Before You Begin

To complete the lessons in this chapter, you must have:

- Installed Microsoft Windows NT Server 4.0 with TCP/IP.
- An understanding of the NetBIOS concepts presented in Chapter 8, "NetBIOS over TCP/IP."

Lesson 1: WINS Overview

The Windows Internet Name Service, or WINS, eliminates the need for broadcasts to resolve computer names to IP addresses, and provides a dynamic database that maintains mappings of computer names to IP addresses. In this lesson, you learn the function and purpose of WINS.

After this lesson, you will be able to:
- Explain how a WINS server resolves NetBIOS names.
- Describe the benefits of using WINS.

Estimated lesson time: 5 minutes

WINS is an enhanced NetBIOS Name Server (NBNS) designed by Microsoft to eliminate broadcast traffic associated with the B-node implementation of NetBIOS over TCP/IP. It is used to register NetBIOS computer names and resolve them to IP addresses for both local and remote hosts.

There are several advantages of using WINS. The primary advantage is that client requests for computer name resolution are sent directly to a WINS server. If the WINS server can resolve the name, it sends the IP address directly to the client. As a result, a broadcast is not needed and network traffic is reduced. However, if the WINS server is unavailable, the WINS client can still use a broadcast in an attempt to resolve the name.

Another advantage of using WINS is that the WINS database is updated dynamically, so it is always current. This eliminates the need for an LMHOSTS file. In addition, WINS provides network and interdomain browsing capabilities.

Before two NetBIOS-based hosts can communicate, the destination NetBIOS name must be resolved to an IP address. This is necessary because TCP/IP requires an IP address rather than a NetBIOS computer name to communicate. Resolution uses the following process:

1. In a WINS environment, each time a WINS client starts, it registers its NetBIOS name/IP address mapping with a configured WINS server.
2. When a WINS client initiates a Windows NT command to communicate with another host, the name query request is sent directly to the WINS server instead of broadcasting it on the local network.

3. If the WINS server finds a NetBIOS name/IP address mapping for the destination host in this database, it returns the destination host's IP address to the WINS client. Because the WINS database obtains NetBIOS name/IP address mappings dynamically, it is always current.

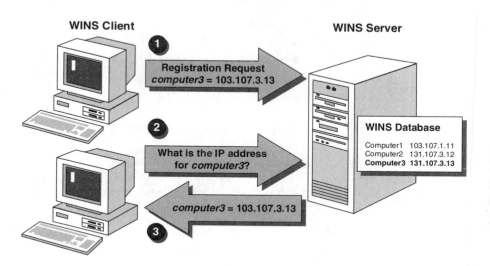

Summary

There are several advantages to using WINS. The primary advantage is that broadcast traffic is reduced because requests for name resolution are sent directly to the WINS server.

Lesson 2: The WINS Resolution Process

WINS uses standard methods of name registration, name renewal, and name release. This lesson introduces the different phases used to resolve a NetBIOS name to an IP address using WINS.

After this lesson, you will be able to:
- Explain how WINS processes name registration, name renewal, and name release.

Estimated lesson time: 25 minutes

The process WINS uses to resolve and maintain NetBIOS names is similar to the B-node implementation. The method used to renew a name is unique to NetBIOS node types that use a NetBIOS name server. WINS is an extension of RFCs 1001 and 1002. The following illustration shows the process of resolving a NetBIOS name.

Note   RFCs 1001 and 1002 describe NetBIOS over TCP/IP. For a copy of these RFCs, see the *Course Materials* Web page on the course compact disc.

Name Registration

Each WINS client is configured with the IP address of a primary WINS server and optionally, a secondary WINS server. When a client starts, it registers its NetBIOS name and IP address with the configured WINS server. The WINS server stores the client's NetBIOS name/IP address mapping in its database.

Name Renewal

All NetBIOS names are registered on a temporary basis, which means that the same name can be used later by a different host if the original owner stops using it.

Name Release

Each WINS client is responsible for maintaining the lease on its registered name. When the name will no longer be used, such as when the computer is shut down, the WINS client sends a message to the WINS server to release it.

Name Query and Name Resolution

After a WINS client has registered its NetBIOS name and IP address with a WINS server, it can communicate with other hosts by obtaining the IP address of other NetBIOS-based computers from a WINS server.

All WINS communications are done using directed datagrams over UDP port 137 (NetBIOS Name Service).

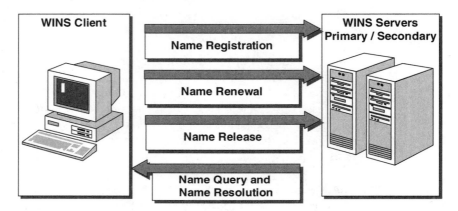

Name Registration

Unlike the B-node implementation of NetBIOS over TCP/IP, which broadcasts its name registration, WINS clients register their NetBIOS names with WINS servers.

When a WINS client initializes, it registers its NetBIOS name by sending a name registration request directly to the configured WINS server. NetBIOS names are registered when services or applications start, such as the Workstation, Server, and Messenger.

If the WINS server is available and the name is not already registered by another WINS client, a successful registration message is returned to the client. This message contains the amount of time the NetBIOS name is registered to the client, specified as the Time to Live (TTL). The following illustration shows the name registration process.

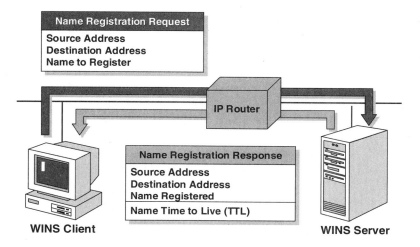

When a Duplicate Name Is Found

If there is a duplicate name registered in the WINS database, the WINS server sends a challenge to the currently registered owner of the name. The challenge is sent as a name query request. The WINS server sends the challenge three times at 500-millisecond intervals.

If the registered computer is a multihomed computer, the WINS server tries each IP address it has for the computer until it receives a response, or until all of the IP addresses have been tried.

If the current registered owner responds successfully to the WINS server, the WINS server sends a negative name registration response to the WINS client that is attempting to register the name. If the current registered owner does not respond to the WINS server, the WINS server sends a successful name registration response to the WINS client that is attempting to register the name.

When the WINS Server Is Unavailable

A WINS client will make three attempts (using ARP) to find the primary WINS server. If it fails after the third attempt, the name registration request is sent to the secondary WINS server, if configured. If neither server is available, the WINS client may initiate a broadcast to register its name.

Name Renewal

To continue using the same NetBIOS name, a client must renew its lease before it expires. If a client does not renew the lease, the WINS server makes it available for another WINS client.

Name Refresh Request

A WINS client first attempts to refresh its name registrations after one-eighth of the TTL has expired. If the WINS client does not receive a name refresh response, it will keep attempting to refresh its registrations every two minutes, until half of the TTL has expired.

At this point, the WINS client will then attempt to refresh its registrations with the secondary WINS server with whose IP address it has been configured. On switching to the secondary WINS server, the WINS client attempts to refresh its registrations as if it were the first refresh attempt—every one-eighth of the TTL until successful, or until half of the TTL has expired, which is four attempts. It then reverts to the primary WINS server.

After a client has successfully refreshed its registration one time, it starts subsequent name registration requests when half of the TTL has expired. The following illustration shows how a WINS client renews its lease to use the same NetBIOS name.

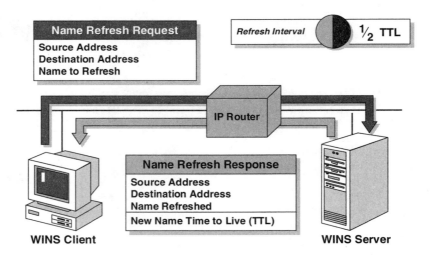

Name Refresh Response

When a WINS server receives the name refresh request, it sends the client a name refresh response with a new TTL.

Name Release

Name Release Request

When a WINS client is properly shut down, it sends a name release request directly to the WINS server for each registered name. The name release request includes the client's IP address and the NetBIOS name to be removed from the WINS database. This allows the name to be available for another client, as shown in the following illustration.

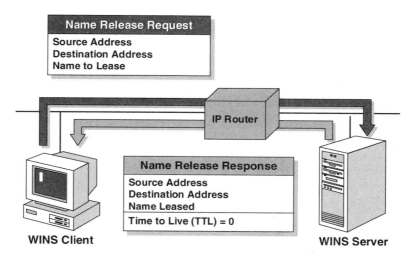

Name Release Response

When the WINS server receives the name release request, it checks its database for the specified name. If the WINS server encounters a database error, or if a different IP address maps the registered name, it sends a negative name release to the WINS client.

Otherwise, the WINS server sends a positive name release and then designates the specified name as inactive in its database. The name release response contains the released NetBIOS name and a TTL value of zero.

Name Query and Name Response

A common method of resolving NetBIOS names to IP addresses is with a NetBIOS name server, such as WINS. When a WINS client is configured, by default, the H-node type of NetBIOS over TCP/IP is implemented. The NetBIOS name server is always checked for a NetBIOS name/IP address mapping before initiating a broadcast. The following steps and illustration demonstrate the process:

1. When a user initiates a Windows NT command, such as **net use**, the NetBIOS name cache is checked for the NetBIOS name/IP address mapping of the destination host.

2. If the name is not resolved from cache, a name query request is sent directly to the client's primary WINS server.

   If the primary WINS server is unavailable, the client resends the request two more times before switching to the secondary WINS server.

   When either WINS server resolves the name, a success message with the IP address for the request NetBIOS name is sent to the source host.

3. If no WINS server can resolve the name, a name query response is sent back to the WINS client with the message "Requested name does not exist," and broadcast is implemented.

If the name is not resolved from cache by a WINS server, or broadcast, the name may still be resolved by parsing the LMHOSTS or HOSTS file, or by using a Domain Name System (DNS).

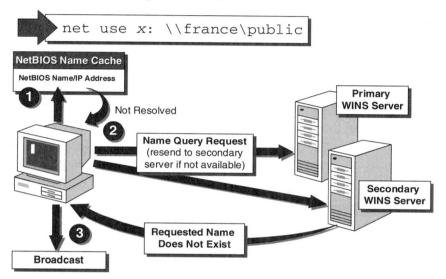

Summary

WINS uses standard name registration, name renewal, and name release methods. To continue using the same NetBIOS name, a client must renew its lease before it expires. When a WINS client is shut down, it notifies the WINS server that it no longer needs its NetBIOS name.

Lesson 3: Implementing WINS

This lesson outlines the considerations for implementing WINS. This lesson shows you how to install the WINS Server service, configure static mappings, and configure a WINS proxy agent.

After this lesson, you will be able to:

- Describe the client and server requirements for implementing WINS.
- Explain how to configure static mappings of non-WINS clients.
- Configure a WINS proxy agent and a DHCP server for WINS.

Estimated lesson time: 60 minutes

Before you implement WINS in an internetwork, consider the number of WINS servers you will need on an internetwork. Only one WINS server is required for an internetwork, because requests for name resolution are directed datagrams that can be routed. Two WINS servers ensure a backup system for fault tolerance. If one server becomes unavailable, the second server can be used to resolve names.

You should also consider the following WINS server recommendations:

- There is no built-in limit to the number of WINS requests that can be handled by a WINS server, but typically it can handle 1,500 name registrations and about 4,500 name queries per minute.
- A conservative recommendation is one WINS server and a backup server for every 10,000 WINS clients.
- Computers with multiple processors have demonstrated performance improvements of approximately 25 percent for each additional processor, as a separate WINS thread is started for each processor.
- If logging of database changes is turned off (through WINS Manager), name registrations are much faster, but if a crash occurs, there is a risk of losing the last few updates.

WINS Requirements

Before you install WINS, you should determine that your server and clients meet the configuration requirements.

WINS Server Requirements

The WINS Server service must be configured on at least one computer within the TCP/IP internetwork running Windows NT Server (it does not have to be a domain controller).

The server must have an IP address, subnet mask, default gateway, and other TCP/IP parameters. These parameters can be assigned by a DHCP server, but statically assigned parameters are recommended.

WINS Client Requirements

WINS is implemented by configuring clients to use WINS and installing and configuring the WINS Server service.

The client can be a computer running any of the following supported operating systems:

- Windows NT Server 4.0 or 3.5*x*
- Windows NT Workstation 4.0 or 3.5*x*
- Windows 95
- Windows for Workgroups 3.11 running Microsoft TCP/IP-32
- Microsoft Network Client 3.0 for MS-DOS
- LAN Manager 2.2c for MS-DOS

The client must have an IP address of a WINS server configured, for a primary WINS server, or for primary and secondary WINS servers.

WINS Server Configuration

- Install WINS.
- Configure a static mapping for all non-WINS clients to enable the WINS clients on remote networks to communicate with the non-WINS clients.
- Configure a WINS proxy agent to extend the name resolution capabilities of the WINS server to non-WINS clients.
- Configure WINS support on a DHCP server.

WINS Client Configuration

The client is configured on the **WINS** tab of the **Microsoft TCP/IP Properties** dialog box. To configure the client, type the IP address of a primary WINS server, and, optionally, the IP address of a secondary WINS server.

Practice

This procedure installs a WINS server to automatically resolve NetBIOS names to IP addresses for WINS clients.

Note Perform this procedure from the computer you designate as the WINS server (Server1).

▶ **To install the WINS Server service**

1. Click the **Start** button, point to **Settings**, and then click **Control Panel**.

2. In Control Panel, double-click the Network icon, click the **Services** tab, and then click **Add**.

   The **Select Network Service** dialog box appears.

3. Select **Windows Internet Name Service**, and then click **OK**.

   The **Windows NT Setup** dialog box appears, prompting for the full path of the Windows NT distribution files.

4. Type the full path to the Windows NT distributions files, and then click **Continue**.

   The appropriate files are copied to your computer, and then the **Network** dialog box appears.

5. Click **Close**.

   A **Network Settings Change** dialog box appears, indicating that the computer needs to be restarted to initialize the new configuration.

6. Click **Yes**.

7. Log on as Administrator.

Configuring Static Entries for Non-WINS Clients

If you have DHCP clients that require a static mapping, you must reserve an IP address for the DHCP client so that its IP address will always be the same.

On an internetwork that has non-WINS clients, it can be beneficial to configure a static IP address/NetBIOS name mapping for each non-WINS client. This ensures that NetBIOS names of non-WINS clients can be resolved by a WINS client without maintaining a local LMHOSTS file. For example, if a WINS client tries to **net use** to a non-WINS client on a remote network, the name cannot be resolved because the non-WINS client is not registered with the WINS server.

▶ **To configure a static mapping**

1. Click the **Start** button, point to **Programs**, point to **Administrative Tools**, and then click **WINS Manager**.

2. On the **Mappings** menu, click **Static Mappings**.

   The **Static Mappings** dialog box appears.

3. Click **Add Mappings**.

   The **Add Static Mappings** dialog box appears.

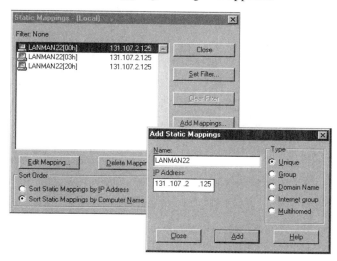

4. In the **Name** box, type the computer name of the non-WINS client.

5. In the **IP Address** box, type the IP address of the non-WINS client.

6. Under **Type**, the options in the following table are available to indicate whether this entry is a unique name or a kind of group with a special name.

Type option	Description
Unique	A unique name maps to a single IP address.
Group	Also referred to as a "Normal" group. When adding an entry to a group by using WINS Manager, you must enter the computer name and IP address. However, the IP addresses of individual members of a group are not stored in the WINS database. Because the member addresses are not stored, there is no limit to the number of members that can be added to a group. Broadcast name packets are used to communicate with group members.
Domain Name	A NetBIOS name-to-address mapping that has 0x1C as the 16th byte. A domain group stores up to a maximum of 25 addresses for members. For registrations after the 25th address, WINS overwrites a replica address or, if none is present, it overwrites the oldest registration.

(*continued*)

Type option	Description
Internet Group	Internet groups are user-defined groups that enable you to group resources, such as printers, for easy reference and browsing. An Internet group can store up to a maximum of 25 addresses for members. A dynamic member, however, does not replace a static member added by using WINS Manager or importing the LMHOSTS file.
Multihomed	A unique name that can have more than one address. This is used for multihomed computers. Each multihomed group name can contain a maximum of 25 addresses. For registrations after the 25th address, WINS overwrites a replica address or, if none is present, it overwrites the oldest registration.

7. Click **Add**.

   The mapping is immediately added to the database for that entry, and then the boxes are cleared so that you can add another entry.

8. Repeat this process for each static mapping, and then click **Close**.

Important Each static mapping is added to the database when you click the **Add** button; you cannot cancel work in this dialog box. If you make a mistake in typing a name or IP address for a mapping, you must return to the **Static Mappings** dialog box and delete the mapping there.

Configuring a WINS Proxy Agent

If you have computers on your internetwork that are not supported as WINS clients, they can resolve NetBIOS names on a WINS server using a WINS proxy agent. A WINS proxy agent extends the name resolution capabilities of the WINS server to non-WINS clients by listening for broadcast name registrations and broadcast resolution requests, and then forwarding them to a WINS server. The following illustration shows how a WINS proxy agent forwards broadcasts to a WINS server.

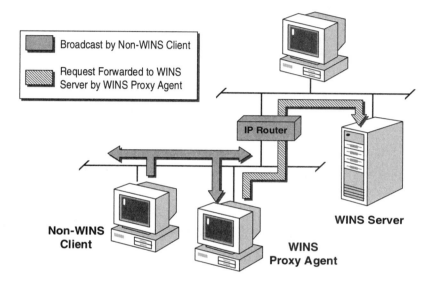

Configuring the WINS proxy agent is accomplished by using the Registry Editor to open HKEY_LOCAL_MACHINE \SYSTEM\CurrentControlSet\Services\ NetBT\Parameters and then setting the **EnableProxy** parameter to **1** (REG_DWORD).

NetBIOS Name Registration

When a non-WINS client broadcasts a name registration request, the WINS proxy agent forwards the request to the WINS server to verify that no other WINS client has registered that name. The NetBIOS name is not registered, only verified.

NetBIOS Name Resolution

When a WINS proxy agent detects a name resolution broadcast, it checks its NetBIOS name cache and attempts to resolve the name. If the name is not in cache, the request is sent to a WINS server. The WINS server sends the WINS proxy agent the IP address for the requested NetBIOS name. The WINS proxy agent returns this information to the non-WINS client.

Implementation Requirements

To use a WINS proxy agent to extend name resolution capabilities of a WINS server requires the following:

- At least one proxy agent on each subnet that has non-WINS clients. This is not required if the routers are configured to forward broadcasts (UDP ports 137 and 138 enabled), but it is recommended to reduce broadcast traffic.
- A maximum of two proxy agents per subnet.
- The proxy agent must be a WINS client but cannot be a WINS server.

▶ **To configure a WINS proxy agent**

This procedure configures a WINS proxy agent. To be a WINS proxy, the client must first be configured as a WINS client.

1. Click the **Start** button, and then click **Run**.
2. In the **Open** box, type **regedt32.exe** and then click **OK**.

   The Registry Editor window appears.
3. Maximize the HKEY_LOCAL_MACHINE window.
4. Open the following registry key:

   SYSTEM\CurrentControlSet\Services\NetBT\Parameters
5. Double-click the **EnableProxy** value.

   The **DWORD Editor** dialog box appears.
6. In the **Data** box, type **1**
7. Click **OK**.
8. Close the **Registry Editor**.
9. Access the **Microsoft TCP/IP Properties** dialog box.
10. Click the **WINS Address** tab.
11. In the **Primary WINS Server** box, type the IP address of your primary WINS server.
12. Click **OK**.
13. Click **Close**.

    You will be prompted to restart the computer.
14. Click **Yes**.
15. Log on as Administrator.

▶ **To remove the WINS proxy agent**

In preparation for the procedures in next lesson, you remove the WINS proxy agent.

1. Click the **Start** button, and then click **Run**.
2. In the **Open** box, type **regedt32.exe** and then click **OK**.

   The Registry Editor window appears.
3. Maximize the HKEY_LOCAL_MACHINE window.
4. Open the following registry key:

   SYSTEM\CurrentControlSet\Services\NetBT\Parameters
5. Double-click the **EnableProxy** parameter.

   The **DWORD Editor** dialog box appears.
6. In the **Data** box, type **0**
7. Click **OK**.
8. Close the Registry Editor.
9. Access the **Microsoft TCP/IP Properties** dialog box.
10. Click the **WINS Address** tab.
11. In the **Primary WINS Server** box, clear the IP address.
12. Click **OK**.
13. Click **Close**.

    You will be prompted to restart the computer.
14. Click **Yes**.
15. Log on as Administrator.

Configuring a DHCP Server for WINS

If the computer is a DHCP client, WINS support can be configured by using DHCP Manager to add and configure the following two DHCP scope options:

- **044 WINS/NBNS Servers**. Configure the address of primary and secondary servers.
- **046 WINS/NBT Node**. Configure to 0x8 (H-node).

When the DHCP client leases or renews an address lease, it will receive these two DHCP scope options, and the client will be configured for WINS support.

Important The IP addresses that you configure in the primary WINS server and secondary WINS server boxes take precedence over the same parameters configured using DHCP.

Practice

In this procedure, you configure the DHCP server to supply the appropriate WINS server addressing information to DHCP clients.

▶ **To start the DHCP Server service**

Note Complete this procedure only from the DHCP server.

1. Click the **Start** button, point to **Settings**, and then click **Control Panel**.
2. Double-click the **Services** icon.

    The **Services** dialog box appears.
3. Click **Microsoft DHCP Server**, and then click **Start**.
4. Click **Startup**.

    The **Service** dialog box appears.
5. Click **Automatic**, and then click **OK**.
6. Click **Close**.
7. Close Control Panel.

▶ **To configure the DHCP server to assign WINS server addresses**

In this procedure, you configure the DHCP server to automatically assign the WINS server address and NetBIOS node types to DHCP clients.

Note Complete this procedure only from the DHCP server.

1. Click the **Start** button, point to **Programs**, point to **Administrative Tools**, and then click **DHCP Manager**.

    The DHCP Manager window appears.
2. Double-click ***Local Machine***.

    The local scope IP address appears.
3. Click the local scope's IP address.

    The local scope options appear under **Option Configuration**.
4. On the **DHCP Options** menu, click **Scope**.

    The **DHCP Options: Scope** dialog box appears.
5. Under **Unused Options**, select **044 WINS/NBNS Servers**, and then click **Add**.

    A **DHCP Manager** message box appears, indicating that for WINS to function properly, you must add the **046 WINS/NBT Node Type** option.

6. Click **OK**.

   The **044 WINS/NBNS Servers** option moves under **Active Options**.

7. Click **Value**.

   The **DHCP Scope: Options** dialog box expands.

8. Click **Edit Array**.

   The **IP Address Array Editor** dialog box appears.

9. Under **New IP Address**, type your server's IP address, and then click **Add**.

   The new IP address appears under **IP Addresses**.

10. To return to the **DHCP Options: Scope** dialog box, click **OK**.

11. Under **Unused Options**, select **046 WINS/NBT Node Type**, and then click **Add**.

    The **046 WINS/NBT Node Type** option moves under **Active Options**, and the **Byte** option box appears.

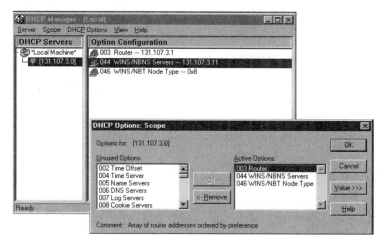

12. In the **Byte** option box, type **0x8** and then click **OK**.

    The DHCP Manager window appears with active scope options of **003 Router**, **044 WINS/NBNS Servers**, and **046 WINS/NBT Node Type** listed under **Option Configuration**.

13. Exit DHCP Manager.

▶ **To update the DHCP client**

In this procedure, you renew your DHCP lease, which automatically assigns the new DHCP scope options of WINS server addresses and node type to the client.

Note Complete this procedure only from the DHCP client.

---

1. At a command prompt, type **ipconfig /all** and then press ENTER.

   The **Windows IP Configuration** settings appear. The **Node Type** is listed as **broadcast**, and the primary WINS server is not listed.

2. Switch to the **Microsoft TCP/IP Properties** dialog box.

3. Click **Obtain an IP address from a DHCP Server**.

   A message box asks you to confirm the installation of DCHP.

4. Click **Yes**.

5. Click **OK** twice.

6. At a command prompt, type **ipconfig /all** and then press ENTER.

   The **Windows IP Configuration** settings appear. The **Node Type** and **primary WINS server** parameters are updated.

▶ **To use WINS for name resolution**

In this procedure, you use WINS for NetBIOS name resolution. Resolution will be limited to the local subnet, because no remote hosts have registered themselves in the local WINS server database.

1. At a command prompt, verify that the NetBIOS name cache is empty. Type **nbtstat -c** and then press ENTER.

2. If entries appear, clear the NetBIOS name cache. Type **nbtstat -R** and then press ENTER.

3. Start Windows NT Explorer and attempt to browse your other computer.

   Was browsing successful?

   _____

   If you were to browse a remote host computer, would you be successful?

   _____

Summary

To implement WINS, both the server and client require configuration. Configuring a static mapping for non-WINS clients allows WINS clients on remote networks to communicate with them. To resolve a NetBIOS name on a non-WINS client, the WINS proxy agent checks its name cache. If the name is not resolved, the request is sent to the WINS server. At least one, and a maximum of two, proxy agents are required on each subnet with non-WINS clients.

Lesson 4: Database Replication Between WINS Servers

All WINS servers on an internetwork can be configured to fully replicate database entries with other WINS servers. This ensures that a name registered with one WINS server is eventually replicated to all other WINS servers. This lesson explains how WINS database entries are replicated to other WINS servers.

After this lesson, you will be able to:

- Explain when a WINS server should be configured as a push or pull partner.
- Configure a WINS server to replicate database entries.

Estimated lesson time: 40 minutes

Database replication occurs whenever the database changes, including when a name is released. Replicating databases enables a WINS server to resolve NetBIOS names of hosts registered with another WINS server. For example, if a host on Subnet 1 is registered with a WINS server on the same subnet, but wants to communicate with a host on Subnet 2 and that host is registered with a different WINS server, the NetBIOS name cannot be resolved unless the two WINS servers have replicated their databases with each other.

To replicate database entries, each WINS server must be configured as either a pull or a push partner with at least one other WINS server. A *push partner* is a WINS server that sends a message to its pull partners notifying them when its WINS database has changed. When a WINS server's pull partners respond to the message with a replication request, the WINS server sends a copy of its new database entries (replicas) to its pull partners.

A *pull partner* is a WINS server that requests new database entries (replicas) from its push partners. This is done by requesting entries with a higher version number than the last entry it received during the last replication.

Note WINS servers replicate only new entries in their database. The entire WINS database is not replicated each time replication occurs.

Configuring a WINS Server as a Push or Pull Partner

Determining whether to configure a WINS server as a pull partner or push partner depends on your network environment. Keep the following rules in mind when configuring WINS server replication:

- Configure a push partner when servers are connected by fast links, because push replication occurs when the configured number of updated WINS database entries is reached.

- Configure a pull partner between sites, especially across slow links, because pull replication can be configured to occur at specific intervals.

- Configure each server to be both a push and pull partner to replicate database entries between them.

These rules are depicted in the following example and illustration:

- In both Sydney and Seattle, all WINS servers at each site push their new database entries to a single server at their site.

- The servers that receive the push replication are configured for pull replication between each other because the network link between Sydney and Seattle is relatively slow. Replication should occur when the link is the least used, such as late at night.

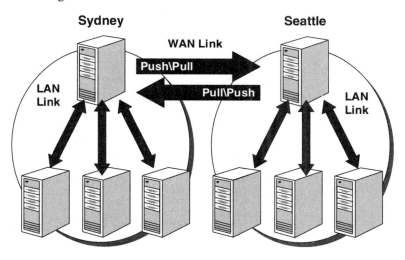

Note You configure a WINS server as a push or pull partner with the WINS Administration tool.

Configuring Database Replication

Database replication requires that you configure at least one push partner and one pull partner. There are four methods of starting the replication of the WINS database:

1. At system start-up. Once a replication partner is configured, by default, WINS automatically pulls database entries each time the WINS Server service is started. The WINS server can also be configured to push on system start-up.

2. At a configured interval, such as every five hours.

3. When a WINS server has reached a configured threshold for the number of registrations and changes to the WINS database. When the threshold (the update count setting) is reached, the WINS server notifies all of its pull partners, who will then request the new entries.

4. By forcing replication through the **WINS Manager Replication Partners** dialog box.

Practice

In these procedures, you configure your WINS server to perform database replication with another WINS server.

Note In order to complete this procedure you first need to configure your second computer (Server2) as a WINS server. Follow the procedure for installing the WINS Server service.

▶ **To configure WINS replication partners**

In this procedure, you configure your second computer (WINS server) as a replication partner.

1. In the WINS Manager window, select the **Server** menu, and then click **Replication Partners**.

   The **Replication Partners** dialog box appears showing the local WINS server.

2. Click **Add**.

   The **Add WINS Server** dialog box appears.

3. In the **WINS Server** box, type **131.107.2.200** and then click **OK**.

   The **Replication Partners** dialog box appears with your IP address added to the list of WINS servers.

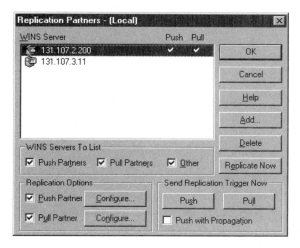

Important   From this computer, you must add your primary WINS server as a replication partner.

---

4. Under **WINS Server**, click your IP address.

5. Under **Replication Options**, click the **Configure** button next to **Pull Partner**.

   The **Pull Partner Properties** dialog box appears.

   The replication interval is set for 30 minutes.

Note   If this were a push partner, you would type a number in the **Update Count** box for the number of new database entries the WINS server must reach before it will send a push message. An appropriate update count should be based on the number of registrations a server handles. A WINS server that receives hundreds of name registrations when users first log on should not be configured to replicate a small number of registrations.

You might also select the **Push with Propagation** check box. This causes the selected WINS servers to obtain any new database entries from the WINS server that sent the message. If the selected WINS servers received any new entries, they propagate the push message to all of their pull partners. If the selected WINS servers did not receive any new entries, they do not propagate the push message.

---

6. Click **OK**.

▶ **To force replication**

In this procedure, you force WINS to replicate the WINS database with the WINS server.

1. In the **Replication Partners** dialog box, click **Replicate Now**.

   A **WINS Manager** message box appears indicating the replication request has been queued.

2. Click **OK**.

3. Click **OK** to return to the WINS Manager window.

   The WINS Manager window appears with your IP address added as a WINS server.

4. Under **WINS Server**, select the local WINS server.

5. On the **Mappings** menu, click **Show Database**.

   The **Show Database** dialog box appears. Under **Select Owner**, notice the addition of all WINS servers that the replication partner knows about.

   Note If the replicated WINS database shows a version ID of 0, repeat steps 1 through 3 to force replication.

   ---

6. Under **Select Owner**, select your IP address.

   Under **Mappings**, the listing of registered names for the WINS server appears.

7. View the information in other WINS server databases, and then click **Close** to return to **WINS Manager**.

WINS Automatic Replication Partners

If your network supports multicasting, the WINS server can be configured to automatically find other WINS servers on the network by multicasting to the IP address 224.0.1.24. This multicasting occurs by default every 40 minutes. Any WINS servers found on the network are automatically configured as push and pull replication partners, with pull replication set to occur every two hours. If network routers do not support multicasting, the WINS server will find only other WINS servers on its subnet.

Automatic WINS server partnerships are turned off by default. To manually disable this feature, use the Registry Editor to set **UseSelfFndPnrs** to **0** and **McastIntvl** to a large value.

Summary

All of the WINS servers on a given network can be configured to communicate with each other so that a name registered with one WINS server will eventually be known by all WINS servers. A pull partner requests WINS new database entries. A push partner sends a message to its pull partners notifying them that its WINS database has changed.

Lesson 5: Maintaining the WINS Server Database

In this lesson, you learn how to view the WINS database and search for specific entries. You also review how to back up and restore the WINS database.

After this lesson, you will be able to:
- Configure WINS to automatically remove obsolete database entries.
- Back up and restore the WINS database.
- Use the Jetpack utility to compact the WINS database.

Estimated lesson time: 40 minutes

WINS Manager provides the ability to view the contents of the WINS database and search for specific entries.

Practice

In this procedure, you view the NetBIOS name-to-address mappings that have been registered in the WINS database.

Note Complete this procedure only from the WINS server.

▶ **To start WINS Manager**

1. At a command prompt, type **nbtstat -R** to purge the NetBIOS name cache (the **-R** is case sensitive).

   This verifies that any names in the cache have been removed prior to using WINS for name resolution.

2. In Control Panel, double-click the **Services** icon.

   The Services dialog box appears.

3. Scroll down the list of services to verify that WINS has started.

4. Close the **Services** dialog box.

5. Click the **Start** button, point to **Programs**, point to **Administrative Tools**, and then click **WINS Manager**.

   The WINS Manager window appears.

▶ **To open the WINS database and view IP address mappings**

1. On the WINS Manager **Mappings** menu, click **Show Database**.

   The **Show Database** dialog box appears listing all of the NetBIOS names that have been registered in WINS.

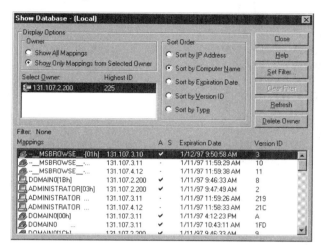

2. To view mappings for a specific WINS server, select **Show Only Mappings from Selected Owner**, and then from the **Select Owner** list, select the WINS server you want to view.

3. Select the **Sort Order** option to sort by IP address, computer name, timestamp for the mapping, version ID, or type. Under **Sort Order**, select how you want mappings sorted.

4. If you want to view only a range of mappings, click **Set Filter**, and then specify the IP addresses or NetBIOS names.

5. View the mappings in the **Mappings** box. Each mapping includes the elements in the following table.

Element	Description
🖳	Indicates that the entry is a unique name.
🖳	Represents a group, internet group, or multihomed computer.
Name	The registered NetBIOS name.
IP Address	The IP address that corresponds to the registered name.
A or S	Indicates whether the mapping is active (dynamic) or static. If there is a cross symbol in the A column, it indicates that the name is no longer active and will soon be removed from the database.

(continued)

Element	Description
Expiration Date	Shows when the entry will expire. When a replica is stored in the database, its expiration data is set to the current time on the receiving WINS server, plus the renewal interval.
Version ID	A unique hexadecimal number assigned by the WINS server during name registration, which is used by the server's pull partner during replication to find new records.

6. What NetBIOS names have been registered at the WINS server by the client?

7. How long will it be before the names expire?

8. Are there any mappings for remote hosts?

9. To delete a WINS server and all database entries owned by that server, select a WINS server in the **Select Owner** list, and then click **Delete Owner**.
10. Click **Close**.

Configuring the WINS Server

Each WINS database should be periodically cleared of entries that were released and entries that were registered at another WINS server but were never removed. This process can be done manually by selecting **Initiate Scavenging** on the **Mappings** menu. The WINS administrator can also automatically clean up the database at configured intervals.

▶ **To configure the length of time a NetBIOS name is in each phase**

1. On the **WINS Manager Server** menu, click **Configuration**.

   The **WINS Server Configuration** dialog box appears.

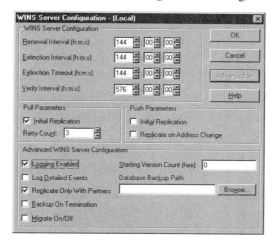

2. To view all of the options in the dialog box, click **Advanced**.

3. Under **WINS Server Configuration**, specify the intervals for each option as described in the following table.

Interval	Description
Renewal Interval	The frequency at which a WINS client will renew its name registration with the WINS server. The default value is 144 hours.
Extinction Interval	The interval between the time an entry in the WINS database is marked as *released* (no longer registered) and the time it is marked as *extinct*. The default value is 144 hours.
Extinction Timeout	The interval between the time an entry is marked *extinct* and the time the entry is scavenged (removed) from the WINS database. The default is the same as the renewal interval, and cannot be less than 24 hours.
Verify Interval	The time after which the WINS server will verify that names it does not own (those replicated from other WINS servers) are still active. The default value is 576 hours (24 days). This is the minimum value that WINS Manager will save.

> **Note** The default values listed in this table are correct; your version of the product documentation or Help may contain incorrect default values for the renewal and extinction intervals.

The WINS server pulls replicas of new WINS database entries from its partners when the computer initializes. By default, **Initial Replication** under **Pull Parameters** is selected.

4. To inform partners of the database status when the computer is initialized, select **Initial Replication** under **Push Parameters**.

5. When finished, click **OK**.

> **Note** The *Microsoft Windows NT Server Resource Kit* includes the Winscl.exe utility, which allows you to delete individual dynamic entries from the WINS database.

Advanced WINS Server Configuration Options

The options in the following table specify how push and pull partners act on start-up as well as perform additional configurations.

Advanced option	Description
Logging Enabled	Specifies whether logging of database changes should be turned on.
Log Detailed Events	Specifies whether logging of events is verbose. If you are tuning for performance, this should be turned off.
Replicate Only With Partners	Specifies that replication will be done only with WINS pull or push partners, and not with a non-listed WINS server partner. This is selected by default.
Backup On Termination	Specifies that the database will be backed up automatically when WINS Manager is closed.
Migrate On/Off	Specifies that static unique and multihomed entries are treated as dynamic when they conflict with a new registration or replica. This means that if they are no longer valid, they will be overwritten by the new registration or replica. Check this option if you are upgrading non–Windows NT computers to Windows NT.
Starting Version Count	Specifies the highest version ID number for the database. Usually, you will not need to change this value unless the database becomes corrupted and needs to be recreated.
Database Backup Path	Specifies the directory where the WINS database backup will be stored. This directory is also used for automatic restoration of the database. Do not specify a network directory.

Backing Up and Restoring the WINS Database

It is important to back up the WINS database in the event of system failure or database corruption. Once you specify a backup directory, the WINS database is automatically backed up every 24 hours.

▶ **To specify the backup directory**

1. On the **WINS Manager Mappings** menu, click **Back Up Database**.

   The **Select Backup Directory** dialog box appears.

2. Specify the location for saving backup files.

3. Click **OK**.

Backing Up the WINS Registry

You should also periodically back up the registry entries for the WINS server.

▶ **To back up the WINS registry entries**

1. Use the Registry Editor to open HKEY_LOCAL_MACHINE\SYSTEM\CurrentControlSet\Services\WINS

2. On the **Registry** menu, click **Save Key**.

3. In the **Save Key** dialog box, specify the path where you store backup versions of the WINS database file.

Restoring a Corrupt WINS Database

In the event that the WINS database becomes corrupt, use one of the following methods to restore the backup database:

- Stop and restart the WINS Server service. If the WINS Server service detects a corrupt database, it automatically restores a backup copy.

- On the **WINS Manager Mappings** menu, click **Restore Database**.

   You then specify the directory where the backup copy is located. The database is restored from the backup copy.

The WINS Database Files

The files in the following table are stored in the *systemroot*\System32\Wins directory.

File	Description
Wins.mdb	The WINS database file.
Winstmp.mdb	A temporary file that WINS creates when you set up a WINS server. This file may remain in the \WINS directory after a software or hardware failure.
J50.log	A log of all transactions processed with the database. This file is used by WINS to recover data, if necessary.
J50.chk	A checkpoint file.

Caution Because these files are necessary for maintaining the WINS database, do not tamper with or remove them, except to manually restore a corrupt WINS database.

Compacting the WINS Database

Because Windows NT Server 4.0 is designed to automatically compact the WINS database, you should not need to run this procedure. If necessary, you can use the Jetpack utility provided with Windows NT Server to compact a WINS database.

▶ **To compact the WINS database**

1. Stop the WINS Server service from **Control Panel**, **Services**, **Windows Internet Name Service**, or at a command prompt. To stop the service from a command prompt, use the following command syntax:

   net stop wins

2. From the *systemroot*\System32\Wins directory, run the Jetpack utility using the following command syntax (assign any file name to *temporary_name*):

   jetpack wins.mdb *temporary_name***.mdb**

   The contents of Wins.mdb are compacted in *temporary_name*, the temporary file is copied to Wins.mdb, and then the temporary name is deleted.

3. Restart the WINS Server service from **Control Panel**, **Services**, **Windows Internet Name Service**, or at a command prompt. To restart the service from a command prompt, use the following command syntax:

   net start wins

Summary

You can view the contents of the WINS database and search for specific entries through WINS Manager. You can manually remove obsolete database entries, or configure WINS to remove them automatically. Windows NT Server 4.0 is designed to automatically compact the WINS database.

Review

The following questions are intended to reinforce key information presented in this chapter. If you are unable to answer a question, review the appropriate lesson and then try the question again.

1. What are two benefits of WINS?

   _____

   _____

2. What two methods can be used to enable WINS on a client computer?

   _____

   _____

3. How many WINS servers are required in an internet of 12 subnets?

   _____

4. What methods can non-WINS clients use to resolve NetBIOS names?

   _____

   _____

5. When should you use a WINS proxy agent?

   _____

   _____

6. After a default installation of WINS, how often is the WINS database backed up?

   _____

   _____

7. What types of names are stored in the WINS database?

   _____

8. How would WINS replication be configured in an environment with a slow WAN link with limited bandwidth?

_____

_____

9. How would WINS replication be configured in a LAN environment without network traffic problems?

_____

_____

10. When does WINS use multicasting?

_____

_____

C H A P T E R   1 0

IP Internetwork Browsing and Domain Functions

Lesson 1   Browsing Overview . . . 226

Lesson 2   Browsing an IP Internetwork . . . 230

Lesson 3   Domain Functions in an IP Internetwork . . . 235

Review . . . 240

About This Chapter

Previous chapters discussed NetBIOS name resolution using the LMHOSTS file and WINS. In this chapter, you learn about browsing for NetBIOS resources in a TCP/IP internetwork. The lessons in this chapter cover browsing for NetBIOS resources, domain logon, account password changes, and domain synchronization processes. During the lessons, you plan an LMHOSTS implementation to ensure internetwork browsing and domain activity.

Before You Begin

To complete the lessons in this chapter, you must have:

- Installed Microsoft Windows NT Server 4.0 with TCP/IP.

- An understanding of the concepts presented in Chapter 8, "NetBIOS over TCP/IP."

Lesson 1: Browsing Overview

To share resources across a network efficiently, users must be able to find out what resources are available. Windows NT provides the Computer Browser service to display a list of currently available resources. This lesson reviews the operation of the Windows NT Computer Browsing service.

After this lesson, you will be able to:

- Explain the Windows NT Computer Browsing service in terms of collection, distribution, and the servicing of client requests.

Estimated lesson time: 15 minutes

The Computer Browser service is a distributed series of lists of available network resources. These lists are distributed to specially assigned computers that perform browsing services on behalf of browsing clients.

Computers designated as *browsers* eliminate the need for all computers to maintain a list of all of the shared resources on the network. By assigning the browser role to specific computers, the Computer Browser service lowers the amount of network traffic required to build and maintain a list of all shared resources on the network.

The types of browsers differ according to their roles in the overall browsing service.

Computer role	Function
Master browser	The computer that collects and maintains the master list of available servers within its domain or workgroup and a list of other domains or workgroups. It also distributes this list, referred to as the *browse list*, to the backup browsers.
Backup browser	A computer that receives a copy of the browse list from the master browser. It then distributes the list to the browser clients upon request.
Domain master browser	The domain master browser has an additional role besides always being a master browser for its domain. If there are other master browsers for the domain on remote networks, the domain master browser synchronizes the browse list from all of the master browsers within the domain.

Computers running Windows NT Workstation, Windows NT Server, Windows for Workgroups, or Windows 95 can perform the master browser and backup browser roles. Only a computer running Windows NT Server acting as a primary domain controller (PDC) can perform the domain master browser role.

Browsing Collection and Distribution

The browsing services in Windows NT can be understood in terms of three key processes:

- Collection of browsing information
- Distribution of browsing information
- Servicing of browser client requests

The Collection Process

The collection process is performed by the master browser computer. The master browser collects information in its master browse list on an ongoing basis as shown in the following illustration. The information includes a list of servers within its domain, or workgroup, and a list of other domains or workgroups.

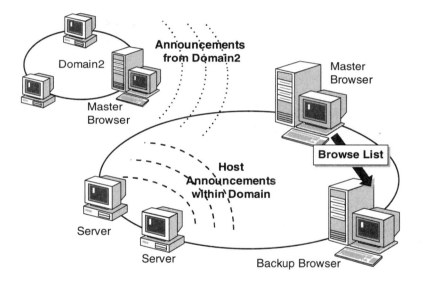

The Distribution Process

The distribution process occurs when the browse lists gathered during the collection process are distributed to the computers that will service the requests from clients. The distribution process occurs through the following:

- Master Browser Announcement

  Periodically, the master browser broadcasts a master browser announcement packet. This packet informs the backup browsers that a master browser still exists. If the master browser does not reply, the election process is initiated to elect a new master browser.

- Browse List Pull Operation from Master Browser to Backup Browser

  Periodically, each backup browser contacts the master browser in its domain and downloads the browse list being kept at the master browser.

Servicing Client Browsing Requests

Once the browse list has been built by the master browser and distributed to the backup browsers, it is ready to begin servicing client requests, as shown in the following process and illustration.

1. When a client attempts to access a domain or workgroup from Windows NT Explorer, it contacts the master browser of the domain or workgroup to which it is attempting to connect.

2. The master browser forwards the client computer a list of three backup browsers.

3. The client then requests the network resource list from a backup browser.

4. The backup browser responds to the requesting client with a list of servers on that domain or workgroup.

5. The client selects a server and receives a list of the server's available resources.

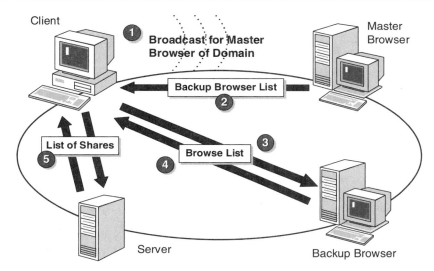

Summary

The Windows NT Computer Browser service provides the ability to view network resources. The types of browsers differ according to their roles in the overall browsing service. The master browser collects a list of servers within its domain and a list of other domains on an ongoing basis. These are compiled in the browse list. Once the browse list has been built by the master browser and distributed to the backup browsers, it is ready to begin servicing client requests.

Lesson 2: Browsing an IP Internetwork

The Computer Browser service uses NetBIOS broadcasts to obtain lists of network resources. This lesson describes the problems associated with browsing an IP internetwork.

After this lesson, you will be able to:
- Describe problems and solutions involved with internetwork browsing.

Estimated lesson time: 15 minutes

Because NetBIOS broadcasts are not routed, it is important that hosts are configured to use WINS or an LMHOSTS file to enable browsing and domain activity across subnets. You can solve browsing problems by using WINS or the LMHOSTS file. However, if your router can forward NetBIOS name broadcasts, it is not necessary to use WINS or the LMHOSTS file.

The Computer Browser service relies on a series of broadcast packets; as a result, browsing across IP routers that do not forward broadcasts can create certain problems. To facilitate client browsing of all network resources in an IP internetwork, there must be mechanisms for the collection, distribution, and servicing of client requests for browse lists.

The IP Router Solution

Some routers can be configured to forward broadcasts from one IP subnet to another. If the IP router is configured to forward these NetBIOS broadcasts, the Browsing service works that same way—as if all of the domains or workgroups were located on the same subnet. All master browsers are aware of all servers in their domains or workgroups—and all other domains or workgroups—and all client browsing requests can be satisfied.

If these settings are enabled on all IP routers in the internetwork, the following information is irrelevant. However, this broadcast forwarding solution is not recommended because it propagates all NetBIOS over TCP/IP broadcast traffic across an internetwork, leading to decreased performance by all nodes on the internetwork. Enabling broadcast forwarding can cause browser election conflicts that report errors in the system log.

Windows NT Solutions

Typically, the IP routers are not configured to forward NetBIOS broadcasts. This means the browsing, collection, distribution, and the servicing of client requests must now take place over *directed* IP traffic rather than *broadcast* IP traffic. There are two ways to facilitate this in Windows NT:

- *WINS.* WINS is used in the collection of browse lists and the servicing of client requests.

- *LMHOSTS Entries.* Special entries in the LMHOSTS file will help facilitate the distribution of browsing information and the servicing of client requests.

Browsing with WINS

WINS solves NetBIOS name broadcast problems by dynamically registering a computer's NetBIOS name and IP address, and storing them in the WINS database. When WINS clients communicate with TCP/IP hosts across subnets, the destination host's IP address is retrieved from the database rather than using a broadcast.

One enhancement WINS adds to this mechanism of collecting domain or workgroup names is that a domain master browser running as a WINS client will periodically query the WINS server to get a list of all of the domains listed in the WINS database.

The advantage of browsing with WINS is that the domain master browser for a given domain now has a list of all domains, including those on remote subnets that are not spanned by its domain as shown in the following illustration.

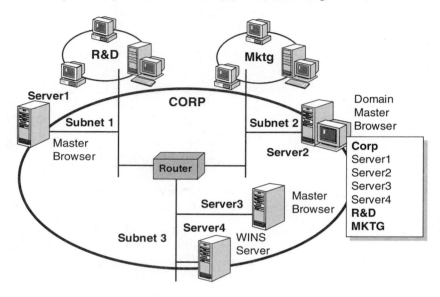

Note The list of domains obtained through the WINS query contains only the domain names and their corresponding IP addresses, but does not include the names of the master browsers that announced those domains.

Browsing Using the LMHOSTS File

To implement direct communication between subnets, non-WINS clients that use broadcasts for NetBIOS name registration and resolution require an LMHOSTS file. The file must be configured with the IP address and NetBIOS name of the domain controllers located on other subnets.

For direct communication between master browsers on remote subnets and the domain master browser, the LMHOSTS file must be configured with the NetBIOS names and IP addresses of the browser computers as shown in the following illustration.

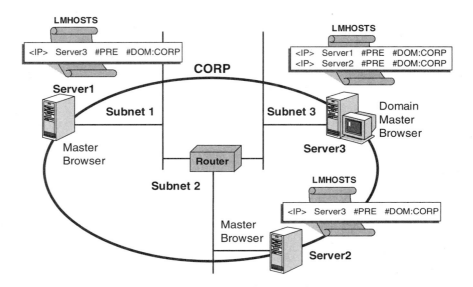

Master Browsers

For computers running Windows NT, the LMHOSTS file on each subnet's master browser should contain the following information:

- IP address and computer name of the domain master browser
- The domain name preceded by the **#PRE #DOM:** tags

For example:

130.20.7.80 *<domain master_browser>* **#PRE #DOM:***<domain_name>*

Domain Master Browsers

At the domain master browser, the LMHOSTS file must be configured with entries for each of the master browsers on remote subnets.

Each master browser computer should have a **#DOM** entry for all of the other master browser in the domain. This way, if one master browser is promoted to the domain master browser, the LMHOSTS files do not need to be changed on the other master browsers.

When multiple LMHOSTS entries exist for the same domain name, the master browser determines which of the entries corresponds to the domain master browser by sending a query to the IP address for each entry. Only the domain master browser will respond. The master browser then contacts the domain master browser to exchange browse lists.

Summary

WINS solves NetBIOS name broadcast problems by dynamically registering a computer's NetBIOS name and IP address, and storing them in the WINS database.

Lesson 3: Domain Functions in an IP Internetwork

This lesson explains how to configure the LMHOSTS file to provide Microsoft domain functions.

After this lesson, you will be able to:

- Describe how domain logon, account password changes, and domain synchronization processes occur in an IP internetwork.
- Plan an LMHOSTS file implementation.

Estimated lesson time: 25 minutes

Besides browsing, some of the other tasks performed by Windows NT network services cause broadcasts to be sent to all computers in a Microsoft domain. These tasks include:

- *Logging on to a domain and password changes.* A broadcast is sent to the domain to locate a domain controller that can authenticate the logon request or to locate the PDC to change the user's password.

- *Domain controllers replicating the domain user account database.* A broadcast is sent from the PDC to the backup domain controllers (BDCs) in the domain instructing them to request replication of the new changes to the domain accounts database.

Because these broadcasts will not cross IP routers, directed traffic must be used to accomplish these tasks. The following illustration shows that when a broadcast is sent to the domain for these tasks, the message is also sent directly to remote domain controllers. The list of computers receiving the direct message is determined by either WINS or LMHOSTS entries.

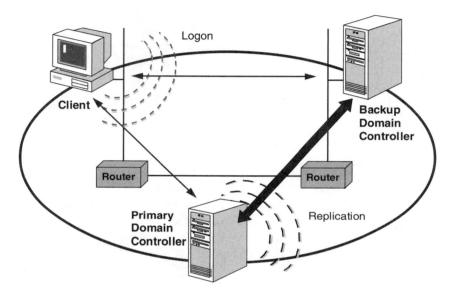

Using the LMHOSTS File

The client broadcasts the message directly to the domain and also looks for any **#DOM** entries in the LMHOSTS file with a matching domain name. If it finds a matching entry, it sends the same message directly to the computer listed.

It is recommended you add remote domain controller **#DOM** entries to each client. This way, if the local domain controllers are offline, the user will still be able to log on. If there are no local domain controllers, a **#DOM** entry is required if the user wants to log on.

A non-WINS PDC must have **#DOM** entries for all BDCs. All of the BDCs must have an entry for the PDC. It is recommended that the domain controllers have **#DOM** entries for each other as well. This way, if a BDC is promoted to a PDC, all of the remaining BDCs will still have a **#DOM** mapping to the new PDC.

Using WINS

Clients contact WINS and ask for the list of domain controllers in the domain. WINS replies with a list of up to 25 domain controllers, called an *Internet group*, registered with that domain. The client then sends the domain message directly to these domain controllers.

Practice

In this practice, you decide which computers require an LMHOSTS file to support browsing, logon validation, domain synchronization, WINS integration, and how each LMHOSTS file must be configured. This practice is based on the following illustration and scenario.

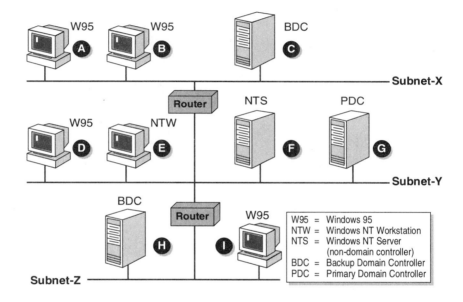

Scenario

As shown in the preceding illustration, the domain spans multiple subnets. Each subnet has a domain controller and various other computers. Hosts on each subnet can only browse and access NetBIOS-based hosts on their own subnets because the routers are not configured to forward broadcasts.

1. Which computers require an LMHOSTS file configured to support internetwork browsing? Which computers should be configured in the LMHOSTS file?

   _____

   _____

   _____

   _____

2. Which computers require an LMHOSTS file to support logon validation? Which computers should be configured in the LMHOSTS file?

   _____

   _____

   _____

   _____

3. Which computers require an LMHOSTS file configured to support domain account synchronization? Which computers should be configured in the LMHOSTS file?

   _____

   _____

   _____

   _____

4. If a WINS server was installed on Subnet-Y, and all computers were configured to use WINS, which computers would require an LMHOSTS file?

_____

_____

_____

_____

Summary

Some of the tasks performed by Windows NT network services cause broadcasts to be sent to all computers in a Microsoft domain. The client broadcasts the message directly to the domain and also looks for any **#DOM** entries in the LMHOSTS file with a matching domain name.

Review

The following questions are intended to reinforce key information presented in this chapter. If you are unable to answer a question, review the appropriate lesson and then try the question again.

1. Why are there problems with browsing in an IP internetwork?

2. How does a master browser on a subnet resolve the IP address of its domain master browser for a domain that spans an internetwork?

3. How does WINS aid in the collection of domains or workgroups?

4. What is required on non-WINS domain controllers to ensure that account synchronization can be accomplished when the domain spans IP internetworks?

C H A P T E R   1 1

Host Name Resolution

Lesson 1   TCP/IP Naming Schemes . . . 242

Lesson 2   Host Names . . . 243

Lesson 3   The HOSTS File . . . 249

Review . . . 252

About This Chapter

This chapter discusses host name resolution concepts and issues. The lessons in this chapter cover how a domain name server, NetBIOS name server, broadcast, and the LMHOSTS file are used to resolve host names. During the lessons, you configure and use the HOSTS file.

Before You Begin

To complete the lessons in this chapter, you must have installed Microsoft Windows NT Server 4.0 with TCP/IP.

Lesson 1: TCP/IP Naming Schemes

Even though TCP/IP hosts require an IP address to communicate, hosts can be referenced by a name rather than an IP address.

After this lesson, you will be able to:

- Explain the different naming schemes used by hosts.

Estimated lesson time: 5 minutes

There are different naming schemes used by Windows NT and UNIX hosts. A Windows NT host can be assigned a host name, but the host name is used only with TCP/IP utilities. UNIX hosts require only an IP address. Using a host or domain name to communicate is optional.

Before communication can take place, an IP address is required on each TCP/IP host. However, the naming scheme affects the way a host is referenced—for example:

- To perform a **net use** command between two computers running Windows NT, a user always specifies the computer's NetBIOS name rather than the IP address, as in the following example:

  net use *x*: *computer_name*

  The NetBIOS name must be resolved to an IP address before ARP can resolve the IP address to a hardware address.

- To reference a UNIX host running TCP/IP, a user specifies the IP address, host name, or domain name. If a host name or domain name is used, the name is resolved to an IP address. If the IP address is used, name resolution is not necessary and the IP address is resolved to a hardware address.

The main difference in the way you reference the two types of hosts is that you must always communicate using the NetBIOS name with Microsoft network commands and not the IP address. Using TCP/IP utilities to reference a UNIX host allows you to use the IP address.

Note Windows NT 4.0 allows a user to connect to another computer running Windows NT by using an IP address. For example,
\net use *x*: *131.107.2.200\share_name*.

Summary

Windows NT and UNIX hosts use different naming schemes. Windows NT and other Microsoft network operating systems require a NetBIOS name to communicate with other Windows NT hosts.

Lesson 2: Host Names

A host name simplifies the way a host is referenced because names are easier to remember than IP addresses. Host names are used in virtually all TCP/IP environments. This lesson describes how host name resolution works.

After this lesson, you will be able to:

- Explain how the HOSTS file resolves a host name to an IP address on a local and a remote network.
- Explain how a host name is resolved to an IP address using a DNS server and Microsoft-supported methods.

Estimated lesson time: 20 minutes

A host name is an alias assigned to a computer by an administrator to identify a TCP/IP host. The host name does not have to match the NetBIOS computer name, and can be any 256-character string. Multiple host names can be assigned to the same host.

A host name simplifies the way a user references other TCP/IP hosts. Host names are easier to remember than IP addresses. In fact, a host name can be used in place of an IP address when using PING or other TCP/IP utilities.

A host name always corresponds to an IP address that is stored in a HOSTS file or in a database on a DNS or NetBIOS name server. Windows NT also uses the LMHOSTS file to map host names to IP addresses.

The HOSTNAME utility will display the host name assigned to your system. By default, the host name is the computer name of your computer running Windows NT.

Host Name Resolution

Host name resolution is the process of mapping a host name to an IP address. Before the IP address can be resolved to a hardware address, the host name must be resolved to an IP address.

Windows NT can resolve host names using several methods. These methods are also discussed in Chapter 8, "NetBIOS over TCP/IP."

Microsoft TCP/IP can use any of the methods shown in the following tables to resolve host names. The methods that Windows NT can use to resolve a host name are configurable.

Standard methods of resolution	Description
Local host name	The configured host name for the computer. This name is compared to the destination host name.
HOSTS file	A local text file in the same format as the 4.3 Berkeley Software Distribution (BSD) UNIX\Etc\Hosts file. This file maps host names to IP addresses. This file is typically used to resolve host names for TCP/IP utilities.
Domain Name System (DNS) server	A server that maintains a database of IP address/computer name (host name) mappings.

Microsoft methods of resolution	Description
NetBIOS Name Server (NBNS)	A server implemented under RFCs 1001 and 1002 to provide name resolution of NetBIOS computer names. The Microsoft implementation of this is WINS.
Local broadcast	A broadcast on the local network for the IP address of the destination NetBIOS name.
LMHOSTS file	A local text file that maps IP addresses to the NetBIOS computer names of Windows networking computers on remote networks.

Resolving Names with a HOSTS File

Unlike the LMHOSTS file, which is used for remote hosts only, the HOSTS file maps host names of both local and remote hosts to their IP addresses. As shown in the illustration, the process is as follows:

1. Host name resolution begins when a user types a command using the host name assigned to the destination host.

   Windows NT checks to see if the host name is the same as the local host name. If the two names are different, the HOSTS file is parsed. If the host name is found in the HOSTS file, it is resolved to an IP address.

   If the host name cannot be resolved and no other resolution methods—such as DNS, a NetBIOS name server, or the LMHOSTS file—are configured, the process stops and the user receives an error message.

2. After the host name is resolved to an IP address, an attempt is made to resolve the destination host's IP address to its hardware address.

If the destination host is on the local network, ARP obtains its hardware address by consulting the ARP cache or by broadcasting the destination host's IP address.

If the destination host is on a remote network, ARP obtains the hardware address of a router and the request is routed to the destination host.

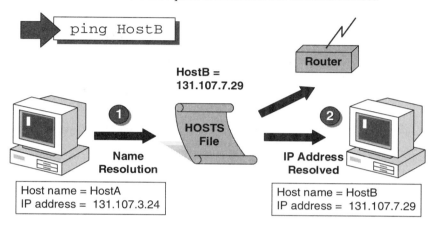

Resolving Names with a DNS Server

A Domain Name System (DNS) server is a centralized online database that is used in UNIX environments to resolve fully qualified domain names (FQDNs) and other host names to IP addresses. Windows NT 4.0 can use a DNS server and provides DNS server services. Resolving a domain name using a DNS server is very similar to using a HOSTS file.

If Windows NT is configured to resolve host names using a DNS server, it uses two steps to resolve a host name as shown in the following process and illustration:

1. When a user types a command using an FQDN or a host name, the DNS server looks up the name in its database and resolves it to an IP address.

If the DNS server does not respond to the request, additional attempts are made at intervals of 5, 10, 20, 40, 5, 10, and 20 seconds. If the DNS server does not respond to any of the attempts, and there are no other resolution methods configured such as a NetBIOS name server or LMHOSTS, the process stops and an error is reported.

2. After the host name is resolved, ARP obtains the hardware address. If the destination host is on the local network, ARP obtains its hardware address by consulting the ARP cache or by broadcasting the IP address. If the destination host is on a remote network, ARP obtains the hardware address of a router that can deliver the request.

If the DNS server is on a remote network, ARP must obtain the hardware address of a router before the name can be resolved.

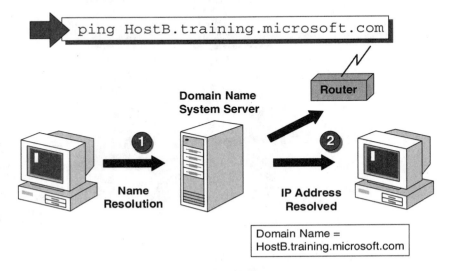

Microsoft Methods of Resolving Host Names

Windows NT can be configured to resolve host names using a NetBIOS name server, broadcast, and LMHOSTS in addition to the HOSTS file and DNS server. If one of these methods fails, the other methods provide a backup, as shown in the following example and illustration.

If NBNS and LMHOSTS are configured, the order of resolution is as follows:

1. When a user types a command referencing a host name, Windows NT checks to see if the host name is the same as the local host name. If they are the same, the name is resolved and the command is carried out, without generating network activity.

2. If the host name and local host name are not the same, the HOSTS file is parsed. If the host name is found in the HOSTS file, it is resolved to an IP address and address resolution occurs. The HOSTS file must reside on the local system.

3. If the host name cannot be resolved using the HOSTS file, the source host sends a request to its configured domain name servers. If the host name is found by a DNS server, it is resolved to an IP address and address resolution occurs.

   If the DNS server does not respond to the request, additional attempts are made at intervals of 5, 10, 20, 40, 5, 10, and 20 seconds.

4. If the DNS server cannot resolve the host name, the source host checks its local NetBIOS name cache before it makes three attempts to contact its configured NetBIOS name servers. If the host name is found in the NetBIOS name cache or found by a NetBIOS name server, it is resolved to an IP address and address resolution occurs.

5. If the host name is not resolved by the NetBIOS name server, the source host generates three broadcast messages on the local network. If the host name is found on the local network, it is resolved to an IP address and address resolution occurs.

6. If the host name is not resolved using broadcasts, the local LMHOSTS file is parsed. If the host name is found in the LMHOSTS file, it is resolved to an IP address and address resolution occurs.

If none of these methods resolve the host name, the only way to communicate with the other host is to specify the IP address.

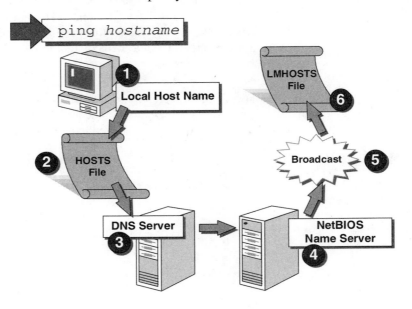

Summary

A host name is used to identify a TCP/IP host or default gateway. Host name resolution is the process of mapping a host name to an IP address. This is necessary before ARP can resolve the IP address to a hardware address.

Lesson 3: The HOSTS File

Now that you have learned the concepts of how host names are solved using different methods, you will look at the HOSTS file. In this lesson, you modify the HOSTS file so that host names are resolved correctly.

After this lesson, you will be able to:
- Configure and use the HOSTS file.

Estimated lesson time: 15 minutes

The HOSTS file is a static file used to map host names to IP addresses. This file provides compatibility with the UNIX HOSTS file. The HOSTS file is used by PING and other TCP/IP utilities to resolve a host name to an IP address on both local and remote networks. The HOSTS file can be used to resolve NetBIOS names (Microsoft TCP/IP-32-specific).

A HOSTS file must reside on each computer. A single entry consists of an IP address corresponding to one or more host names. By default, the host name *localhost* is an entry in the HOSTS file.

The HOSTS file is parsed whenever a host name is referenced. Names are read in a linear fashion. The most commonly used names should be near the beginning of the file.

Note The HOSTS file can be edited with any text editor. It is located in a directory with a name in the following form: *\systemroot*\System32\Drivers\Etc

Each host entry is limited to 255 characters, and entries in the HOSTS file are not case sensitive.

The following is an example of the HOSTS file:

```
#This file is used by Microsoft TCP/IP utilities
#
 127.0.0.1.     localhost loopback

 102.54.94.97   rhino.microsoft.com

 131.107.2.100  unixhost UNIXHOST # LAN Manager UNIX Host

 131.107.3.1    gateway  GATEWAY  # Default Gateway
```

Practice

In this procedure, you configure and use the HOSTS file, configure Windows NT to use a DNS, and identify problems associated with host name and domain name resolution. In the first part of the procedure, you add host name/IP address mappings to your HOSTS file, and then use the file to resolve host names.

▶ **To determine the local host name**

In this procedure, you determine the local host used for TCP/IP utilities, such as PING.

1. Open a command prompt.
2. Clear the NetBIOS name cache.
3. Type **hostname** and then press ENTER.

   The local host name is displayed.

▶ **To ping local host names**

In this procedure, you ping the name of the local host to verify that Microsoft TCP/IP can resolve local host names without entries in the HOSTS file.

1. Type **ping Server1** (where *Server1* is the name of your computer) and then press ENTER.

   What was the response?

   _____

2. Type **ping Server2** (where *Server2* is your second computer) and then press ENTER.

   What was the response?

   _____

▶ **To attempt to ping a local computer name**

Note Perform this procedure from Server1.

- Type **ping computertwo** and then press ENTER.

   What was the response?

   _____

▶ **To add an entry to the HOSTS file**

Note Perform this procedure from Server1.

1. Change to the following directory by typing:

    cd *%systemroot%***\system32\drivers\etc**

2. Use a text editor to modify a file called HOSTS by typing:

    edit HOSTS

3. Add the entry in the following table to the HOSTS file.

Computer IP address	Use this host name
131.107.2.211	computertwo

4. Save the file, and then exit **Edit**.

▶ **To use HOSTS for name resolution**

- Type **ping computertwo** and then press ENTER.

  What was the response?

  _____

  _____

Summary

The HOSTS file maps host names to IP addresses and provides compatibility with the UNIX HOSTS file.

Review

The following questions are intended to reinforce key information presented in this chapter. If you are unable to answer a question, review the appropriate lesson and then try the question again.

1. What is a host name?

   _____

   _____

2. What is the purpose of a host name?

   _____

   _____

3. What does a HOSTS file entry consist of?

   _____

   _____

4. During resolution, what occurs first, IP address resolution or host name resolution?

   _____

C H A P T E R   1 2

Domain Name System (DNS)

Lesson 1   Domain Name System (DNS) . . . 254

Lesson 2   Name Resolution . . . 261

Lesson 3   Configuring the DNS Files . . . 264

Lesson 4   Planning a DNS Implementation . . . 269

Review . . . 278

About This Chapter

This chapter covers the structure and components of the Domain Name System
(DNS), including how to resolve TCP/IP addresses, how to configure DNS files,
and how to register a DNS server with the parent domain. During the lessons, you
design a Domain Name System for various scenarios. This includes making
decisions about the number of domains, name servers, zones, and associated DNS
files.

Before You Begin

To complete the lessons in this chapter, you must have installed Microsoft
Windows NT Server 4.0 with TCP/IP.

Lesson 1: Domain Name System (DNS)

The Domain Name System (DNS) is similar to a telephone book. In DNS, the host computer contacts the name of a computer and a domain name server cross-references the name to an IP address. This lesson describes the architecture and structure of DNS.

After this lesson, you will be able to:

- Describe the structure, architecture, and components of DNS.
- Explain how DNS is used to resolve names and IP addresses.

Estimated lesson time: 30 minutes

Before 1980, the ARPANET had only a few hundred networked computers. The computer name-to-address mapping was contained in a single file called Hosts.txt. This file was stored on the host computer of the Stanford Research Institute's Network Information Center (SRI-NIC) in Menlo Park, California. As the following illustration shows, other host computers on the ARPANET copied the Hosts.txt file from the SRI-NIC to their sites as needed.

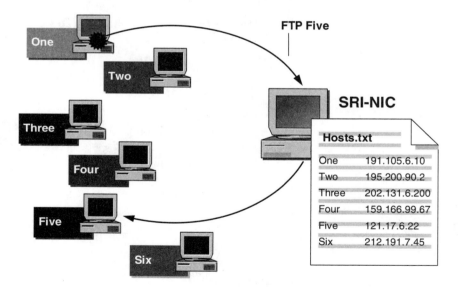

Initially, this scheme worked well because the Hosts.txt list needed to be updated only one or two times a week. However, after a few years, problems arose due to the ever-increasing size of the ARPANET. The problems included the following:

- The Hosts.txt file became too large.

- The file needed to be updated more than once a day.

- Because all network traffic had to be routed through SRI-NIC, maintaining Hosts.txt became a restriction point for the entire network.

- Network traffic on the SRI-NIC host became almost unmanageable.

- Hosts.txt uses a *flat name* structure (name space). This required every computer name to be unique across the whole network.

These and other problems led the governing body of the ARPANET to find a solution to the mechanism surrounding the Hosts.txt file. The decision led to the creation of the Domain Name System (DNS), which is a distributed database using a *hierarchical name* structure (hierarchical name space).

Note The Domain Name System is described in RFCs 1034 and 1035. For copies of these RFCs, see the *Course Materials* Web page on the course compact disc.

How DNS Works

The Domain Name System works using three main components: resolvers, name servers, and the domain name space.

With basic DNS communication, a DNS client, or *resolver*, sends queries to a name server. The server returns the requested information, or a pointer to another name server, or a failure message if the request can not be satisfied.

The Domain Name System is a hierarchical client/server-based distributed database management system. DNS maps to the application layer and uses UDP and TCP as the underlying protocols.

The purpose of the DNS database is to translate computer names into IP addresses as shown in the following illustration. In the DNS, the clients are called *resolvers* and the servers are called *name servers*.

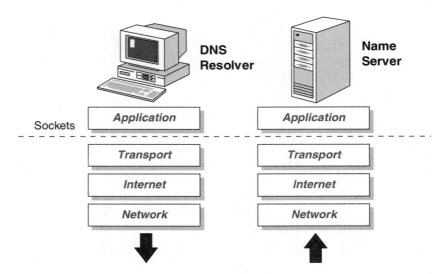

The Domain Name System is analogous to a telephone book. The user looks up the name of the person or organization that he wants to contact and cross-references the name to a telephone number. Similarly, a host computer contacts the name of a computer and a domain name server cross-references the name to an IP address.

Resolvers first send UDP queries to servers for increased performance and resort to TCP only if truncation of the returned data occurs.

Resolvers

The function of the resolvers is to pass name requests between applications and name servers. The name request contains a query. For example, the query might ask for the IP address of a Web site. The resolver is often built into the application or is running on the host computer as a library routine.

Name Servers

Name servers take name requests from resolvers and resolve computer (or domain) names to IP addresses. If the name server is not able to resolve the request, it may forward the request to a name server that can resolve it. The name servers are grouped into different levels that are called *domains*.

Domain Name Space

The domain name space is a hierarchical grouping of names in an inverted-tree-like structure as shown in the following illustration.

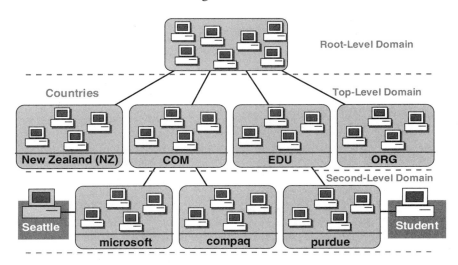

Root-Level Domains

Domains define different levels of authority in a hierarchical structure. The top of the hierarchy is called the *root* domain. The root domain uses a null label, but references to the root domain can be expressed by a period (**.**).

Top-Level Domains

The following are the present top-level domains:

- com   Commercial organizations
- edu   Educational institutions and universities
- org   Not-for-profit organizations
- net   Networks (the backbone of the Internet)
- gov   Non-military government organizations
- mil   Military government organizations
- num   Phone numbers
- arpa   Reverse DNS
- *xx*   Two-letter country code

Top-level domains can contain second-level domains and hosts.

Note An Internet Society committee is planning several additional top-level domains such as .firm and .web.

Second-Level Domains

Second-level domains can contain both hosts and other domains called *subdomains*. For example, the Microsoft domain, microsoft.com, can contain computers such as ftp.microsoft.com and subdomains such as dev.microsoft.com. The subdomain dev.microsoft.com can contain hosts such as ntserver.dev.microsoft.com.

Host Names

Host names inside domains are added to the beginning of the domain name and are often referred to by their fully qualified domain name (FQDN). For example, a host named fileserver in the microsoft.com domain would have the fully qualified domain name of fileserver.microsoft.com.

Zones of Authority

A *zone of authority* is the portion of the domain name space for which a particular name server is responsible. The name server stores all address mappings for the domain name space within the zone and answers client queries for those names.

The name server's zone of authority encompasses at least one domain This domain is referred to as the zone's *root domain*. The zone of authority may also include subdomains of the zone's root domain. However, a zone does not necessarily contain all of the subdomains under the zone's root domain.

In the following illustration, microsoft.com is a domain, but the entire domain is not controlled by one zone file. Part of the domain is located in a separate zone file for dev.microsoft.com. Breaking up domains across multiple zone files may be needed for distributing management of the domain to different groups, or for data replication efficiency.

A single DNS server can be configured to manage one or multiple zone files. Each zone is anchored at a specific domain node called the zone's root domain.

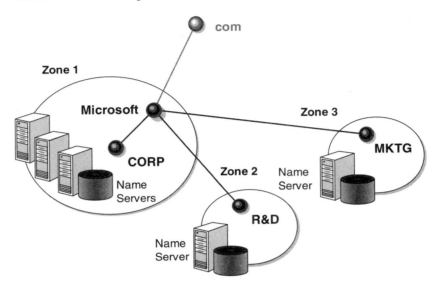

Name Server Roles

DNS name servers can be configured in different roles. DNS servers can store and maintain their database of names in several different ways. Each of the following roles describes a different way a DNS name server can be configured to store its zone data.

Primary Name Servers

The primary name server obtains zone data from local files. Changes to a zone, such as adding domains or hosts, are made at the primary name server level.

Secondary Name Servers

A secondary name server obtains the data for its zones from another network name server that has authority for that zone. Obtaining this zone information across the network is referred to as a *zone transfer*.

There are three reasons to have secondary name servers:

- *Redundancy.* You need at least one primary and one secondary name server for each zone. The computers should be as independent as possible.

- *Faster access for remote locations.* If you have a number of clients in remote locations, having secondary name servers (or other primary name servers for subdomains) prevents these clients from communicating across slow links for name resolution.

- *Reduction of load.* Secondary name servers reduce the load on the primary server.

Because information for each zone is stored in separate files, this primary or secondary designation is defined at a zone level. In other words, a particular name server may be a primary name server for certain zones and a secondary name server for other zones.

Master Name Servers

When you define a zone on a name server as a secondary zone, you must designate another name server from which to obtain the zone information. The source of zone information for a secondary name server in a DNS hierarchy is referred to as a *master name server.* A master name server can be either a primary or secondary name server for the requested zone. When a secondary name server starts up, it contacts its master name server and initiates a zone transfer with that server.

Caching-Only Servers

Although all DNS name servers cache queries that they have resolved, caching-only servers are DNS name servers that only perform queries, cache the answers, and return the results. In other words, they are not authoritative for any domains (no zone data is kept locally) and they only contain information that they have cached while resolving queries.

When trying to determine when to use such a server, keep in mind that when the server is initially started it has no cached information and must build this information up over time as it services requests. Much less traffic is sent across the slow link because the server is not doing a zone transfer. This is important if you are dealing with a slow link between sites.

Summary

Due to the increasing size of the ARPANET, the Domain Name System was created. In DNS, a client, called a resolver, sends queries to a name server. Name servers then take name requests and resolve computer names to IP addresses. The domain name space is a hierarchical grouping of root-level domains, top-level domains, second-level domains, and host names. Specific servers are responsible for a portion of the domain name space called zones of authority.

Lesson 2: Name Resolution

There are three types of queries that a client (resolver) can make to a DNS server: *recursive, iterative,* and *inverse.*

After this lesson, you will be able to:
- Explain how recursive, iterative, and inverse queries work.
- Explain how queries are placed in a cache for future requests.

Estimated lesson time: 10 minutes

Recursive Queries

In a recursive query, the queried name server is petitioned to respond with the requested data, or with an error stating that data of the requested type does not exist or that the domain name specified does not exist. The name server cannot refer the request to a different name server.

Iterative Queries

In an iterative query, the queried name server gives the best answer it currently has back to the requester. This answer may be the resolved name or a referral to another name server that may be able to answer the client's original request.

The following illustration shows an example of both recursive and iterative queries. In this example a client within a corporation is querying its DNS server for the IP address for "www.whitehouse.gov."

1. The resolver sends a recursive DNS query to its local DNS server asking for the IP address of "www.whitehouse.gov." The local name server is responsible for resolving the name and cannot refer the resolver to another name server.

2. The local name server checks its zones and finds no zones corresponding to the requested domain name. It then sends an iterative query for www.whitehouse.gov to a root name server.

3. The root name server has authority for the root domain and will reply with the IP address of a name server for the .gov top-level domain.

4. The local name server sends an iterative query for "www.whitehouse.gov" to the .gov name server.

5. The .gov name server replies with the IP address of the name server servicing the whitehouse.gov domain.

6. The local name server sends an iterative query for "www.whitehouse.gov" to the whitehouse.gov name server.

7. The whitehouse.gov name server replies with the IP address corresponding to www.whitehouse.gov.

8. The local name server sends the IP address of "www.whitehouse.gov" back to the original resolver.

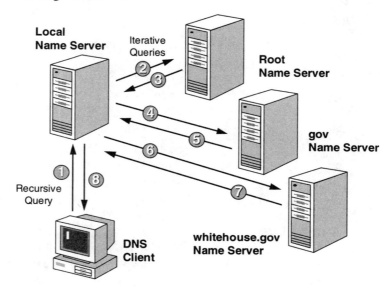

Inverse Queries

In an inverse query, the resolver sends a request to a name server to resolve the host name associated with a known IP address. There is no correlation between host names and IP addresses in the DNS name space. Therefore, only a thorough search of all domains guarantees a correct answer.

To prevent an exhaustive search of all domains for an inverse query, a special domain called "in-addr.arpa" was created. Nodes in the in-addr.arpa domain are named after the numbers in the dotted decimal representation of IP addresses. Because IP addresses get more specific from left to right and domain names get less specific from left to right, the order of IP address octets must be reversed when building the in-addr.arpa domain. With this arrangement, administration of lower limbs of the in-addr.arpa domain can be delegated to organizations as they are assigned their class A, B, or C IP addresses.

Once the in-addr.arpa domain is built, special resource records called *pointer records* (PTR) are added to associate the IP addresses and the corresponding host name. For example, to find a host name for the IP address 157.55.200.51, the resolver queries the DNS server for a pointer record for 51.200.55.157.in-addr.arpa. The pointer record found contains the host name and corresponding IP address 157.55.200.51. This information is sent back to the resolver. Part of the administration of a DNS name server is ensuring that pointer records are created for hosts.

Caching and TTL

When a name server is processing a recursive query, it may be required to send out several queries to find the answer. The name server caches all of the information that it receives during this process for a time that is specified in the returned data. This amount of time is referred to as the *Time to Live* (TTL). The name server administrator of the zone that contains the data decides on the TTL for the data. Smaller TTL values help ensure that data about the domain is more consistent across the network if this data changes often. However, this also increases the load on name servers.

Once data is cached by a DNS server, it must start decreasing the TTL from its original value so that it will know when to flush the data from its cache. If a query comes in that can be satisfied by this cached data, the TTL that is returned with the data is the current amount of time left before the data is flushed from the DNS server cache. Client resolvers also have data caches and honor the TTL value so that they know when to expire the data.

Summary

A client (resolver) can make recursive, iterative and inverse queries to a DNS server. As queries are resolved by the name server, the information is placed in a cache for future requests.

Lesson 3: Configuring the DNS Files

There are four configuration files used by a typical DNS name server. This lesson describes these files in detail.

After this lesson, you will be able to:
- Describe the contents of the DNS database files.

Estimated lesson time: 25 minutes

A typical DNS name server has a database file, reverse lookup file, cache file, and boot file. These configuration files perform a variety of functions on the server.

The Database File

The database file (Zone.dns) stores resource records for a domain. For example, if your zone is "microsoft.com," then this file will be called "microsoft.com.dns." Windows NT 4.0 supplies a sample database file called Place.dns as a template you can work with. This file should be edited and renamed before you use it on a production DNS server. It is generally a good idea to name this file the same as the zone it represents. This is the file that will be replicated between master name servers and secondary name servers.

There are several types of resource records defined in DNS. RFC 1034 defines SOA, A, NS, PTR, CNAME, MX, and HINFO record types. Microsoft has added the WINS and WINS-R Microsoft-specific record types.

Start of Authority Record

The first record in any database file must be the Start of Authority (SOA) record. The SOA defines the general parameters for the DNS zone. The following is an example of an SOA record:

```
@ IN SOA nameserver1.microsoft.com. glennwo.microsoft.com. (
     1        ; serial number
     10800    ; refresh [3 hours]
     3600     ; retry [1 hour]
     604800   ; expire [7 days]
     86400 )  ; time to live [1 day]
```

The following rules apply to all SOA records:

- The at symbol (@) in a database file indicates "this server."
- IN indicates an Internet record.
- Any host name not terminated with a period (.) will be appended with the root domain.
- The @ symbol is replaced by a period (.) in the e-mail address of the administrator.
- Parentheses (( )) must enclose line breaks that span more than one line.

Name Server Record

The name server (NS) record lists the additional name servers. A database file may contain more than one name server record. The following is an example of a name server record:

```
@ IN NS nameserver2.microsoft.com
```

Host Record

A Host (A) record statically associates a host name to its IP address. Host records will comprise most of the database file and will list all hosts within the zone. The following are examples of host records:

```
rhino       IN A 157.55.200.143
localhost   IN A 127.0.0.1
```

CNAME Record

A Canonical Name (CNAME) record enables you to associate more than one host name with an IP address. This is sometimes referred to as *aliasing*. The following is an example of a CNAME record:

```
FileServer1 CNAME rhino
www         CNAME rhino
ftp         CNAME rhino
```

Note Database record types are defined in RFCs 1034, 1035, and 1183. For copies of these RFCs, see the *Course Materials* Web page on the course compact disc.

The Reverse Lookup File

The reverse lookup file (*z.y.x.w*.in-addr.arpa) allows a resolver to provide an IP address and request a matching host name. A reverse lookup file is named like a zone file according to the in-addr.arpa zone for which it is providing reverse lookups. For example, to provide reverse lookups for the IP network 157.57.28.0, a reverse lookup file is created with a file name of 57.157.in-addr.arpa. This file contains SOA and name server records similar to other DNS database zone files, as well as pointer records.

This DNS reverse-lookup capability is important because some applications provide the capabilities to implement security based on the connecting host names. For instance, if a client tries to link to a network file system (NFS) volume with this security arrangement, the NFS server would contact the DNS server and do a reverse name lookup on the client's IP address. If the host name returned by the DNS server is not in the access list for the NFS volume or if the host name was not found by DNS, then the NFS request would be denied.

The Pointer Record

Pointer (PTR) records provide an address-to-name mapping within a reverse lookup zone. IP numbers are written in backward order and "in-addr.arpa" is appended to the end to create this pointer record. As an example, looking up the name for "157.55.200.51" requires a pointer query for the name "51.200.55.157.in-addr.arpa." An example might read:

```
51.200.55.157.in-addr.arpa. IN PTR mailserver1.microsoft.com.
```

The Cache File

The Cache.dns file contains the records of the root domain servers. The cache file is essentially the same on all name servers and must be present. When the name server receives a query outside its zone, it starts resolution with these root domain servers. An example entry might read:

```
.                       3600000 IN      NS      A.ROOT-SERVERS.NET.
A.ROOT-SERVERS.NET.     3600000 A               198.41.0.4
```

The cache file contains host information that is needed to resolve names outside of authoritative domains. It contains names and addresses of root name servers. The default file provided with the Windows NT 4.0 DNS Server has the records for all of the root servers on the Internet. For installations not connected to the Internet, the file should be replaced to contain the name server's authoritative domains for the root of the private network.

Note For a current Internet cache file see ftp://rs.internic.net/domain/named.cache.

The Boot File

The boot file is the start-up configuration file on the Berkeley Internet Name Daemon (BIND)-specific implementation of DNS. This file contains host information needed to resolve names outside of authoritative domains. The file is not defined in an RFC and is not needed in order to be RFC compliant. The Windows NT 4.0 DNS Server can be configured to use a boot file—if administration is to be done through changes to the text files—rather than by using DNS Manager.

The boot file controls the start-up behavior of the DNS server. Commands must start at the beginning of a line and no spaces may precede commands. Recognized commands are: **directory**, **cache**, **primary**, and **secondary**.

The syntax for the boot file is as shown in the following table.

Command	Description
Directory command	Specifies a directory where other files referred to in the boot file can be found.
Cache command	Specifies a file used to help the DNS service contact name servers for the root domain. This command and the file it refers to must be present. A cache file suitable for use on the Internet is provided with Windows NT 4.0.
Primary command	Specifies a domain for which this name server is authoritative and a database file that contains the resource records for that domain (that is, the zone file). Multiple primary command records can exist in the boot file.
Secondary command	Specifies a domain for which this name server is authoritative and a list of master server IP addresses from which to attempt to download the zone information, rather than reading it from a file. It also defines the name of the local file for caching this zone. Multiple secondary command records could exist in the boot file.

The following table shows examples of the commands in a boot file.

Syntax	Example
directory [*directory*]	`directory c:\winnts\system32\dns`
cache.[*file_name*]	`cache.cache`
primary [*domain*] [*file_name*]	`primary microsoft.com.microsoft.dns` `primary dev.microsoft.com dev.dns`
secondary [*domain*] [*hostlist*] [*local_file_name*]	`secondary test.microsoft.com` `157.55.200.100 test.dns`

Summary

Four configuration files used by a typical DNS name server. The database file stores resource records for a domain. For the name server to resolve inverse queries, a reverse lookup file is required. The cache file contains the names and addresses for the name servers that maintain the root domain. The boot file is the start-up configuration file on a Berkeley Internet Name Daemon DNS server.

Lesson 4: Planning a DNS Implementation

The configuration of your DNS servers depends on factors such as the size of your organization, organization locations, and fault-tolerance requirements. This lesson gives you an idea of how to configure DNS for your site. It contains scenarios that measure your network planning knowledge prior to installing DNS.

After this lesson, you will be able to:
- Register a DNS server with the parent domain.
- Estimate the number of DNS name servers, domains, and zones needed for a network.

Estimated lesson time: 40 minutes

Rather than maintain a DNS server, an organization with a small network may find it simpler and more efficient to have DNS clients query a DNS name server maintained by an Internet service provider (ISP). Most ISPs will maintain domain information for a fee. Organizations that want to control their domain or cut the costs of using an ISP should maintain their own DNS servers.

If an organization, regardless of size, wants to connect to the Internet as a second-level domain, the InterNIC must be informed of the domain name of the organization and the IP addresses of at least two DNS servers that service the domain. An organization could set up DNS servers within itself independent of the Internet.

For reliability and redundancy, Microsoft recommends that at least two DNS servers be configured per domain—a primary and a secondary name server. The primary name server maintains the database of information, which is replicated to the secondary name server. This replication allows name queries to be serviced even if one of the name servers is unavailable. The replication scheduled can be configured depending on how often names change in the domain. Replication should be frequent enough so that changes are known to both servers. However, excessive replication can tie up the network and name servers unnecessarily.

Registering with the Parent Domain

Once you have your DNS server or servers configured and installed, you need to register with the DNS server that is above you in the hierarchical naming structure of DNS. The following illustration provides an example of registering your DNS server with the domain level above it. The parent system needs the name and addresses of your name servers and may require other information, such as the date that the domain becomes available and the names and mailing addresses of contact people.

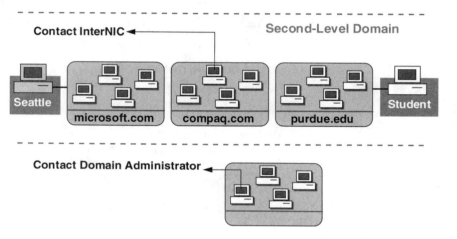

If you are registering with a parent below the second-level domain, check with the administrator of that system to determine the information you need to supply.

Note If you are registering at the subdomain or higher, visit InterNIC's online registration services at http://internic.net. If you have any questions, call their registration help line at (703) 742-477.

Practice

In this practice, you work through three DNS implementation scenarios. In each scenario, you estimate the number of DNS name servers, domains, and zones needed for a network.

Each scenario describes a company that is migrating to Windows NT Server and wants to implement directory services. You will answer some questions involved in drafting a DNS network design for each company using unique criteria.

The purpose of these practices is to measure your network planning knowledge prior to installing DNS. This will serve as a baseline to measure how much you have learned at the completion of this course and will help you start thinking about DNS network design.

Scenario 1: Designing DNS for a Small Network

The XYZ Company is in the process of replacing their older midrange computer with a computer running Windows NT Server 4.0.

Most employees access the midrange system through terminal devices. Some users have 486 computers and a few have Pentium computers; these computers are not networked. The company has already purchased the hardware for the migration.

The network will be used for basic file and print sharing and will also have one Windows NT server running SQL Server. The majority of users will need access to the computer running Microsoft SQL Server. Desktop applications will be installed on the local computers, but data files will be saved on the servers.

The XYZ Company would like to be connected to the Internet so they can receive e-mail.

Draft a network design using the following criteria

Environmental components	Detail
Users	100
Location(s)	Single office.
Administration	One full-time administrator.
Servers	3 computers, 2 Pentium 120s with 32 MB RAM, 3.2 GB hard disk. 1 Pentium 150 with 128 MB RAM dedicated to Exchange Server.
Clients	All Pentium and 486 computers, running Windows NT 4.0 or Windows 95.
Microsoft BackOffice applications	Exchange Server and DNS.
Server usage	Basic file and print.

The design will take into account:

- Number of users
- Number of administrative units
- Number of sites

1. How many DNS domains will you need to configure?

2. How many subdomains will you need to configure?

3. How many zones will you need to configure?

_____

4. How many primary name servers will you need to configure?

_____

5. How many secondary name servers will you need to configure?

_____

6. How many DNS cache-only servers will you need to configure?

_____

Scenario 2: Designing DNS for a Medium-Size Network

You are consulting for the WXY Company, which has 8,795 users. There are 8,000 users located in four primary sites, with the remaining employees located in 10 branch offices in major U.S. cities. The company has decided to upgrade their existing LANs to Windows NT servers. The organization has also decided to centralize all user accounts in a single location at the corporate headquarters.

The four primary sites are connected by T1 lines. The branch offices are connected to the nearest primary site by 56 Kbps lines.

Three of the four primary sites are independent business units and operate independently of the others. The fourth is corporate headquarters. Branch offices have between 25 and 250 users needing access to all four of the primary sites but seldom needing access to the other branch offices.

In addition to the 10 branch offices, you have discovered that the company has a temporary research location employing 10 people. The site has one server that connects to Boston using dial-on-demand routers. This site is expected to be shut down within six months. They are a stand-alone operation requiring connectivity for messaging only.

Primary sites will continue to maintain their own equipment and the equipment of the branch offices connected to them. Currently, bandwidth utilization is at 60 percent during peak times. Future network growth is expected to be minimal for the next 12 to 18 months.

Draft a network design using the following criteria

Environmental components	Detail
Users	8,795
Location(s)	Four primary sites, with 10 branch sites in major cities in the U.S. No plans for opening any international locations.
Administration	Full-time administrators at each of the four primary sites. Some of the smaller sites have part-time administrators.
Number of name servers	To be determined.
Number of cache servers	DNS cache servers are needed in each of the remote locations for the same zone.
Clients	386, 486, and Pentium computers running Windows NT and Windows 95.
Server applications	SQL Server, Exchange Server, and DNS.

Primary Site: Portland
Users: 1500
SQL Server
Messaging

Corporate HQ
Primary Site: Boston
Users: 2500
SQL Server, SNA Server
Messaging

Primary Site: Chicago
Users: 2000
SNA Server
Messaging

Primary Site: Atlanta
Users: 2000
Messaging

Branch Office:
San Francisco
Users: 25
Messaging

Branch Office:
Dallas
Users: 250
Messaging

Other branch offices include: Los Angeles, 40 users; Salt Lake City, 25 users; Montreal, 30 users; New Orleans, 25 users; Kansas City, 25 users; Washington, D.C., 100 users; Denver, 200 users; Miami, 75 users.

The design must take into account:

- Number of users
- Number of administrative units
- Number of sites
- Speed and quality of links connecting sites
- Available bandwidth on links
- Expected changes to network
- Line of business applications

1. How many DNS domains will you need to configure?

_____

2. How many subdomains will you need to configure?

_____

3. How many zones will you need to configure?

_____

4. How many primary name servers will you need to configure?

_____

5. How many secondary name servers will you need to configure?

_____

6. How many DNS cache-only servers will you need to configure?

_____

7. Use the following mileage chart to design a zone/branch office configuration based on the geographical proximity between each primary site and branch office. Branch offices should be in the same zone as the nearest primary site.

Portland, OR	Boston	Chicago	Atlanta

Mileage chart	Atlanta	Boston	Chicago	Portland, OR
Dallas	807	1,817	934	2,110
Denver	1,400	1,987	1,014	1,300
Kansas City	809	1,454	497	1,800
Los Angeles	2,195	3,050	2,093	1,143
Miami	665	1,540	1,358	3,300
Montreal	1,232	322	846	2,695
New Orleans	494	1,534	927	2,508
Salt Lake	1,902	2,403	1,429	800
San Francisco	2,525	3162	2,187	700
Washington, D.C.	632	435	685	2,700

Scenario 3: Designing DNS for a Large Network

The ABC Company has 60,000 users located around the world. The corporate headquarters is in Geneva, Switzerland. North and South America headquarters are located in New York City. The Australia and Asia headquarters are located in Singapore. Each of the regional headquarters will maintain total control of users within their areas.

Users require access to resources in the other regional headquarters. The three regional headquarters sites are connected by T1 lines.

Each of the three regional headquarters have lines of business applications that need to be available to all sites within their areas, as well as the other regional headquarters. The Malaysian and Australian subsidiaries have major manufacturing sites to which all regional subsidiaries need access.

These line of business applications are all running on Windows NT servers. These computers will be configured as servers within the domains.

The links between Singapore, Australia, and Malaysia are typically operating at 90 percent utilization. The Asia and Australia region has 10 subsidiaries comprising Australia, China, Indonesia, Japan, Korea, Malaysia, New Zealand, Singapore, Taiwan, and Thailand.

Due to import restrictions with some of the subsidiaries, it has been decided to give control of the equipment to each subsidiary, and to have a resource domain in each subsidiary. Lately most of the computers the subsidiaries have purchased are running Windows NT Workstation. The company has authorized redundant hardware where you can justify it.

In order to keep this scenario reasonable, the questions and answers deal only with the Asia-Australia region.

Draft a network design using the following criteria

Environmental components	Detail
Users in Asia-Australia domain	25,000 evenly distributed across all of the subsidiaries.
Location(s)	Regional headquarters in Singapore, 10 subsidiaries in Australia, China, Indonesia Japan, Korea, Malaysia, New Zealand, Singapore, Taiwan, Thailand.
Administration	Full-time administrators at the regional headquarters and each of the subsidiaries.
Number of domains	To be determined.
Clients	386, 486 and Pentium computers running Windows 95 or Windows NT Workstation.
Server applications	SQL Server, SNA Server, Systems Management Server, Messaging, DNS.
Number of cache servers	To be determined.

The design for the Asia-Australia region must take into account:

- Number of users
- Number of administrative units
- Number of sites
- Speed and quality of links connecting sites
- Available bandwidth on links
- Expected changes to network
- Line of business applications

1. How many DNS domains will you need to configure?

_____

2. How many subdomains will you need to configure?

_____

3. How many zones will you need to configure?

_____

4. How many primary name servers will you need to configure?

_____

5. How many secondary name servers will you need to configure?

_____

6. How many DNS cache-only servers will you need to be configure?

_____

Summary

Depending on the size of your organization and configuration, you may want to configure DNS for your site. However, an organization with a small network may want to have DNS clients query a DNS name server maintained by an ISP. If your organization wants to connect to the Internet, you must inform InterNIC.

Review

The following questions are intended to reinforce key information presented in this chapter. If you are unable to answer a question, review the appropriate lesson and then try the question again.

1. Name the three components of the Domain Name System.

    _____

    _____

2. Describe the difference between primary, secondary, and master name servers.

    _____

    _____

    _____

    _____

3. List three reasons to have a secondary name server.

    _____

    _____

    _____

    _____

4. Describe the difference between a domain and a zone.

    _____

    _____

5. Describe the difference between recursive and iterative queries.

_____

_____

_____

_____

6. List the files required for a Windows NT DNS implementation.

_____

_____

7. Describe the purpose of the boot file.

_____

_____

For More Information

- Read *DNS and BIND* by Paul Albitz and Cricket Liu, published by O'Reilly & Associates.
- Read the white paper titled *DNS and Microsoft Windows NT 4.0.*

CHAPTER 13

Implementing DNS

Lesson 1 The Microsoft DNS Server . . . 282

Lesson 2 Administering the DNS Server . . . 286

Lesson 3 Integrating DNS and WINS . . . 296

Review . . . 301

About This Chapter

This chapter addresses installing and configuring DNS, integrating DNS and WINS, and using NSLOOKUP, the DNS diagnostic tool. In the lessons, you install and configure a Domain Name System, configure DNS files, and use DNS servers to resolve host names into IP addresses.

Before You Begin

To complete the lessons in this chapter, you must have:

- Installed Microsoft Windows NT Server 4.0 with TCP/IP.
- An understanding of the concepts presented in Chapter 12, "Domain Name System (DNS)."

Lesson 1: The Microsoft DNS Server

Windows NT 4.0 includes an interoperable, standards-based DNS service. This lesson introduces the Microsoft DNS server implementation.

After this lesson, you will be able to:

- Install the Microsoft DNS Server service.
- Troubleshoot DNS with NSLOOKUP.

Estimated lesson time: 25 minutes

Microsoft DNS is an RFC-compliant DNS server; as a result, it creates and uses standard DNS zone files and supports all standard resource record types. It is interoperable with other DNS servers and includes the DNS diagnostic utility, NSLOOKUP. Microsoft DNS is tightly integrated with WINS and is administered through the graphical administration utility called DNS Manager.

Installing Microsoft DNS Server

Before installing the Microsoft Windows NT DNS Server service, it is important that the Windows NT 4.0 server's TCP/IP protocol be configured correctly. The DNS Server service obtains the default settings for the host name and domain name through the **Microsoft TCP/IP properties** dialog box. The DNS Server service will create default SOA, A, and NS records based on the specified domain name and host name. If the host name and domain name are not specified, only the SOA record is created.

Practice

Note If you have not already installed the Windows NT 4.0 Service Pack 2, you should do so now. To install the service pack, follow the procedure outlined in the Setup Instructions section of About This Book. This procedure shows you how to install the service pack from the course compact disc.

In this procedure, you install the Microsoft DNS Server service. You configure DNS in a later lesson.

Note Complete this procedure from the computer you designate as the DNS server.

▶ **To configure the DNS Server service search order**

1. Log on as Administrator.

2. At a command prompt, type **ipconfig** and then press ENTER.

3. Record the IP address for your computer.

---

4. Switch to the **Microsoft TCP/IP Properties** dialog box, and then click the **DNS** tab.

5. In the **Domain** box, type **Domain1** (or your domain name)

6. Under **DNS Service Search Order**, click **Add**.

7. In the **DNS Server** box, type in the IP address for your computer, and then click **Add**.

8. Click **OK**.

   The **Network** dialog box appears.

9. Click **OK** to close the **Network** dialog box.

▶ **To install the DNS Server service**

1. In Control Panel, double-click the Network icon, and then click **Services**.

2. Click **Add**.

   The **Select Network Service** dialog box appears.

3. In the **Network Service** list, click **Microsoft DNS Server**, and then click **OK**.

   Windows NT Setup displays a dialog box asking for the full path to the Windows NT distribution files.

4. Type the path to the Windows NT distribution files, and then click **Continue**.

   All necessary files, including the sample files, are copied to your hard disk.

5. In the **Network** dialog box, click **Close**.

6. When prompted, click **Yes** to restart your computer.

Troubleshooting DNS with NSLOOKUP

The NSLOOKUP utility, the primary diagnostic tool for DNS, enables users to interact with a DNS server. NSLOOKUP can be used to display resource record on DNS servers, including UNIX DNS implementations. NSLOOKUP is installed with the TCP/IP protocol.

NSLOOKUP Modes

NSLOOKUP has two modes: interactive and non-interactive. If a single piece of data is needed, use non-interactive or command-line mode. If more than one piece of data is needed, interactive mode can be used.

NSLOOKUP Syntax

nslookup [*–option* ...] [*computer-to-find* | – [*server*]]

Syntax	Description
–option ...	Specifies one or more NSLOOKUP commands. For a list of commands, use the **Help** option inside NSLOOKUP.
computer-to-find	If *computer-to-find* is an IP address and the query type is A or PTR, the name of the computer is returned. If *computer-to-find* is a name and does not have a trailing period, the default DNS domain name is appended to the name. To look up a computer outside of the current DNS domain, append a period to the name.
	If a hyphen (–) is typed instead of *computer-to-find*, the command prompt changes to NSLOOKUP interactive mode.
server	Use this server as the DNS name server. If the server is omitted, the currently configured default DNS server is used.

▶ **To use NSLOOKUP in command mode**

1. At a command prompt, modify the properties so that it has a screen buffer size of 50.

   Use the **Layout** property page to do this.

2. If the command prompt is not full-screen, press ALT+ENTER.

3. Type the following command:

   nslookup *hostx*

   where *hostx* is a host in your domain.

   NSLOOKUP will return the IP address of the computer *hostx* because the information is stored in the DNS database.

4. Exit the command prompt.

NSLOOKUP Command Help

You can find NSLOOKUP commands using Windows NT Help. To find the commands, start Windows NT Help and search for nslookup. You can then click NSLOOKUP commands to see a list of all commands.

▶ **To use NSLOOKUP in interactive mode**

1. At a command prompt, type **nslookup** and then press ENTER.

   A > prompt appears.

2. Type **set all** at the > prompt.

   This command lists all of the current values of the NSLOOKUP options.

3. Use Windows NT Help and the **set** commands to change the **time-out** to **1 second** and the **number of retries** to **7**. Use **set all** to verify that the defaults were changed.

   Set ti=1

   Set ret=7

4. Switch to DNS Manager and note the number of hosts in your domain.
5. Switch back to the command prompt.
6. Type the names of the other computers, one at a time, at the > prompt. Press ENTER after each name.
7. Switch to DNS Manager, and then press F5.

   All of the computer names that could be resolved are added to the zone database.

8. Exit the command prompt.
9. Close Windows NT Help and DNS Manager.

Summary

Microsoft DNS is interoperable with other DNS servers. Before installing the DNS Server service, you should make sure that the Windows NT 4.0 server's TCP/IP protocol is configured correctly.

The NSLOOKUP utility is the primary diagnostic tool for DNS. It lets you display resource records on DNS servers.

Lesson 2: Administering the DNS Server

There are two ways to administrate the Microsoft DNS server: use the DNS Manager or manually edit the DNS configuration files. This lesson reviews the tools used to administer a DNS server.

After this lesson, you will be able to:

- Administer a DNS server.
- Create a zone file and populate it with resource records.

Estimated lesson time: 60 minutes

Configuring DNS Server Properties

You can use DNS Manager to configure the Microsoft Windows NT DNS server. Because the DNS server has no initial information about a user's network, the DNS server installs as a caching-only name server for the Internet. This means that the DNS server contains only information on the Internet root servers. For most DNS server configurations, additional information must be supplied to obtain the preferred operation, as shown in the following illustration and table.

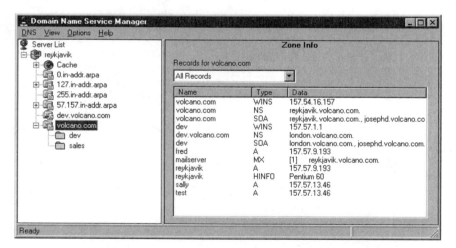

Property	Description
Interfaces	Specifies which interfaces DNS operates over on a multihomed computer. By default, all interfaces are used.
Forwarders	Configures your server to use another name server as a forwarder. The name server can also be configured as a slave to the forwarder.
Boot method	Displays what boot method the name server is using—either from the registry or from the data files.

Practice

In these procedures, you configure DNS, configure DNS files, and use the DNS service to resolve host names into IP addresses.

Note   You need two computers for these procedures. One computer functions as a DNS server and the other computer functions as a DNS client.

In this procedure, you view the default installation of the Windows NT DNS Server service.

▶ **To view the default DNS server installation**

Note   Complete this procedure from the DNS server computer.

1. Log on as Administrator.
2. Click the **Start** button, point to **Programs**, point to **Administrative Tools**, and then click **DNS Manager**.
3. On the **DNS** menu, click **New Server**.

   The **Add DNS Server** dialog box appears.
4. In the **Add DNS Server** box, type **Server1** and click **OK**.
5. Double-click **Cache**.

   This displays all of the information your DNS server currently has in the cache. All root servers for the Internet are contained in the cache.
6. On the **Options** menu, click **Preferences**.

   The **Preferences** dialog box appears.
7. Click **Show Automatically Created Zones**, and then click **OK**.
8. Click your computer name and then press F5 to refresh the DNS Manager window.

   The three reverse lookup zones appear: **0.in-addr.arpa**, **127.in-addr.arpa**, and **255.in-addr.arpa**.
9. Double-click each of the reverse lookup zones.

   What type of records does each of them contain?

10. Double-click 127.in-addr.arpa.

    A **0** folder appears.

11. Double-click the **0** folder.

    A second **0** folder appears.

12. Double-click the second **0** folder.

    The PTR record for local host appears. This entry is used when the loopback IP address of 127.0.0.1 is looked up.

    At this point, the DNS Server service installed on your computer is configured as a caching-only name server.

Manually Configuring DNS

The DNS server can be configured manually by editing files in the default installation path *system_root*\System32\Dns. Administration is identical to administration of traditional DNS. These files can be modified using a text editor. The DNS service must then be stopped and restarted.

Adding DNS Domains and Zones

The first step in configuring the DNS server is to determine the hierarchy for your DNS domains and zones. Once the domain and zone information has been determined, this information must be entered into the DNS configuration using the DNS Manager.

Adding Primary or Secondary Zones

You add primary and secondary zones through DNS Manager, as shown in the following illustration. After entering your zone information, DNS Manager will construct a default zone file name. If the zone file already exists in the DNS directory, DNS Manager will automatically import these records.

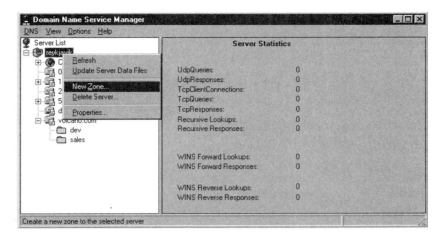

A primary zone stores name-to-address mappings locally. When you configure a primary zone, you need no information other than the zone name.

Secondary zones obtain name-to-address mappings from a master server by zone transfer. When you configure a secondary zone, you must supply the names for the zone and master name server.

Note The Microsoft Windows NT convention is to create a file called *zonename*.dns, which differs from other DNS servers that create files called Db.zone.

Adding Subdomains

Once all zones have been added to the server, subdomains under the zones can be added. To add a subdomain, on the shortcut menu of the preferred zone, click **New Domain**. Enter the name of the new subdomain, and then click **OK**.

If multiple levels of subdomains are needed, create each successive subdomain through the **New Domain** shortcut menu option for the immediate parent.

There is a key written to the DNS registry entry for each zone for which the DNS will be authoritative. The keys are located under:

HKEY_LOCAL_MACHINE\SYSTEM\ CurrentControlSet\Services\DNS\Zones

Each zone has its own key and the key contains the name of the database file, which indicates whether the DNS server is a primary or secondary name server. For example, for the zone "dev.volcano.com," there is the following registry entry:

HKEY_LOCAL_MACHINE\SYSTEM\\CurrentControlSet\Services\DNS\
Zones\dev.volcano.com

Configuring Zone Properties

Property	Description
General	Configures the zone file in which the resource records are stored, and specifies whether this is a primary or secondary name server.
SOA record	Configures zone transfer information and the name server administrator mailbox.
Notify	Specifies the secondary servers to be alerted when the primary server database changes. Also, additional security can be applied to the name server by specifying that only the listed secondary servers can contact this server.
WINS lookup	Enables the name server to query WINS to resolve names. A list of WINS servers can be configured in this dialog. The WINS servers can be set on a per-name-server basis by selecting the **Settings Only Affect Local Server** check box. If this is not selected, secondary servers will also use the configured WINS servers.

Practice

In this procedure, you configure the DNS server by adding primary zone.

▶ **To add a zone to a server**

Note Complete this procedure from the DNS server computer.

1. Right-click your computer name, and then click **New Zone**.

   The **Creating New Zone for Server1** dialog box appears.
2. Click **Primary**, and then click **Next**.
3. In the **Zone Name** box, type **zone1.com** (where zone1.com is your *zone name*).
4. Press the TAB key.

   zone1.com.dns is automatically entered in the **Zone File** box.
5. Click **Next**, and then click **Finish**.

   The **Server List** now has a zone name, and the **Zone Info** entries have been added.

6. Click each of the resource records.

   What type of records does each of them contain?

   _____

7. Click your zone name.
8. On the **DNS** menu, click **Properties**.

   The **Zone Properties** dialog box appears.

9. Click the **Notify** tab.

   Note If you were configuring a secondary DNS server for your domain, you would indicate it in the **Notify List** box and then click **Add**.

10. Click **OK**.

Adding Resource Records

Once the zones and subdomains are configured, resource records can be added. To add a resource record, select a zone or subdomain and then click **DNS–New Host** or select **New Record** from the menu bar.

New Host

To create a new host, type the host name and IP address, and then select **Create Associated PTR Record** in the associated reverse lookup domain, as shown in the following illustration.

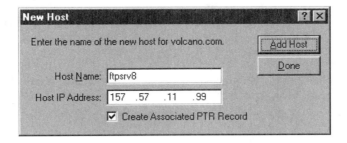

New Record

To create a new record, select which resource record type to create. A dialog box displays various fields specific to record type, as shown in the following illustration. The TTL field displays the default TTL from the SOA record for the zone file. A TTL value will be stored in the record only if it is changed from the default. Enter the information and then click **OK** to add the resource record.

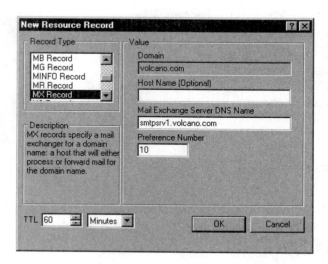

Configuring Reverse Lookup

To find a host name, given the host's IP address, a reverse lookup zone must be created for each network on which hosts in the DNS database reside. Adding a reverse lookup zone is procedurally identical to adding any other type of zone, except for the zone name.

For example, if a host has an address of 198.231.25.89, it would be represented in the in-addr.arpa domain as 89.25.231.198.in-addr.arpa. Furthermore, to enable this host to appear to a client who has its IP address, a zone would need to be added to the DNS for 25.231.198.in-addr.arpa, as shown in the following example.

All pointer records for the network 198.231.25.0 would be added to this reverse lookup zone.

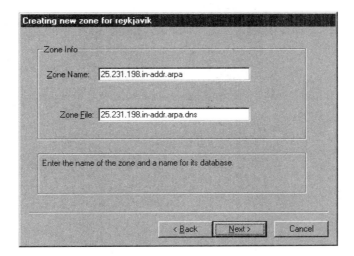

Practice

In this procedure, you create a reverse lookup zone that allows the DNS service to return a name when queried with an IP address from a client.

▶ **To configure a reverse lookup zone for the primary DNS server**

Note Complete this procedure from the DNS server computer.

1. Determine the reverse lookup zone name for your primary DNS server by using one of these three methods:

   - For class A addresses, use your first octet and append to it **.in-addr.arpa** (for example: A class A IP address of 29.122.15.88 would have a reverse lookup zone name of **29.in-addr.arpa**).

   - For class B addresses, use your first two octets in reverse order and append to them **.in-addr.arpa** (for example: A class B IP address of 129.122.15.88 would have a reverse lookup zone name of **122.129.in-addr.arpa**).

   - For class C addresses, use your first three octets in reverse order and append to them **.in-addr.arpa** (for example: A class C IP address of 229.122.15.88 would have a reverse lookup zone name of **15.122.129.in-addr.arpa**).

   What is your reverse lookup zone name?

2. Open the DNS Manager, and then click on your computer name.

3. On the **DNS** menu, click **New Zone**.

   The **Creating New Zone** dialog box appears.

4. Click **Primary**, and then click **Next**.

5. Type your reverse lookup zone name in the **Zone Name** box.

6. Tab to the **Zone File** box.

   The file name is automatically generated.

7. Click **Next**, and then click **Finish**.

Note If you were to configure zone properties for a secondary DNS server, you would enter its IP address using the **Notify** tab in the **Zone Properties** dialog box.

In this procedure, you add a host name to your domain.

▶ **To add your other computer as a host in your domain**

Note Complete this procedure from the DNS server computer.

---

1. Right-click your zone name.

2. On the menu that appears, click **New Host**.

   The **New Host** dialog box appears.

3. In the **Host Name** box, type your second computer name.

4. In the **Host IP Address** box, type the IP address of your second computer.

5. Click **Create Associated PTR Record**, and then click **Add Host**.

6. Click **Done**.

7. Click the **107.131.in-addr.arpa** zone, and then press F5.

   A plus sign (+) precedes **107.131.in-addr.arpa**.

8. Double-click **107.131.in-addr.arpa**.

   A folder appears beneath **107.131.in-addr.arpa**.

9. Double-click the folder.

   A **PTR** record appears in the **Zone Info** box.

10. Double-click the **PTR** record, examine the contents of the record, and then click **OK**.

    This is the reverse lookup record that is automatically generated when the **Create Associated PTR Record** option is selected.

11. Repeat steps 1 through 10 to add a host record for your computer and refresh the listings.

12. Verify that there are two A records (one record for your first computer, one record for your second computer) in your zone.

13. Verify that there are two PTR records (one record for your first computer, one record for your second computer) in the reverse lookup (107.131.in-addr.arpa) zone.

Summary

The first step in configuring Microsoft Windows NT DNS server is to determine the hierarchy for your DNS domains and zones. Once the zones and subdomains are configured, resource records can be added. To find a host name given the host's IP address, a reverse lookup zone must be created for each network on which hosts in the DNS database reside.

Lesson 3: Integrating DNS and WINS

WINS requires less management than DNS because it dynamically registers name-to-address mappings. This lesson explains why WINS is used and how to use it with DNS.

After this lesson, you will be able to:
- Explain how to integrate DNS with WINS.
- Configure the WINS client.
- Configure WINS host name resolution and reverse lookup resolution.
- Configure an alias for a host name.

Estimated lesson time: 45 minutes

DNS is a static database of name-to-address mappings that must be manually updated. DNS implements a hierarchical model, which allows the administration and replication of the database to be broken into zones.

WINS, on the other hand, allows machines to dynamically register their name-to-address mappings and therefore requires less administration. WINS is a flat name space and requires each WINS server to maintain a complete database of entries through replication.

The WINS Record

A new WINS data record is defined as part of the database file and is unique to the Microsoft DNS server. It is entered into the zone's root domain by placing the record in the database file. If a name-to-address mapping is not found in the database file, DNS queries the WINS database. For example:

1. A client contacts its DNS server and requests an IP address of another host.

   The DNS server searches its database and does not find an address record for the host.

2. Because the database file contains a WINS record, the DNS server converts the host portion of the name to a NetBIOS name and sends a request for this NetBIOS name to the WINS server.

3. If the WINS server is able to resolve the name, it returns the IP address to the DNS server.

4. The DNS server returns the IP address to the requesting client.

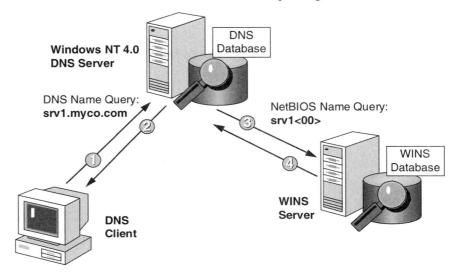

Note If a zone is configured for WINS resolution, all DNS servers that are authoritative for that zone must be configured for WINS resolution.

Enabling WINS Lookup

By enabling WINS Lookup, DNS can be configured to submit queries to a WINS server when a name-to-address mapping cannot be resolved by the DNS server.

You enable WINS Lookup with the DNS Manager by selecting the zone, opening its **Shortcut** menu, and then selecting **Properties**. Click the **WINS Lookup** tab, select the **Use WINS Resolution** check box, and then enter the IP addresses of the preferred WINS servers, as shown in the following illustration.

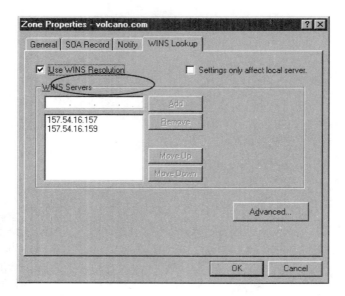

WINS Reverse Lookup

The presence of a WINS-R record at the zone root instructs the DNS server to use a NetBIOS node adapter status lookup. This lookup is for any reverse lookup requests for IP addresses in the zone root which are not statically defined with PTR records.

With DNS Manager, enabling WINS reverse lookup is accomplished by obtaining properties on the appropriate in-addr.arpa zone and selecting the **WINS Reverse Lookup** property page. Enter the **Use WINS Reverse Lookup** check box and enter the **DNS Host Domain** to be appended to the NetBIOS name before returning the response to the resolver.

WINS Time to Live

The WINS TTL can be configured from the **Advanced** dialog box found in the **WINS Lookup** property page of the properties of a zone. When a name-to-address mapping is resolved by the WINS server, the address is cached for the **Cache Timeout Value**. By default, this value is set to 10 minutes. If this address is forwarded to another DNS server, the TTL is also forwarded.

Practice

In these procedures, you configure a Windows NT server to use WINS for host name resolution. In the first procedure, you configure the WINS client so that it uses the primary WINS server.

▶ **To configure the WINS client**

Note   Complete this procedure from the DNS client computer.

---

1. Switch to the **Microsoft TCP/IP Properties** dialog box.
2. Click the **WINS Address** tab.
3. In the **Primary WINS Server** box, type the IP address for your DNS server.
4. Click **OK**, and then click **Close**.

   The **Network Settings Change** message box appears, prompting you to restart the computer.
5. Click **Yes**.

   The computer restarts.
6. Log on as Administrator.

In this procedure, you configure DNS so that it uses WINS to resolve any host names it cannot resolve.

▶ **To configure WINS resolution**

Note   Complete this procedure from the DNS server computer.

---

1. Start DNS Manager.
2. Right-click your zone name, and then click **Properties**.

   The **Zone Properties** dialog box appears.
3. Click the **WINS Lookup** tab.
4. Click **Use WINS Resolution**.
5. In the **WINS Servers** box, type the IP address of your DNS server.
6. Click **Add**, and then click **OK**.

In this procedure, you configure DNS so that it uses WINS to resolve any IP addresses it cannot resolve.

▶ **To configure WINS reverse lookup**

Note Complete this procedure from the DNS server computer.

1. Switch to DNS Manager.
2. Right-click your reverse lookup zone: **107.131.in-addr.arpa**, and then click **Properties**.

   The **Zone Properties** dialog box appears.
3. Click the **WINS Reverse Lookup** tab.
4. Click **Use WINS Reverse Lookup**.
5. Type your zone name in the **DNS Host Domain** box, and then click **OK**.

▶ **To test WINS reverse lookup**

Note Complete this procedure from the DNS server computer.

1. At a command prompt, type:

   nslookup 131.107.2.211

   where *131.107.2.211* is your client IP address.

   The NSLOOKUP utility returns your computer's host name because your host has a record in your reverse lookup database.
2. Type:

   nslookup 131.107.2.200

   where *131.107.2.200* is your server IP address.

   The NSLOOKUP utility returns the host name at 131.107.2.200 because WINS reverse lookup has been configured. DNS automatically adds an address record into the DNS database when it resolves the IP address.

Summary

By enabling WINS lookup, DNS can be configured to submit queries to a WINS server when a name-to-address mapping cannot be resolved. You enable WINS lookup through the **Zone Properties** dialog box in DNS Manager.

Review

The following questions are intended to reinforce key information presented in this chapter. If you are unable to answer a question, review the appropriate lesson and then try the question again.

1. What is the purpose of entering a host name and domain name in the DNS configuration dialog box of the TCP/IP protocol *before* installing the Microsoft DNS Server service?

2. What is the function of the NSLOOKUP utility?

3. Describe the WINS lookup process.

4. Describe a situation where WINS lookup is useful.

For More Information
- Read *DNS and BIND* by Paul Albitz and Cricket Liu, published by O'Reilly and Associates.
- Read the white paper titled *DNS and Microsoft Windows NT 4.0*.

CHAPTER 14

Connectivity in Heterogeneous Environments

Lesson 1   Connectivity in Heterogeneous Environments . . . 304

Lesson 2   Remote Execution Utilities . . . 307

Lesson 3   Data Transfer Utilities . . . 309

Lesson 4   Printing Utilities . . . 316

Review . . . 323

About This Chapter

In this chapter, you review connectivity with NetBIOS-based hosts and foreign hosts. You also review the different connectivity tools provided with Microsoft Windows NT. The lessons in this chapter provide information on installing and configuring Microsoft FTP server software and TCP/IP printing support.

Before You Begin

To complete the lessons in this chapter, you must have:

- Installed Windows NT Server 4.0 with TCP/IP.
- A shared printer to perform the TCP/IP print procedure (optional).

Lesson 1: Connectivity in Heterogeneous Environments

A primary benefit of using TCP/IP is that it provides the ability to connect to and interoperate with different types of hosts, such as a UNIX host. This lesson explains the different requirements for connecting to foreign hosts and connecting to and interoperating with RFC-compliant NetBIOS-based hosts.

After this lesson, you will be able to:

- Explain the connectivity requirements for Microsoft networking.

Estimated lesson time: 10 minutes

Microsoft TCP/IP allows connectivity to many foreign computer systems because it is a common network protocol used by all of them. To communicate with any foreign computer such as OS/2, UNIX, Solaris, or VMS, you need a common network protocol such as TCP/IP. You also need applications (usually client/server) on both ends that communicate using this common network protocol.

Connecting to a Remote Host with Microsoft Networking

In order to use standard Microsoft networking commands and functions (for example, **net use**, Windows NT Explorer, or File Manager) to connect to a remote host, the following requirements must be met:

- *Transport Driver Connectivity.* Both computers must be able to communicate with each other using the same transport driver, such as TCP/IP, NBF, or IPX.

- *SMB Connectivity.* The Workstation service communicates with an *SMB server* process at the remote host. SMB is the file-sharing protocol used on all MS®-Net products.

Note If the NetBIOS scope parameter is configured on the remote host, the scope ID must match the scope ID on your Microsoft clients or they will not be able to communicate with NetBIOS.

Many vendors have implemented NetBIOS over TCP/IP and SMB servers on their operating systems. Examples of these vendors are Digital Equipment Corporation's PATHWORKS on VMS, IBM LAN Server on OS/2, and LAN Manager for UNIX.

Connecting to Windows NT Server from a Remote Host

Windows NT Server provides file services to personal computers through the server message block (SMB) protocol. File service for UNIX clients is available through the network file system (NFS) protocol, the FTP service, or by installing an SMB-based client.

Third-party NFS servers are available for Windows NT. These servers enable Windows NT Server to provide file service for personal computers, UNIX workstations, or other systems acting as NFS clients. They provide support for the Windows NT File System (NTFS), file allocation table (FAT), CD-ROM file system (CDFS), and high-performance file system (HPFS).

Microsoft TCP/IP Utilities

The following Microsoft TCP/IP utilities provide several options for connecting to foreign TCP/IP-based hosts using Windows Sockets.

TCP/IP utility	Function
REXEC	Runs a process on a remote host running REXEC server software. This provides password protection security.
RSH (Remote Shell)	Enables execution of commands on a remote RSH server without logging on. This does not provide password protection.
Telnet	Provides terminal emulation (DEC VT 100, DEC VT 52, and TTY). This provides user and password authentication.
RCP (Remote Copy)	Copies files between a computer running Windows NT and a server running the RCP daemon without logging on, thus providing no user authentication security.
FTP	Provides bidirectional file transfers between a computer running Windows NT and any TCP/IP host running FTP server software. This gives user and password authentication.
TFTP	A subset of FTP that uses the User Datagram Protocol (UDP) instead of TCP; provides bidirectional file transfers between a computer running Windows NT and a TCP/IP host running TFTP server software, and provides no user authentication.
Web Browser	Web browsers access documents stored on a WWW server, and can provide user and password authentication.
LPD	Services LPR requests and submits print jobs to a printer device, and provides user and password authentication.
LPR	Provides the ability to send a print job to a printer connected to a server running the LPD service, and provides user and password authentication.
LPQ	Provides the ability to view the print queue on an LPD server, and provides user and password authentication.

Summary

TCP/IP gives Windows NT the ability to connect to and interoperate with many foreign TCP/IP-based hosts. Microsoft TCP/IP utilities provide several options for connecting to foreign hosts.

Lesson 2: Remote Execution Utilities

Several TCP/IP utilities provide the ability to connect to remote hosts. This lesson explains the requirements for usage of each remote execution utility.

After this lesson, you will be able to:

- Understand how to connect to a remote host with Microsoft networking.

Estimated lesson time: 10 minutes

REXEC

Remote Execution (REXEC) provides remote execution facilities with authentication based on user names and passwords. When the **rexec** command is carried out, it prompts the user for a password on the remote host. After connecting the user to the remote host, it verifies the password. If the password is valid, it then executes the specified command. REXEC normally terminates when the remote command ends. The syntax of REXEC is:

rexec *tcpiphost command*

RSH

Remote Shell (RSH) is used to run commands on a remote server running the RSH daemon (in most cases, a UNIX host). RSH is useful for compiling programs. A user does not have to log on to the UNIX host to run a command. The only security is that the user's name must be configured in the .rhosts file on the UNIX host. RSH does not prompt for passwords. The following is an example of RSH syntax:

rsh *unixhost command*

Telnet

Telnet is a remote terminal emulation protocol that provides Digital Equipment Corporation VT 100, Digital Equipment Corporation VT 52, or TTY emulation. Telnet uses the connection-oriented services of TCP. Any programs or commands you run are processed by the Telnet server and not by the local host.

In order to run Telnet, the host system must be configured with a Telnet server program, also called a daemon. Microsoft does not provide this program. You must also have a user account for the computer running Windows NT.

The client computer must be configured with Telnet client software (provided with Windows NT), and a user account on the Telnet server.

▶ **To make a terminal connection with Telnet**

1. At a command prompt, start Telnet.exe.

   The Telnet window opens.

2. On the **Connect** menu, choose **Remote System**.

   The **Connect** dialog box appears.

3. In the **Host Name** box, type the host name or IP address of the Telnet server, and then click **OK**.

4. When prompted, log on to the Telnet server using the user account and password located on the Telnet server.

   Once you are connected, you can use host commands as if you were at a terminal connected to that host. Any programs or commands you run are processed by the Telnet server and not by the local host.

Note   Telnet is defined in RFC 854. For a copy of this RFC, see the *Course Materials* Web page on the course compact disc.

Summary

TCP/IP has several remote execution utilities. Remote Execution starts a process on the remote host and requires a user account. Remote Shell runs commands on a remote host and requires a user name in the .rhosts file on a UNIX host. Telnet runs commands interactively in a terminal emulation application.

Lesson 3: Data Transfer Utilities

TCP/IP provides several data transfer utilities, including the widely-used FTP. This lesson explains the requirements and usage of each data transfer utility.

After this lesson, you will be able to:

- Understand how to use data transfer utilities to connect to and access resources on a TCP/IP-based host.
- Install Microsoft® Internet Information Server (IIS) FTP services.
- Use FTP client software to transfer files.

Estimated lesson time: 25 minutes

RCP

Like RSH, Remote Copy Protocol (RCP) does not require the user to log on to a server running the RCP daemon (in most cases, a UNIX host). However, the user must have a name configured in the .rhosts file on the UNIX host and have remote command execution privileges. RCP is used to copy files between a local and remote UNIX host or two remote hosts. RCP does not prompt for passwords. An example of the syntax for RCP:

rcp *host1.user1:source host2.user2:destination*

FTP

The FTP utility, which uses TCP as its transport, is one of the most commonly used utilities. It provides binary and text file transfers with an FTP server. The FTP server could be a UNIX host or a computer running Windows NT configured with the FTP server daemon. FTP is frequently used to transfer files from the worldwide Internet.

A user account is required on the FTP server, unless the FTP server is configured to all anonymous connections. (A detailed discussion of the Windows NT FTP server follows.) There are many servers on the Internet that allow anonymous connections. The syntax of FTP is:

ftp [*options*] *host command*

The destination host must be configured with FTP server daemon (provided with Windows NT), and a user account for the Windows NT user.

The client computer must be configured with FTP client software (provided with Windows NT), and a user account on the FTP server.

FTP Commands

An FTP command can be entered on one line or through a command interpreter. If the command is entered on one line, FTP immediately attempts to establish a connection with an FTP server. If it is not entered on one line, FTP enters its command interpreter, from which a user can type an FTP command.

The most common FTP commands are shown in the following table.

Command	Function
binary	Changes the file transfer type to binary
get	Copies a remote file to a local host
put	Copies a local file to a remote host
!	Temporarily returns the user to the command prompt
quit or **bye**	Exits FTP

TFTP

Trivial File Transfer Protocol (TFTP) is used to transfer files to and from a remote or local host. TFTP uses the connectionless services of UDP. The TFTP does not support any user authentication. Files must be world-readable and writable (UNIX permissions) on the remote system.

Microsoft provides only TFTP client software. You must use a third-party TFTP server service (daemon) in order to use TFTP to connect to a computer running Windows NT. An example of the TFTP syntax would be:

tftp -i host get file-one file-two

Note FTP is defined in RFC 959. TFTP is defined in RFC 1350. For copies of these RFCs, see the *Course Materials* Web page on the course compact disc.

Practice

In these procedures, you install the Windows NT FTP server on your workstation and then with a second computer, access the FTP server with FTP. You then use **netstat** to check the status of FTP ports.

Note It is recommended that you have two computers to complete these procedures. However, in many cases you can start an FTP session with your own server by typing **ftp 127.0.0.1**

Use this first procedure to determine if you have installed Microsoft Internet Information Server (IIS) with the FTP service.

▶ **To examine the Windows NT Server environment**

1. Log on as Administrator.
2. Click the **Start** button, point to **Settings**, and then click **Control Panel**.
3. In Control Panel, double-click the Services icon.

   The **Services** dialog box appears.
4. Determine if the **FTP Publishing Service** is listed.

   If the FTP Publishing Service is not listed, you should install Internet Information Server with the FTP service using the following procedure.
5. Close the **Services** dialog box.
6. Close Control Panel.

In this procedure, you install Internet Information Server with the FTP service. Use this procedure if you have not previously installed IIS with the FTP service.

▶ **To install Internet Information Server**

1. Log on as Administrator.
2. On the desktop, double-click the Install Internet Information Server icon.

   The **Internet Information Server Installation** dialog box appears.
3. In the **Installed from** box, type the path to your Windows NT installation files.

   The **Microsoft Internet Information Server 2.0 Setup** dialog box appears.
4. Read the information in the **Microsoft Internet Information Server 2.0 Setup** dialog box, and then click **OK**.

   The following installation options appear:
   - Internet Service Manager
   - World Wide Web Service
   - WWW Service Samples
   - Internet Service Manager (HTML)
   - Gopher Service
   - FTP Service
   - ODBC Drivers and Administration
5. Make sure that at least the **Internet Service Manager** and **FTP Service** options are selected, and then click **OK**.

6. When prompted to create the **C:\Winnt\System32\Inetsrv** directory, click **Yes**.

   The **Publishing Directories** dialog box appears, listing the default directory:

   FTP Publishing Directory   **C:\Inetpub\Ftproot**

7. Click **OK** to accept the default directory.

8. When prompted to create the default directory, click **Yes**.

   Setup installs the **Internet Information Server FTP Service** software.

9. When Setup is complete, click **OK**.

In this procedure you use FTP client software to copy a file from the FTP server to the FTP client.

▶   **To transfer files using FTP**

1. At a command prompt, type:

   Copy C:\Winnt*.bmp C:\Inetpub\Ftproot

2. Create a temporary directory on your computer named **C:\Ftptemp**.

3. Change to the C:\Ftptemp directory.

4. Start an FTP session with your second computer and ping the computer using the following command:

   ftp server2

5. Log on as Anonymous.

6. When prompted for a password, press ENTER.

   An **ftp>** prompt will appear.

7. Type the following command at the **ftp>** prompt:

   dir

   A listing of all of the files available at the FTP site appears.

8. Use the **get** command to retrieve a single file. Type:

   get lanma256.bmp

9. To view the transferred file on your computer, type the following:

   !dir

   and then press ENTER.

10. Use the **mget** command to retrieve the rest of the files. Type:

    mget *

11. To exit the FTP session, type:

    Bye

    and then press ENTER.

In this procedure you start **netstat** inside an FTP session to check the status of the TCP ports.

▶ **To start an FTP session**

1. At a command prompt, start an FTP session with the second computer by typing the following command:

   ftp server2

2. Log on as Anonymous.

3. When prompted for a password, press ENTER.

   An **ftp>** prompt appears.

4. Type the following command at the **ftp>** prompt:

   !netstat

   This displays the current TCP network connections.

5. Type the following command at the **ftp>** prompt:

   !netstat -n

   This displays the current TCP network connections and the current TCP port connections.

   What TCP port does FTP use on the server side?

   _____

6. To exit the FTP session, type:

   Bye

   and then press ENTER.

Web Browsers

The World Wide Web (WWW) has become one of the most popular ways to transfer data on the Internet. Web browsers access documents stored on a World Wide Web server. The WWW follows a client/server model and uses the Hypertext Transfer Protocol (HTTP) between the client and the server as shown in the following illustration.

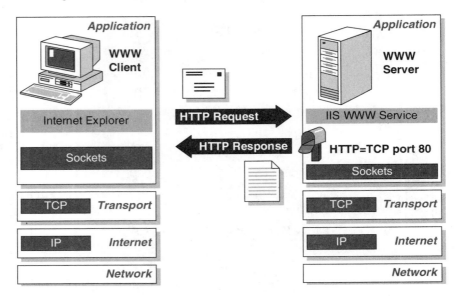

The client must be configured with a Web browser. There are several World Wide Web clients available, some of which can be freely downloaded from the Internet. The server must be configured with the World Wide Web service.

The server responds with the status of the transaction, successful or failed, and the data for the request. After the data is sent, the connection is closed and no state is retained by the server. Each object in an HTTP document requires a separate connection.

Web browsers provide two distinct data transfer benefits. First, Web browsers support many data types. A Web browser can automatically download and display text files and graphics, play video and sound clips, and launch helper applications for known file types.

The second benefit of Web browsers is that they support several data transfer protocols, including FTP, Gopher, HTTP, and Network News Transfer Protocol (NNTP).

Summary

RCP copies files to and from a remote host with no authentication. FTP copies files to and from a remote host reliably over TCP but has user-level authentication. Web browsers such as Microsoft Internet Explorer use HTTP to transfer pages of data from a Web server. TFTP copies files to and from a remote host quickly over UDP. It does not use user-level authentication.

Lesson 4: Printing Utilities

Once you have installed and configured TCP/IP printer support, you can connect to the printer using Print Manager or the LPR command, depending on whether the printer is attached to a computer running Windows NT or a UNIX host. This lesson provides an overview of TCP/IP printing support.

After this lesson, you will be able to:
- Install and configure TCP/IP network printing support.
- Connect and print to a TCP/IP-based printer.
- Use LPQ to view TCP/IP print queues, and use LPR to print a file.

Estimated lesson time: 45 minutes

LPR and LPQ are client applications that communicate with LPD on the server, as shown in the following illustration. These three applications provide the following functions:

- The LPD runs as a service on the computer running Windows NT (LPDSVC) and enables any computer with TCP/IP and LPR to send print jobs to the computer running Windows NT.

- LPR is the client printing application, and enables the Windows NT client to print to any host running LPD.

- LPQ can be used to query the printer once print jobs have been submitted.

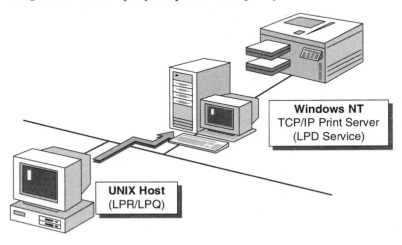

Windows NT
TCP/IP Print Server
(LPD Service)

UNIX Host
(LPR/LPQ)

Note Microsoft TCP/IP printing support is RFC 1179-compliant. For a copy of this RFC, see the *Course Materials* Web page on the course compact disc.

Using the TCP/IP Print Server (LPD)

For Windows NT to accept print jobs from LPR clients, the TCP/IP Printer Server service (LPDSVC) needs to be installed and running. The TCP/IP Printer Server service can be started from the Services program in Control Panel, a command prompt, or Server Manager.

Tip It is recommended that the TCP/IP Print Server service be configured to start automatically, either through the Services program in Control Panel or Server Manager.

TCP/IP Print Server Registry Entries

The configuration parameters for the TCP/IP Print Server are located under the following registry key:

HKEY_LOCAL_MACHINE\SYSTEM\CurrentControlSet\Services\LPDSVC \Parameters

Using LPR and LPQ

Submitting Print Jobs (LPR)

The method you use to print to a TCP/IP-based printer varies according to the environment you are printing from.

- For Windows-based applications, use Print Manager.
- For command-line situations, or when printing from a UNIX host, use the LPR (Lpr.exe) command-line utility.

The LPR utility submits print files to the LPD service running on a Windows NT server or a UNIX host with the following syntax:

lpr –S*ip_address* **–P***printer_name filename*

To send the print job, LPR makes a TCP connection to the LPD service using ports 512 to 1023.

Checking the Print Status (LPQ)

Once a file has been sent to a printer using LPR, you can use the LPQ (Lpq.exe) utility to check the status of the print queue. Use the following syntax:

lpq -S*ip_address* -P*printer_name* -**l**

Note   The -**S** and -**P** in both commands are case sensitive, and must be typed in uppercase. The -**l** (the letter l) can be typed in uppercase or lowercase.

Configuring Print Manager with the LPR Print Monitor

To configure Windows NT Print Manager to use an LPD print server, you must add the Microsoft TCP/IP Printing support and configure a printer to use the LPR print monitor. An example of a configuration is shown in the following illustration.

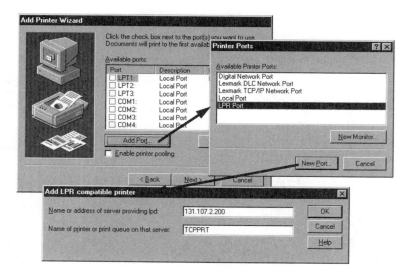

Note   Microsoft TCP/IP Printing must be installed before **LPR Port** will appear in the **Printer Port** dialog box of Print Manager.

Using Windows NT as a Print Gateway

A computer running Windows NT with TCP/IP Print services (LPD) installed can perform two gateway functions as shown in the following illustration. First, the computer running Windows NT can receive print jobs from Microsoft clients and then forward them automatically to a TCP/IP-based print server running LPD. The client does not require LPR or TCP/IP.

In addition, the computer running Windows NT can receive print jobs from any LPR client and then forward them to any printer visible to the computer running Windows NT.

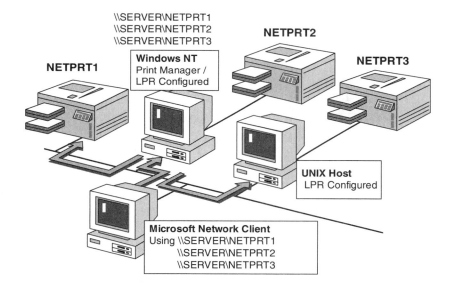

Practice

In these procedures, you install the TCP/IP Print service, create a TCP/IP printer, and then use the LPR utility to print to a printer. You must have a shared printer available to you in order to complete the procedures. You must also know the printer name, printer server IP address, and printer type.

In this procedure, you install the Microsoft TCP/IP Printing service, and then use Print Manager to install a TCP/IP-based printer.

▶ **To install the TCP/IP-based printer**

1. In Control Panel, double-click the Network icon.

   The **Network** dialog box appears.

2. Click the **Services** tab.

   The **Services** property sheet appears.

3. Click **Add**.

   The **Select Network Service** dialog box appears.

4. Click **Microsoft TCP/IP Printing**, and then click **OK**.

   The **Windows NT Setup** box appears, prompting you for the full path of the Windows NT distribution files.

5. Type the path to the Windows NT distribution files, and then click **Continue**.

   The appropriate files are copied to your workstation, and then the **Network** dialog box appears.

6. Click **Close**.

   A **Network Settings Change** message box appears, indicating that the computer needs to be restarted.

7. Click **Yes**.

8. Log on as Administrator.

9. In Control Panel, double-click the Services icon.

   The **Services** dialog box appears.

10. Select **TCP/IP Print Server**, and then click **Start**.

11. Click **Close**.

▶ **To create a TCP/IP-based printer**

1. In Control Panel, double-click the Printers icon.

   The Printers window appears.

2. Double-click **Add Printer**.

   The **Add Printer Wizard** dialog box appears.

3. Click **My Computer**, and then click **Next**.

4. Click **Add Port**.

   The **Printer Ports** dialog box appears.

5. Click **LPR Port**, and then click **New Port**.

   The **Add LPR compatible printer** dialog box appears.

6. In the **Name or address of server providing lpd** box, type your own IP address.

7. In the **Name of printer or print queue on that server** box, type the printer name, and then click **OK**.

8. Click **Close**.

9. Click **Next**.

10. Complete the **Add Printer Wizard** dialog box using the information in the following table.

When prompted for	Use this information
Printer manufacturer and model	*Printer type*
Printer name	*Printer Name*
Shared / Not shared	Shared
Share name	*Printer Name*
Test page	No

An **Insert Disk** message box prompts you for a floppy disk.

11. Click **OK**.

A **Windows NT Setup** dialog box appears, prompting you for the location of the Windows NT Server distribution files.

12. Type the path to the Windows NT Server distribution files, and then click **OK**.

A *printername* icon appears with the TCP/IP printer created.

In this procedure, you connect and print to the TCP/IP-based printer. You use Notepad to send files to be printed. You then use the LPQ command-line utility to view the status of the remote print queue.

▶ **To use Print Manager to connect to a TCP/IP-based printer**

1. In the Printers window, double-click **Add Printer**.

The **Add Printer Wizard** dialog box appears.

2. Click **Network printer server**, and then click **Next**.

The **Connect to Printer** dialog box appears.

3. In the **Printer** box, type the path and name of the printer, and then click **OK**.

The Add Printer wizard prompts you to make this printer the default printer.

4. Click **Yes**, and then click **Next**.

5. Click **Finish**.

An icon representing the shared computer is created in the Printers window.

6. Double-click the new printer icon.

The *printername* on *share* window appears.

7. Start Notepad, and then create and print a short document on the shared printer.

8. Switch back to the *printername* on *share* window.

A **Messenger Service** dialog box appears, notifying you that your print job has finished printing.

9. Click **OK**.

10. Close the *printername* on *share* window.

▶ **To use LPR and LPQ to access a TCP/IP-based printer**

1. At a command prompt, view the remote print queue. Type:

lpq -S*xxx.xxx.xxx.xxx* -P*printername* -l

where *xxx.xxx.xxx.xxx* is the printer server IP address, and *printername* is the printer name.

Important The **-S** and **-P** switches must be in uppercase.

The **Windows NT LPD Server print queue status** dialog box appears.

2. Send a new job to the print queue. Type:

lpr -S*xxx.xxx.xxx.xxx* -P*printername* c:\config.sys

The job is sent to the print queue on *\\printershare*.

3. View the remote print queue to view new jobs spooled.

Notice that the new job lists LPR client document as the job name.

4. Exit the command prompt.

Summary

LPD responds to LPR/LPQ requests and sends print job data to the printer device. LPR submits a print job to an LPD print server. LPQ queries the print job list of an LPD print server. Windows NT can gateway traffic among TCP/IP and non-TCP/IP print hosts.

Review

The following questions are intended to reinforce key information presented in this chapter. If you are unable to answer a question, review the appropriate lesson and then try the question again.

1. List the requirements for a computer running Windows NT to connect to a foreign host.

2. List the requirements for a computer running Windows NT to connect to and interoperate with an RFC-compliant NetBIOS-based host, such as LAN Manager for UNIX.

3. List two differences between accessing resources on a TCP/IP-based host using Windows NT commands versus TCP/IP utilities.

4. Which TCP/IP utilities are used to copy files?

5. Which TCP/IP utilities enable you to run commands on a foreign host?

6. What functions does the TCP/IP network printing support provide?

CHAPTER 15

Implementing the Microsoft SNMP Services

Lesson 1   SNMP Defined . . . 326

Lesson 2   The MIB . . . 330

Lesson 3   Installing and Configuring the SNMP Service . . . 333

Review . . . 346

About This Chapter

This chapter reviews the Simple Network Management Protocol (SNMP)—another protocol in the TCP/IP suite. The lessons provide an overview of SNMP, including the functions performed by an SNMP management station and the Microsoft SNMP service (SNMP agent). During the lessons, you install, configure, and test the SNMP service.

Before You Begin

To complete the lessons in this chapter, you must have:

- Installed Microsoft Windows NT Server 4.0 with TCP/IP.
- The Snmputil.exe file from the course compact disc.

Lesson 1: SNMP Defined

Simple Network Management Protocol (SNMP) provides the ability to monitor and communicate status information between a variety of hosts. This lesson defines SNMP and explains management systems and agents.

After this lesson, you will be able to:
- Explain and describe the Microsoft SNMP service.
- Describe the operations performed by an SNMP agent and management system.

Estimated lesson time: 20 minutes

SNMP is part of the TCP/IP protocol suite. It was originally developed in the Internet community to monitor and troubleshoot routers and bridges. SNMP provides the ability to monitor and communicate status information between:

- Computers running Windows NT
- LAN Manager servers
- Routers or gateways
- Minicomputers or mainframe computers
- Terminal servers
- Wiring hubs

SNMP uses a distributed architecture consisting of management systems and agents. With the Microsoft SNMP service, a computer running Windows NT can report its status to an SNMP management system on a TCP/IP network.

The SNMP service sends status information to one or more hosts when the host requests it or when a significant event occurs—for example, when a host is running out of hard disk space.

Note SNMP is defined in RFC 1157. For a copy of this RFC, see the *Course Materials* Web page on the course compact disc.

Management Systems and Agents

SNMP monitors various hosts using management systems and agents as shown in the following illustration.

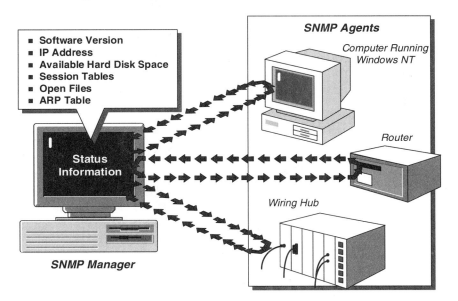

SNMP Management System

The primary function of a management system is to request information from an agent. A management system is any computer running SNMP management software. A management system can initiate the **get**, **get-next**, and **set** operations.

- The **get** operation is a request for a specific value, such as the amount of hard disk space available.

- The **get-next** operation is a request for the "next" value. This operation is used to traverse a conceptual table of objects.

- The **set** operation changes a value. This operation is rarely carried out because most values have read-only access and cannot be set.

SNMP Agent

The primary function of an agent is to perform the **get**, **get-next**, and **set** operations requested by a management system as shown in the following illustration. An agent is any computer running SNMP agent software, typically a server or router. The Microsoft SNMP service is SNMP agent software.

The only operation initiated by an agent is a *trap*. The trap operation alerts management systems to an extraordinary event, such as a password violation.

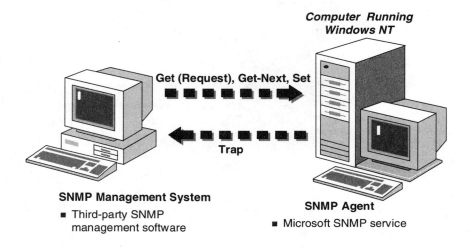

The Microsoft SNMP Service

The Microsoft SNMP service provides SNMP agent services to any TCP/IP host running SNMP management software. The SNMP service:

- Handles requests for status information from multiple hosts.
- Reports significant events (traps) to multiple hosts as they occur.
- Uses host names and IP addresses to identify the hosts to which it reports information and from which it receives requests.
- Can be installed and used on any computer running Windows NT and TCP/IP.
- Enables counters for monitoring TCP/IP performance using Performance Monitor.

The SNMP Architectural Model

The Microsoft SNMP service is written to the Windows Sockets API. This allows calls from management systems written to Windows Sockets. The SNMP service sends and receives messages using the user datagram protocol (UDP Port 161), and uses IP to support routing of SNMP messages.

SNMP provides extension agent dynamic-link libraries (DLLs) for supporting other Management Information Bases (MIBs). Third parties can develop their own MIBs for use with the Microsoft SNMP service. Microsoft SNMP includes a Microsoft Win32® SNMP manager API to simplify the development of SNMP applications.

Summary

SNMP allows computers running Windows NT to be monitored and to alert management systems of events. The Microsoft SNMP service provides agent services, extension agent DLLs, and a Win32 SNMP manager API to simplify the development of SNMP applications.

Lesson 2: The MIB

The information that a management system can request from an agent is contained in a management information base. This lesson defines the management information base and the Management Information Bases (MIBs) supported by the SNMP service.

After this lesson, you will be able to:
- Describe the management information bases supported by SNMP.

Estimated lesson time: 10 minutes

An MIB is a set of manageable objects representing various types of information about a network device, such as the number of active sessions or the version of network operating system software that is running on a host. SNMP management systems and agents share a common understanding of MIB objects.

The SNMP service supports Internet MIB II, LAN Manager MIB II, DHCP MIB, and WINS MIB.

Internet MIB II

Internet MIB II is a superset of the previous standard, Internet MIB I. Internet MIB II defines 171 objects essential for either fault or configuration analysis.

Note Internet MIB II is defined in RFC 1212. For a copy of this RFC, see the *Course Materials* Web page on the course compact disc.

LAN Manager MIB II

LAN Manager MIB II defines approximately 90 objects that include such items as statistical, share, session, user, and logon information. Most LAN Manager MIB II objects have read-only access because of the nonsecure nature of SNMP.

DHCP MIB

Windows NT 4.0 includes a DHCP MIB that defines objects to monitor DHCP server activity. This MIB (Dhcpmib.dll) is automatically installed when the DHCP Server service is installed. It contains approximately 14 objects for monitoring DHCP, such as the number of DHCP discover requests received, the number of declines, and the number of addresses leased out to clients.

WINS MIB

Windows NT 4.0 includes a WINS MIB that defines objects to monitor WINS server activity. This MIB (Winsmib.dll) is automatically installed when the WINS Server service is installed. It contains approximately 70 objects for monitoring WINS, such as the number of resolution requests successfully processed, the number of resolution requests that failed, and the date and time of the last database replication.

The Hierarchical Name Tree

The name space for MIB objects is hierarchical. The following illustration shows how it is structured so that each manageable object can be assigned a globally unique name. Authority for parts of the name space is assigned to individual organizations. This allows organizations to assign names without consulting an Internet authority for each assignment. For example, the name space assigned to LAN Manager is 1.3.6.1.4.1.77. Since the assignment of 1.3.6.1.4.1.77 to LAN Manager, Microsoft as a corporation has been assigned 1.3.6.1.4.1.311, and all new MIBs will be created under that branch. Microsoft has the authority to assign names to objects anywhere below that name space.

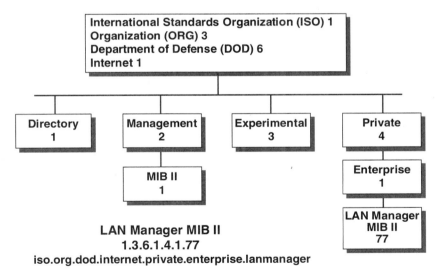

The object identifier in the hierarchy is written as a sequence of labels beginning at the root and ending at the object. Labels are separated with periods. For example, the object identifier for MIB II is:

Object name	Object number
iso.org.dod.internet.management.mibii	1.3.6.1.2.1

The object identifier for LAN Manager MIB II is:

Object name	Object number
iso.org.dod.internet.private.enterprise.lanmanager	1.3.6.1.4.1.77

Note The name space used to map object identifiers is distinct and separate from the hierarchical name space associated with UNIX domain names.

Summary

An MIB is a set of manageable objects that represent information such as the number of sessions on a host.

Lesson 3: Installing and Configuring the SNMP Service

If you want to monitor TCP/IP with Performance Monitor, you need to install the SNMP service. If you want to use a third-party application to monitor a computer running Windows NT, you also need to configure the SNMP service.

After this lesson, you will be able to:

- Define an SNMP community.
- Install and configure the Microsoft SNMP service.
- Use SNMPUTIL to test communications for the Microsoft SNMP service.

Estimated lesson time: 50 minutes

Defining SNMP Communities

Before you install SNMP, you need to define an SNMP community. A *community* is a group to which hosts running the SNMP service belong. Communities are identified by a *community name*. The use of a community name provides primitive security and context checking for agents that receive requests and initiate traps, and for management systems that initiate requests and receive traps. An agent will not accept a request from a management system outside its configured community.

An SNMP agent can be a member of multiple communities at the same time, allowing for communication with SNMP managers from various communities. For example, in the following illustration there are two defined communities—Public and Public2.

Only the agents and managers that are members of the same community can communicate with each other.

- Agent1 can receive and send messages to Manager2 because they are both members of the Public2 community.
- Agent2 through Agent4 can receive and send messages to Manager1 because they are all members of the default community Public.

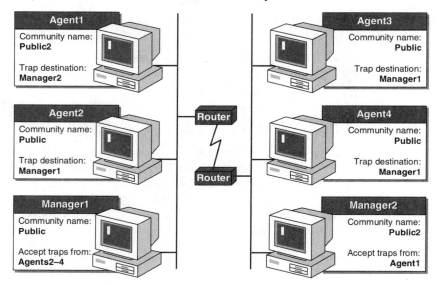

How SNMP Gathers Information

The following steps and illustration outline how the SNMP service responds to management system requests:

1. An SNMP management system sends a request to an agent using the agent's host name (or IP address).

   The request is passed by the application to socket (UDP port) 161.

   The host name is resolved to an IP address using any of the available resolution methods, including HOSTS file, DNS, WINS, broadcast, or LMHOSTS file.

2. An SNMP packet is formed containing the following information:

a. A **get**, **get-next**, or **set** operation for one or more objects.

b. A community name and other validating information.

The packet is routed to socket (UDP port) 161 on the agent.

3. The SNMP agent receives the packet in its buffer.

The community name is verified. If the community name is invalid or the packet is ill-formed, it is discarded.

If the community name is valid, the agent verifies the source host name or IP address. (The agent must be authorized to accept packets from the management system, or the packet will be discarded.)

The request is passed to the appropriate DLL:

If the request is for	This happens
An Internet MIB II object	The TCP DLL retrieves the information.
A LAN Manager MIB II object	The LAN Manager DLL retrieves the information.
A DHCP object	The DHCP MIB DLL retrieves the information.
A WINS object	The WINS MIB DLL retrieves the information.
An extension agent MIB	The DLL for that MIB retrieves the information.

The object identifier is mapped to the appropriate API function, and the API call is made.

The DLL returns the information to the agent.

4. The SNMP packet is sent back to the SNMP manager with the requested information.

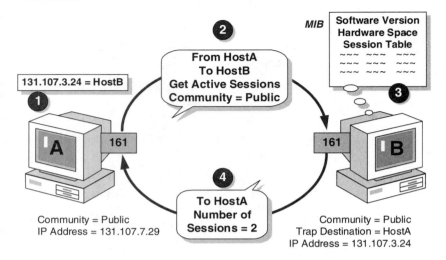

Installing SNMP

When you install the SNMP service, you must determine the Send Trap and Trap Destination parameters.

The Send Trap with Community Names parameter defines the community name to which traps are sent. A management system must belong to the designated community to receive traps. The default community name for all hosts is *Public*.

The Trap Destination parameter consists of names or IP addresses of hosts to which you want the SNMP service to send traps. If you use a host name, make sure it can be resolved so that the SNMP service can map it to the IP address.

Practice

In this procedure, you install and configure the SNMP service.

▶ **To install the SNMP service**

1. In Control Panel, double-click the Network icon.
2. Click the **Services** tab, and then click **Add**.

    The **Select Network Service** dialog box appears.
3. Click **SNMP Service**, and then click **OK**.
4. When prompted, type the path to the Windows NT distribution files.

5. After the appropriate files are copied to the computer, the **Microsoft SNMP Properties** dialog box appears.

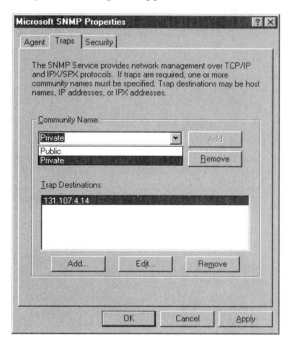

6. Select a Community Name of Public.

7. Click **OK**.

   The **Network** dialog box appears.

8. Click **Close**.

   A **Network Settings Change** message box appears, indicating that you must restart the computer.

9. Click **Yes**.

10. Log on as Administrator.

Configuring SNMP Service Security

The SNMP service provides primitive security and context checking for agents that receive requests and initiate traps, and for management systems that initiate requests and receive traps. An agent will not accept a request from a management system outside the community. Windows NT will send an authentication trap by default.

▶ To configure SNMP security

1. In Control Panel, double-click the Network icon.
2. Click the **Services** tab, click the **SNMP Service**, and then click **Properties**.

   The **Microsoft SNMP Properties** dialog box appears.
3. Click the **Security** tab.
4. Configure the parameters shown in the following table.

Parameter	Description
Send Authentication Trap	When the SNMP service receives a request for information that does not contain the correct community name or does not match an accepted host name for the service, the SNMP service can send a trap to the trap destination(s), indicating that the request failed authentication. Select this check box to specify whether this authentication trap is sent.
Accepted Community Names	A host must belong to a community that appears on this list for the SNMP service to accept requests from that host. Typically, all hosts belong to Public, which is the standard name for the common community of all hosts.
Accept SNMP Packets from Any Host	If this option is selected, no SNMP packets are rejected on the basis of the source host ID and the list of hosts in the box below it.
Only Accept SNMP Packets from These Hosts	If this option is selected, SNMP packets are accepted only from the hosts listed.

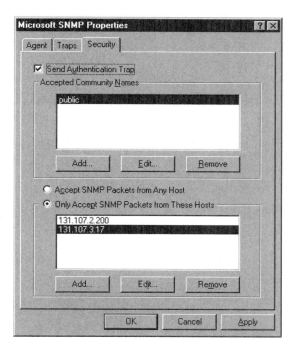

Configuring SNMP Agent Services

SNMP agent services give a computer running Windows NT the ability to provide a management system with information on activity that occurs at different layers of the Internet protocol suite.

▶ **To configure SNMP agent services**

1. In the **Microsoft SNMP Properties** dialog box, click the **Agent** tab.
2. In the **Contact** box, type a contact name.

   This is typically the person who uses the computer.

3. In the **Location** box, type a description for the location of the computer.

4. Under **Service**, select the services to be provided by the agent.

   Each service provides information on activity at the different layers. The default services are Applications, End-to-End, and Internet.

Service	Select this option if
Physical	This computer running Windows NT manages any physical devices, such as repeaters.
Datalink/Subnetwork	This computer running Windows NT manages a bridge.
Internet	This computer running Windows NT acts as an IP gateway (router).
End-to-End	This computer running Windows NT acts as an IP host. This option should always be selected.
Applications	This computer running Windows NT uses any applications that use TCP/IP. This option should always be selected.

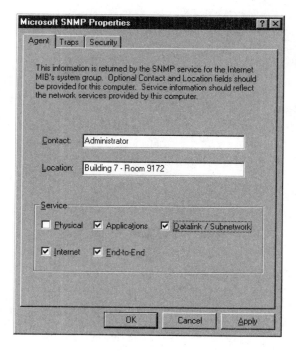

5. Click **OK**.

6. Click **Close**.

Identifying SNMP Service Errors

If the SNMP service fails for any reason, the failure will be documented in the Event Viewer system log as shown in the following illustration. Event Viewer is the first place you should look to identify a problem with the SNMP service.

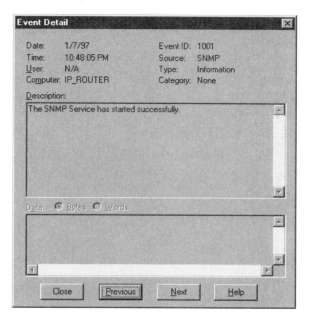

▶ **To see SNMP error messages using Event Viewer**

1. Click the **Start** button, point to **Programs**, point to **Administrative Tools**, and then click **Event Viewer**.

2. Select a message icon to read about an error.

Practice

In these procedures, you use Performance Monitor to view objects added as a result of installing the SNMP service. You then use Performance Monitor to view ICMP and IP counter activity generated by the **ping** command.

Note In order to complete these procedures, you must first install SNMP according to the procedures outlined in this chapter.

▶ **To view the new Performance Monitor objects**

1. Click the **Start** button, point to **Programs**, point to **Administrative Tools**, and then click **Performance Monitor**.

   The Performance Monitor window appears.

2. On the **Edit** menu, click **Add to Chart**.

   The **Add to Chart** dialog box appears.

3. In the **Object** box, click the arrow to display a list of objects.

4. List the TCP/IP-related objects.

   _____

   _____

   _____

▶ **To monitor IP datagrams with Performance Monitor**

1. In the **Object** box, click **ICMP** on the list.

   A list of ICMP counters appears.

2. In the **Counter** box, click **Messages/sec**.

3. In the **Scale** box, set the number to **1.0** and then click **Add**.

4. In the **Object** box, click **IP**.

5. In the **Counter** box, click **Datagrams Sent/sec** from the list.

6. In the **Scale** box, set the number to **1.0** and then click **Add**.

7. Click **Done**.

   Your selections appear in the display area.

8. On the **Options** menu, click **Chart**.

9. Change the **Vertical Maximum** to **10**, and then click **OK**.

10. Move the Performance Monitor window to the top of the screen.

11. At a command prompt, ping your second computer.

12. Return to Performance Monitor, and view the activity that resulted from the ping.

    What activity was recorded as a result of using ping?

    _____

    How many messages per second were recorded for ICMP?

    _____

    How many IP datagrams were sent per second?

    _____

    Why were there twice as many ICMP messages as there were IP datagrams sent?

    _____

13. Close Performance Monitor.

The SNMPUTIL Utility

The *Microsoft Windows NT Resource Kit* includes the SNMPUTIL (Snmputil.exe) utility, which verifies whether the SNMP service has been correctly configured to communicate with SNMP management stations. SNMPUTIL makes the same SNMP calls as an SNMP management station.

The syntax of SNMPUTIL is as follows:

snmputil *command agent community object_identifier_(OID)*

The valid commands are:

get   Get the value of the requested object identifier.

getnext   Get the value of the next object following the specified object identifier.

walk   Step through (walk) the MIB branch specified by the object identifier.

For example, to determine the number of DHCP server addresses leased by a DHCP server named DHCPserver in the Public community, you would issue the following command:

snmputil getnext *DHCPserver* Public .1.3.6.1.4.1.311.1.3.2.1.1.1

This command will respond with the object identifier (OID) and counter value for the object ID in question—in this case, the number of IP leases that are issued.

Practice

In this procedure, you view descriptions of MIB objects, and then access SNMP objects to view the data gathered with an SNMP agent and management program. In the first part of the procedure, you use the Snmputil.exe utility to verify that your SNMP agent is configured to communicate with an SNMP manager.

▶ **To view SNMP data**

1. Copy **C:\LabFiles\Chapt15\Snmputil.exe** to **C:\Winnt**.
2. Open a command prompt.
3. Use Snmputil.exe to determine SNMP objects related to DHCP. Type the following command on one line and then press ENTER:

   snmputil getnext 131.107.2.host_id
   public .1.3.6.1.4.1.311.1.3.2.1.1.1

   How many IP addresses have been leased?

4. Use Snmputil.exe on the WINS object .1.3.6.1.4.1.311.1.2.1.17. Type:

   snmputil getnext 131.107.2.*host_id*
   public .1.3.6.1.4.1.311.1.2.1.17

   How many successful queries have been processed by the WINS server?

5. Use Snmputil.exe on the WINS object **.1.3.6.1.4.1.311.1.2.1.18**. Type:

   snmputil getnext 131.107.2.*host_id*
   public .1.3.6.1.4.1.311.1.2.1.18

   How many unsuccessful queries have been processed by the WINS server?

6. Use Snmputil.exe on the LAN Manager object **.1.3.6.1.4.1.77.1.1.1**. Type:

   snmputil getnext 131.107.2.*host_id* **public .1.3.6.1.4.1.77.1.1.1**

7. Use Snmputil.exe on the LAN Manager Object .1.3.6.1.4.1.77.1.1.2. Type:

   snmputil getnext 131.107.2.*host_id* **public .1.3.6.1.4.1.77.1.1.2**

   What is the version of Windows NT Server running on the computer?

Summary

Before you install SNMP, you must define a community, a group to which SNMP hosts belong. The SNMP service provides basic security and context checking for agents. You can use Event Viewer to monitor SNMP service failures.

Review

The following questions are intended to reinforce key information presented in this chapter. If you are unable to answer a question, review the appropriate lesson and then try the question again.

1. What are the four SNMP operations?

2. Which SNMP operations are initiated by a management system? Which SNMP operations are initiated by an agent?

3. Which MIBs are supported by Windows NT 4.0?

4. Which host name resolution methods does the SNMP employ?

5. What is the purpose of a community name?

CHAPTER 16

Troubleshooting Microsoft TCP/IP

Lesson 1   Windows NT Diagnostic Tools and Guidelines . . . 348

Review . . . 353

About This Chapter

In this chapter, you review guidelines for troubleshooting an IP network. The lesson outlines Microsoft Windows NT and TCP/IP utilities useful in troubleshooting problems. The lesson also covers common TCP/IP-related problems, symptoms, and possible causes.

Before You Begin

There are no prerequisites for completing this chapter.

Lesson 1: Windows NT Diagnostic Tools and Guidelines

There is an orderly process to troubleshooting TCP/IP problems. This lesson explains the process and suggests Windows NT utilities for troubleshooting TCP/IP problems.

After this lesson, you will be able to:
- Identify common TCP/IP-related problems and utilities for troubleshooting.
- Explain the guidelines for troubleshooting TCP/IP.

Estimated lesson time: 20 minutes

Troubleshooting a problem is easiest when you can identify the problem source. TCP/IP-related problems can be grouped into the categories listed in the following table.

Problem source	Common characteristics
Configuration	The host will not initialize or one of the services will not start.
IP addressing	You may not be able to communicate with other hosts. The host could stop responding.
Subnetting	You can ping your workstation, but may not be able to access local or remote hosts.
Address resolution	You can ping your workstation, but not other hosts.
NetBIOS name resolution	You can access a host by its IP address, but not establish a connection with a **net** command.
Host name resolution	You access a host by its IP address, but not by its host name.

Windows NT Utilities

Windows NT includes several utilities that can be helpful for troubleshooting a TCP/IP problem.

Use this tool	To
PING	Verify that TCP/IP is configured correctly and that another host is available.
ARP	View the ARP cache to detect invalid entries.
NETSTAT	Display protocol statistics and the current state of TCP/IP connections.

(continued)

Use this tool	To
NBTSTAT	Check the state of current NetBIOS over TCP/IP connections, update the LMHOSTS cache, or determine your registered name and scope ID.
IPCONFIG	Verify TCP/IP configuration, including DHCP and WINS server addresses.
TRACERT	Verify the route to a remote host.
ROUTE	Display or modify the local routing table.
NSLOOKUP	Display information from DNS name servers.
Microsoft SNMP service	Supply statistical information to SNMP management systems.
Event log	Track errors and events.
Performance Monitor	Analyze performance and detect bottlenecks.
Network Monitor	Capture incoming and outgoing packets to analyze a problem.
Registry Editor	Browse and edit the configuration parameters.

Troubleshooting Guidelines

When troubleshooting TCP/IP, it is recommended that you troubleshoot from the bottom layer of the Internet protocol suite to the top layer as shown in the following illustration. The objective is to verify that protocols at each layer can communicate with protocols at the layers above and below them.

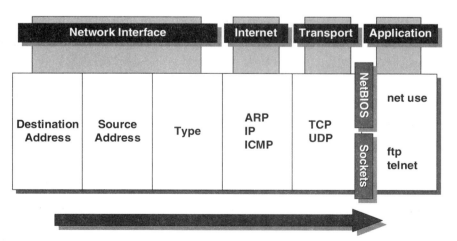

There are two steps in troubleshooting. Make sure you can:

1. Ping successfully.

   If you can ping successfully, you have verified IP communications between the Network Interface layer and the Internet layer. PING uses ARP to resolve the IP address to a hardware address for each echo request and echo reply.

2. Establish a session with a host.

   If you can establish a session, you have verified TCP/IP session communications from the network interface layer through the application layer.

Note   If you are unable to resolve a problem, you may need to use an IP analyzer (such as Microsoft Network Monitor) to view network activity at each layer.

Verifying IP Communications

The first goal in troubleshooting is to make sure you can successfully ping an IP address. This verifies communications between the Network Interface layer and the Internet layer. Ping a host using its host name only after you can successfully ping the host using its IP address. The following procedure and illustration show how to troubleshoot connections using Ping.

▶ **To troubleshoot the Network Interface and Internet layers using PING**

1. Ping the loopback address to verify that TCP/IP was installed and loaded correctly. If this step is unsuccessful, verify that the system was restarted after TCP/IP was installed and configured.

2. Ping your IP address to verify that it was configured correctly. If this step is unsuccessful:

   - View the configuration through the Network program in Control Panel to verify that the address was entered correctly.

   - Verify that the IP address is valid and that it follows addressing guidelines.

3. Ping the IP address of the default gateway to verify that the gateway is functioning and configured correctly and that communication is available on the local network. If this step is unsuccessful, verify that you are using the correct IP address and subnet mask.

4. Ping the IP address of a remote host to verify the connection to the WAN. If this step is unsuccessful:

   - Verify that the IP address of the default gateway is correct.
   - Make sure the remote host is functional.
   - Verify that the link between routers is operational.

5. After you can successfully ping the IP address, ping the host name to verify that the name is configured correctly in the HOSTS file.

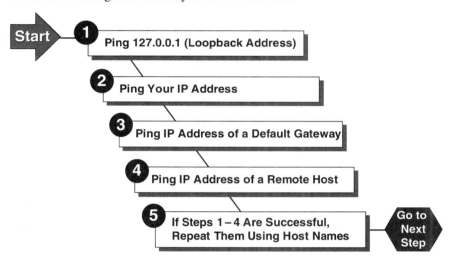

Verifying TCP/IP Session Communications

The next goal during troubleshooting is to verify communications from the Internet layer through the Application layer by successfully establishing a session. Use one of the following methods to verify communications between the Network Interface layer and the Application layer as shown in the following illustration.

To establish a NetBIOS over TCP/IP session with a computer running Windows NT or other RFC-compliant NetBIOS-based host, make a connection with the **net use** or **net view** command. If this step is unsuccessful:

- Verify that the target host is NetBIOS based.
- Confirm that the scope ID on the target host matches that of the source host.
- Verify that you used the correct NetBIOS name.
- If the target host is on a remote network, verify that a name-to-address mapping is available in either WINS or the LMHOSTS file for the correct entry.

To establish a Windows Sockets session with an IP host, use the Telnet or FTP utility to make a connection. If this step is unsuccessful:

- Verify that the target host is configured with the Telnet daemon or FTP daemon.
- Confirm that you have the correct permissions on the target host.
- Check the HOSTS file or a DNS server for a valid entry if you are connecting using a host name.

With an RFC-Compliant NetBIOS-based Host

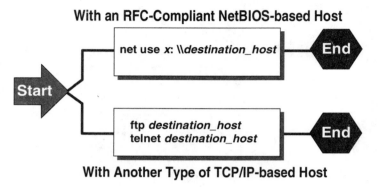

With Another Type of TCP/IP-based Host

Summary

If you can PING successfully, you have verified communications from the Network Interface layer up through the Internet layer. If you can establish a session, you have verified communications from the Internet layer up through the Application layer.

Review

The following questions are intended to reinforce key information presented in this chapter. If you are unable to answer a question, review the appropriate lesson and then try the question again.

1. What are three Windows NT utilities useful in diagnosing TCP/IP-related problems?

   _____

   _____

   _____

2. Which TCP/IP utility is used to verify communications from the Network Interface layer up to the Internet layer?

   _____

3. What are the two procedures for troubleshooting an IP network?

   _____

   _____

Questions and Answers

Chapter 1: Introduction to TCP/IP

Review Answers

Page 8

1. What is TCP/IP?

   TCP/IP is a suite of protocols that provide routing in WANs, and connectivity to a variety of hosts on the Internet.

2. Are all TCP/IP standards published as RFCs? Do all RFCs specify standards?

   Yes, TCP/IP standards are always published as RFCs. However, not all RFCs specify standards.

Chapter 2: Installing and Configuring TCP/IP

Review Answers

Page 22

1. What TCP/IP utilities are used to verify and test a TCP/IP configuration?

   IPCONFIG and PING.

2. What parameters are required on a Windows NT-based computer running TCP/IP on a WAN?

   IP address, subnet mask, and default gateway.

Chapter 3: Architectural Overview of the TCP/IP Protocol Suite

Practice Answers

▶ **To view the ARP request frame details**

Page 36
    5. In the **Detail** window, expand **ETHERNET**.

        The **ETHERNET** frame properties are displayed.

        What is the destination address?

        FFFFFFFFFFFF

        Does the destination address refer to a physical address?

        No, it represents a broadcast address.

        What is the source address?

        The Media Access Control address of the network card in your computer.

        What type of Ethernet frame is this?

        0x0806 – ARP: Address Resolution Protocol

    7. In the **Detail** window, expand **ARP_RARP**.

        What is the sender's hardware address?

        Address will vary.

        What is the target's hardware address?

        000000000000 is the address because this is the request packet and the Media Access Control address is unknown at this time.

        What is the target's protocol address?

        131.107.2.211

▶ **To examine an ARP reply frame details**

Page 37
    2. In the **Detail** window, expand **ETHERNET: ETYPE**.

        The **ETHERNET: ETYPE** frame properties are displayed.

        What is the destination address?

        Address will vary.

        Does the destination address refer to a physical address?

        Yes.

What is the source address?

The Media Access Control address of the network card in your computer.

What type of Ethernet frame is this?

0x0806 – ARP: Address Resolution Protocol

4. In the **Detail** window, expand **ARP_RARP**.

What is the sender's hardware address?

Address will vary.

▶ **To view the ARP cache**

Page 38

2. Document the entry for your default gateway (if configured)—for example: 131.107.2.1 08-00-02-6c-28-93

The entries may vary.

▶ **To ping a local host**

Page 38

2. View the new entry in the ARP cache.

What entry was added?

The host that was pinged (your second computer).

What is the entry's type?

Dynamic.

▶ **To add an ARP entry**

Page 39

2. View the ARP cache to verify that the entry has been added.

What is the entry's type?

Static.

Why was this entry's type different from preceding entries?

Because the entry was added manually, rather than as a result of a broadcast. Entries that are added manually are static until the computer is restarted.

Review Answers

Page 53

1. What are the layers in the four-layer model used by TCP/IP?

Application, Transport, Internet, and Network Interface.

2. What core protocols are provided in the Microsoft TCP/IP transport driver?

TCP, UDP, ICMP, IGMP, IP, and ARP.

3. Which protocol is used to inform a client that a destination network is unreachable?

ICMP.

4. When an IP datagram is forwarded by a router, how is the datagram changed?

Smaller TTL, updated checksum value, and possibly fragmented.

5. When is the User Datagram Protocol used?

When an application needs to send connectionless traffic—typically sending a messaging to multiple receiving stations.

6. When an ARP request is sent out, to what address is it sent?

The broadcast address (FFFFFFFF).

7. What address is requested in the ARP request packet for a local host? For a remote host?

For a local host it is the Media Access Control address of that host. For a remote host it is the Media Access Control address of the gateway to which the IP datagram is being sent (typically your default gateway).

Chapter 4: IP Addressing

Practice Answers

Page 59

1. Convert the following binary numbers to decimal format.

Binary value	Decimal value
10001011	**139**
10101010	**170**
10111111 11100000 00000111 10000001	**191.224.7.129**
01111111 00000000 00000000 00000001	**127.0.0.1**

2. Convert the following decimal values to binary format.

Decimal value	Binary value
250	**11111010**
19	**00010011**
109.128.255.254	**01101101 10000000 11111111 11111110**
131.107.2.89	**10000011 01101011 00000010 01011001**

Practice Answers

Page 63

1. Write the address class next to each IP address.

Address	Class
131.107.2.89	B
3.3.57.0	A
200.200.5.2	C
191.107.2.10	B

2. Which address class(es) allow you to have more than 1,000 hosts per network?

Class A (16,777,214) and class B (65,534).

3. Which address class(es) allow only 254 hosts per network?

Class C.

Practice Answers

Page 67

Identify the IP addresses that would be invalid if it were assigned to a host, and then explain why it is invalid.

a. 131.107.256.80

This is invalid because the highest possible value in an octet is 255.

b. 222.222.255.222

This is a valid address.

c. 231.200.1.1

This is invalid because 231 is a class D address, and is not supported as a host address.

d. 126.1.0.0

This is a valid address.

e. 0.127.4.100

Zero is an invalid address. It indicated "this network only."

f. 190.7.2.0

This is a valid address.

g. 127.1.1.1

This is invalid because 127 addresses are reserved for diagnostics.

    h. 198.121.254.255

    This is invalid because 255 as a host ID indicates a broadcast.

    i. 255.255.255.255

    This is invalid because 255 is a broadcast address.

Practice Answers

Page 67

In this practice, you decide which network components require IP addresses in a TCP/IP network environment. When a protocol is listed, assume it is the only protocol installed on the host. Review the following network components and circle the letter that corresponds to the components that do not require an IP address.

    a. Microsoft Windows NT computer running TCP/IP

    b. LAN Manager workstation that connects to a Windows NT computer running TCP/IP

    c. Computer running Windows 95 that requires access to shared resources on a Windows NT-based computer running TCP/IP

    d. UNIX host that you want to connect to using TCP/IP utilities

    e. Network interface printer running TCP/IP

    f. Router for connecting to a remote IP network

    g. Ethernet port on local router

    h. Microsoft LAN Manager workstation that is attempting to connect to a LAN Manager server running NetBEUI

    i. Computer running Windows for Workgroups that requires access to shared resources on a LAN Manager server running NetBEUI

    j. Serial plotter on a Windows NT-based computer running TCP/IP

    k. Network printer shared off a LAN Manager server running NetBEUI

    l. Communications server providing terminal access to TCP/IP host computers

    m. Your default gateway

    All network components require an IP address except for h, i, j, and k.

Practice Answers

Page 68

In this practice, you decide which class of address will support the following IP network. Next, you assign a valid IP address to each type of host to easily distinguish it from other hosts (for example, UNIX, Windows NT servers, or Windows NT workstations). In this scenario all computers are on the same subnet.

Which address classes will support this network?

Class A or class B.

Which of the following network addresses support this network?

a. 197.200.3.0

b. 11.0.0.0

c. 221.100.2.0

d. 131.107.0.0

B and D will support this network.

Practice Answers

Page 69

Using the network ID that you chose, assign a range of host IDs to each type of host, so that you can easily distinguish the Windows NT Server computers from the Windows NT Workstation computers and the UNIX workstations.

Type of TCP/IP host	IP address range
Windows NT Server computers	**Assign high numbers to all servers, for instance 200–250.**
Windows NT Workstation computers	**Assign low numbers to all UNIX workstations, for instance 150–200.**
UNIX workstations	**Assign numbers to the Windows NT Workstation computers using a different octet than that used by the servers and UNIX workstations.**

Practice Answers

Page 69

In this next practice, you decide how many network IDs and host IDs are required to support this network.

How many network IDs does this network environment require?

2 local networks (E and F) + 3 wide area networks (A, B, and C) = 5 total

How many host IDs does this network environment require?

50 (Windows NT Server computers) + 200 (Windows NT Workstation computers) + 50 (UNIX workstations) + 6 (router interfaces) = 306

Which default gateway (router interface) would you assign to the Windows NT Workstation computers that communicate primarily with the UNIX workstations?

The router interface E.

Practice Answers

Page 73

In this practice, AND the following IP addresses to determine whether the destination IP address belongs to a host on a local network or a remote network.

1. Do the results match?

   No.

2. Is the destination IP address located on a local or remote network?

   Remote.

Review Answers

Page 77

1. In class A, class B, and class C addresses, which octets represent the network ID and which represent the host ID?

   Class A—The network ID uses the first octet. The host ID uses the last three octets.

   Class B—The network ID uses the first two octets. The host ID uses the last two octets.

   Class C—The network ID uses the first three octets. The host ID uses the last octet.

2. Which numbers are invalid as a network ID and why? Which numbers are invalid as a host ID and why?

   As a network ID, 127 is reserved for loopback functions.

   As a network ID and a host ID, all 1's (255) and all 0's are invalid. All 1's are used for broadcasts. All 0's indicate the local network or "this network only."

3. When is a unique network ID required?

A unique network ID is required for each physical network and for the connection between two routers on a WAN.

4. In a TCP/IP internetwork, what components require a host ID besides computers?

Each TCP/IP-based host requires a host ID that is unique to the network ID, including routers.

Review Practice

Page 78

For the following diagram, list all IP addressing problems, and explain how each problem may affect communications. Are the IP addresses and default gateway addresses appropriate for each situation?

Host B has an incorrect default gateway address, so communications will be limited to the local network.

Host D has no default gateway assigned, so communications will be limited to the local network.

Hosts F and I have a common IP address. This could cause problems if a host attempts to access the IP address of 147.103.0.1.

Page 79

For the following diagram, list all IP addressing problems, and explain how each problem may affect communications. Are the IP addresses and default gateway addresses appropriate for each situation?

Hosts C and E have duplicate IP addresses (109.128.5.35). Windows NT will detect the duplicate addresses and fail in initializing TCP/IP. If duplicate IP addresses exist on other types of TCP/IP-based hosts (for example, LAN Manager), hosts C and E cannot communicate with each other, hosts could stop responding, and other hosts may not be able to access hosts C and E.

Host B has a different network ID from the other hosts. Host B will not be able to communicate with any other local host. It will not be able to communicate with remote hosts because the network ID for the default gateway is different from its own.

Host F has the same IP address as its default gateway. It may not be able to communicate with local or remote hosts.

Chapter 5: Subnetting

Practice Answers

Page 88

In this practice, you define a subnet mask for several situations. Remember that not every situation requires subnetting.

1. Class A network address on a local network.

   255.0.0.0

2. Class B network address on a local network with 4,000 hosts.

   255.255.0.0

3. Class C network address on a local network with 254 hosts.

   255.255.255.0

4. Class A address with 6 subnets.

   255.224.0.0

5. Class B address with 126 subnets.

   255.255.254.0

6. Class A network address. Currently, there are 30 subnets that will grow to approximately 65 subnets within the next year. Each subnet will never have more than 50,000 hosts.

   Using 7 bits = 255.254.0.0

   Using 8 bits = 255.255.0.0

7. Using the subnet mask from the preceding scenario, how much growth will this subnet mask provide?

   Using 7 bits will provide up to 126 subnets and 131,070 hosts per subnet.

   Using 8 bits will provide up to 254 subnets and 65,534 hosts per subnet.

8. Class B network address. Currently, there are 14 subnets that may double in size within the next two years. Each subnet will have fewer than 1,500 hosts.

   Using 5 bits = 255.255.248.0

9. Using the subnet mask from the preceding scenario, how much growth will this subnet mask provide?

   Using 5 bits will provide up to 30 subnets and 2,046 hosts per subnet.

Practice Answers

Page 89

In this practice, you review two invalid subnet masks to see what would happen when you try to communicate with a host on a local and remote network.

Using the information below, convert your computer's IP address and the IP address of your default gateway to binary format, and then AND them to the subnet mask to determine why the subnet mask is invalid.

Your IP address	131.107.2.200	1 0 0 0 0 0 1 1 0 1 1 0 1 0 1 1 0 0 0 0 0 0 1 0 1 1 0 0 1 0 0 0
Subnet mask	255.255.255.248	1 1 1 1 1 1 1 1 1 1 1 1 1 1 1 1 1 1 1 1 1 1 1 1 1 1 1 1 1 0 0 0
Result		
Destination IP address	131.107.2.211	1 0 0 0 0 0 1 1 0 1 1 0 1 0 1 1 0 0 0 0 0 0 1 0 1 1 0 1 0 0 1 1
Subnet mask	255.255.255.248	1 1 1 1 1 1 1 1 1 1 1 1 1 1 1 1 1 1 1 1 1 1 1 1 1 1 1 1 1 0 0 0
Result		

Did the result of ANDing indicate that the destination IP address and subnet mask were for a local or remote network?

> **Remote.**

Why would you not be able to successfully ping your default gateway?

> **IP would determine it was on a remote network, and there would be no gateway available.**

Using the information below, convert your IP address and the IP address of the remote host to binary format, and then AND them to the subnet mask to determine why the subnet mask would be invalid.

Your IP address	131.107.2.200	1 0 0 0 0 0 1 1 0 1 1 0 1 0 1 1 0 0 0 0 0 0 1 0 1 1 0 0 1 0 0 0
Subnet mask	255.255.0.0	1 1 1 1 1 1 1 1 1 1 1 1 1 1 1 1 0 0 0 0 0 0 0 0 0 0 0 0 0 0 0 0
Result		
Destination IP address	131.107.2.211	1 0 0 0 0 0 1 1 0 1 1 0 1 0 1 1 0 0 0 0 0 0 1 0 1 1 0 1 0 0 1 1
Subnet mask	255.255.0.0	1 1 1 1 1 1 1 1 1 1 1 1 1 1 1 1 0 0 0 0 0 0 0 0 0 0 0 0 0 0 0 0
Result		

Did the result of ANDing indicate that the destination IP address and subnet mask were for a local or remote network?

> **Local.**

Why would you not be able to successfully ping a remote host?

> **IP tried to route the packet to a host on the local network even though the host was really on a remote network.**

Compare the two results generated using incorrect subnet masks to see how differently TCP/IP responds when the subnet mask indicates a local network versus a remote network. What did you conclude about how TCP/IP uses a subnet mask?

The subnet mask is used to determine whether an IP address is located on a local or a remote network. If the destination IP address is on the local network, the datagram is sent directly to that host. If the destination IP address is on a remote network, the datagram is sent to the source host's default gateway.

Example 1

Page 91

Which hosts have an incorrect subnet mask?

D and E are invalid.

How will an invalid subnet mask affect these hosts?

They will not be able to communicate with any host if the second octet is different from their own.

What is the correct subnet mask?

255.0.0.0

Example 2

Page 92

What is the problem with this subnet mask?

The subnet mask indicates that both hosts are on the same network.

How will it affect communications?

Packets sent by either host to the other host will not be routed to the other network, so the two hosts will not be able to communicate with each other.

What is the correct subnet mask?

A correct subnet mask is 255.255.255.0. Other correct subnet masks include:

255.255.254.0
255.255.252.0
255.255.248.0
255.255.240.0
255.255.224.0

Practice Answers

Page 95

In this additional practice, you determine the appropriate subnet mask for a given range of IP addresses.

1. Address range of 128.71.1.1 through 128.71.254.254.

    255.255.0.0

    The only way to get a network ID of 254 is to use the entire octet, in this case the third octet.

2. Address range of 61.8.0.1 through 61.15.255.254.

    255.248.0.0

    A subnet mask of 248 indicates an incremental value of 8.

3. Address range of 172.88.32.1 through 172.88.63.254.

    255.255.224.0

    An incremental value of 32 indicates a subnet mask of 224.

4. Address range of 111.224.0.1 through 111.239.255.254.

    255.240.0.0

    A network range of 224–239 uses an incremental value of 16.

5. Address range of 3.64.0.1 through 3.127.255.254.

    255.192.0.0

    A network range of 64–127 uses an incremental value of 64 using only 2 bits.

Defining a Range of Network IDs for Two Subnets

Page 97

In this practice, you define a range of network IDs for an internetwork that consists of two subnets, using 2 bits from a class B subnet mask.

1. List all possible bit combinations for the following subnet mask, and then convert them to decimal format to determine the beginning value of each subnet.

255	255	192	0
1 1 1 1 1 1 1 1	1 1 1 1 1 1 1 1	1 1 0 0 0 0 0 0	0 0 0 0 0 0 0 0

Invalid	0 0 0 0 0 0 0 0	=	0
Subnet 1	**0 1 0 0 0 0 0 0**	=	**64**
Subnet 2	**1 0 0 0 0 0 0 0**	=	**128**
Invalid	1 1 0 0 0 0 0 0	=	192 (subnet mask)

2. List the range of host IDs for each subnet.

Subnet	Beginning value	Ending value
Subnet 1	*w.x*.64.1	*w.x*.127.254
Subnet 2	*w.x*.128.1	*w.x*.191.254

Defining a Range of Network IDs for 14 Subnets

Page 98

In this practice, you define a range of network IDs for an internet that consists of 14 subnets, using 4 bits from a class B subnet mask.

1. List all possible bit combinations for the following subnet mask, and then convert them to decimal format to determine the beginning value of each subnet.

255	255	240	0
1 1 1 1 1 1 1 1	1 1 1 1 1 1 1 1	1 1 1 1 0 0 0 0	0 0 0 0 0 0 0 0

Invalid	0 0 0 0 0 0 0 0	=	0
Subnet 1	0 0 0 1 0 0 0 0	=	16
Subnet 2	0 0 1 0 0 0 0 0	=	32
Subnet 3	0 0 1 1 0 0 0 0	=	48
Subnet 4	0 1 0 0 0 0 0 0	=	64
Subnet 5	0 1 0 1 0 0 0 0	=	80
Subnet 6	0 1 1 0 0 0 0 0	=	96
Subnet 7	0 1 1 1 0 0 0 0	=	112
Subnet 8	1 0 0 0 0 0 0 0	=	128
Subnet 9	1 0 0 1 0 0 0 0	=	144
Subnet 10	1 0 1 0 0 0 0 0	=	160
Subnet 11	1 0 1 1 0 0 0 0	=	176
Subnet 12	1 1 0 0 0 0 0 0	=	192
Subnet 13	1 1 0 1 0 0 0 0	=	208
Subnet 14	1 1 1 0 0 0 0 0	=	224
Invalid	1 1 1 1 0 0 0 0	=	240 (subnet mask)

2. List the range of host IDs for each subnet.

Subnet	Beginning value	Ending value
Subnet 1	*w.x.*16.1	*w.x.*31.254
Subnet 2	*w.x.*32.1	*w.x.*47.254
Subnet 3	*w.x.*48.1	*w.x.*63.254
Subnet 4	*w.x.*64.1	*w.x.*79.254
Subnet 5	*w.x.*80.1	*w.x.*95.254
Subnet 6	*w.x.*96.1	*w.x.*111.254
Subnet 7	*w.x.*112.1	*w.x.*127.254
Subnet 8	*w.x.*128.1	*w.x.*143.254
Subnet 9	*w.x.*144.1	*w.x.*159.254
Subnet 10	*w.x.*160.1	*w.x.*175.254
Subnet 11	*w.x.*176.1	*w.x.*191.254
Subnet 12	*w.x.*192.1	*w.x.*207.254
Subnet 13	*w.x.*208.1	*w.x.*223.254
Subnet 14	*w.x.*224.1	*w.x.*239.254

Defining a Range of Network IDs Using a Shortcut

Page 99

In this practice, you use a shortcut to define a range of network IDs for 14 subnets. Compare the results to the results in the preceding practice. The two should match. The first step has been done for you.

1. List the number of bits (in high order) that will be used for the subnet mask.

255	255	240	0
1 1 1 1 1 1 1 1	1 1 1 1 1 1 1 1	**1 1 1 1** 0 0 0 0	0 0 0 0 0 0 0 0

2. Convert the bit with the lowest value to decimal format.

16.

3. Convert the number of bits to decimal format (in low order), and then subtract 1 to determine the number of possible subnets.

0 0 0 0 1 1 1 1 = 15 (8+4+2+1)

15–1=14 (valid subnets)

4. Starting with 0, increment by the value calculated in step 2 the same number of times as the possible bit combinations calculated in step 3.

The results should match the combinations in the preceding practice.

Practice Answers

Page 101

In this additional practice, you define a range of host IDs for each of the following subnets.

1. Network ID of 75.0.0.0, subnet mask of 255.255.0.0, and 2 subnets.

   Network A: 75.x.0.1 – 75.x.255.254

   Network B: 75.y.0.1 – 75.y.255.254

   (Where x and y are any numbers from 1 through 254, as long as they are unique to each network.)

2. Network ID of 150.17.0.0, subnet mask of 255.255.255.0, and 4 subnets.

   Network A: 150.17.w.1 – 150.17.w.254

   Network B: 150 17.x.1 – 150.17.x.254

   Network C: 150.17.y.1 – 150.17.y.254

   Network D: 150.17.z.1 – 150.17.z.254

   (Where w, x, y, and z are any numbers 1 though 254, as long as they are unique to each of the four networks.)

3. Network IDs of 107.16.0.0 and 107.32.0.0, subnet mask of 255.240.0.0, and 2 subnets.

   Network A: 107.16.0.1 – 107.31.255.254

   Network B: 107.32.0.1 – 107.47.255.254

   A subnet mask of 240 allows for a maximum of 14 subnets; each network ID is incremented by a value of 16.

4. Network IDs of 190.1.16.0, 190.1.32.0, 190.1.48.0, and 190.1.64.0, subnet mask of 255.255.248.0, and 4 subnets.

   Network A: 190.1.16.1 – 190.1.23.254

   Network B: 190.1.32.1 – 190.1.39.254

   Network C: 190.1.48.1 – 190.1.55.254

   Network D: 190.1.64.1 – 190.1.71.254

   A subnet mask of 248 allows for a maximum of 30 subnets; each network ID is incremented by a value of 8.

5. Network IDs of 154.233.32.0, 154.233.96.0, and 154.233.160.0, subnet mask of 255.255.224.0, and 3 subnets.

Network A: 154.233.32.1 – 154.233.63.254

Network B: 154.233.96.1 – 154.233.127.254

Network C: 154.233.160.1 – 154.233.191.254

A subnet mask of 224 allows for a maximum of 6 subnets; each network ID is incremented by a value of 32.

Review Answers

Page 106

1. What is the purpose of a subnet mask?

   To mask a portion of the IP address so IP can distinguish the network ID from the host ID.

2. What requires a subnet mask?

   Each host on a TCP/IP network requires a subnet mask.

3. When is a default subnet mask used?

   A default subnet mask is used when a TCP/IP host is not part of a subnetwork.

4. When is it necessary to define a custom subnet mask?

   When you divide your network into subnets.

Practices Answers

Scenario 1

Page 107

You have been assigned one class B address of 131.107.0.0 by the InterNIC. Your intranet currently has 5 subnets. Each subnet has approximately 300 hosts. Within the next year the number of subnets will triple. The number of hosts on three of the subnets could increase to as many as 1,000.

1. How many bits did you use for the subnet mask?
2. How much growth did you allow for additional subnets?
3. How much growth did you allow for additional hosts?

   Using 5 bits for the subnet mask would allow for 30 subnets and 2,046 hosts per subnet.

   Using 6 bits for the subnet mask would allow for 62 subnets and 1,022 hosts per subnet.

Scenario 2

Page 107

You have been assigned one class A address of 124.0.0.0 by the InterNIC. Your private internet currently has 5 subnets. Each subnet has approximately 500,000 hosts. In the near future, you would like to divide the 5 subnets into 25 smaller, more manageable subnets. The number of hosts on the 25 new subnets could eventually increase to 300,000.

1. How many bits did you use for the subnet mask?
2. How much growth did you allow for additional subnets?
3. How much growth did you allow for additional hosts?

Using 5 bits for the subnet mask would allow for 30 subnets and 524,286 hosts per subnet.

Scenario 3

Page 108

You have 5 subnets with approximately 300 hosts on each subnet. Within the next 6 months, the number of subnets could increase to more than 100. The number of hosts on each subnet will probably never be more than 2,000. You do not have any plans to connect to the worldwide public Internet.

1. Which class of address did you use?
2. How many bits did you use for the subnet mask?
3. How much growth did you allow for additional subnets?
4. How much growth did you allow for additional hosts?

In this scenario, subnet addressing is not necessary. You could use a different class A or class B IP address for each network. A class C IP address could not be used because it would only allow 254 hosts per network.

Scenario 4

Page 108

An Internet service provider has just been assigned the block of 2,048 class C network numbers beginning with 192.24.0.0 and ending with 192.31.255.0.

1. What IP address would begin a "supernetted" route to this block of numbers?

192.24.0.0

2. What net mask would be used to supernet this block of numbers?

255.248.0.0

Customers of this Internet service provider have the following requirements:

- Customer 1 will not have more than 2,023 hosts.
- Customer 2 will not have more than 4,047 hosts.
- Customer 3 will not have more than 1,011 hosts.
- Customer 4 will not have more than 500 hosts.

Assign the missing IP and subnet mask values for each customer.

1. Customer 1

Beginning IP address	192.24.0.1
Ending IP address	192.24.7.8
Subnet mask	**255.255.248.0**

2. Customer 2

Beginning IP address	**192.24.16.1**
Ending IP address	192.24.31.254
Subnet mask	255.255.240.0

3. Customer 3

Beginning IP address	192.24.8.1
Ending IP address	**192.24.11.254**
Subnet mask	255.255.252.0

4. Customer 4

Beginning IP address	192.24.14.1
Ending IP address	192.24.15.254
Subnet mask	**255.255.254.0**

Chapter 6: Implementing IP Routing

Practice Answers

▶ **To view the routing table**

Page 118

What address, other than your IP address and the loopback address, is listed under **Gateway Address**? If you are working with a stand-alone machine, the gateway address will not appear.

The address for the default gateway with a network address of 0.0.0.0.

▶ **To view the routing table**

Page 119

Is the default gateway address listed under **Gateway Address**?

No.

▶ **To attempt network communication**

Page 119

- Ping the IP address of a your second computer or a computer on your local network.

Was the ping successful?

Yes.

Without a gateway address in the routing table, would you be able to ping the IP address of a remote host?

No. You would receive an error indicating the destination host is unreachable.

▶ **To add a route entry**

Page 120

3. If you were to ping a host on another network, would the ping be successful? Why or why not?

No, there is no route listed to the other network, and no default gateway configured.

Review Answers

Page 128

1. How is IP routing enabled?

By adding multiple network adapter cards or configuring multiple IP addresses to a computer, and selecting the Enable IP Forwarding check box.

2. Is a routing table required on a multihomed computer connecting a two-subnet internet? Why or why not?

No, because the computer already has an interface to both subnets.

3. When is it necessary to build a static routing table?

When a multihomed computer is not configured with RIP and does not have an interface to a subnet.

4. What information is required in a routing table?

Destination network address, subnet mask used with the address, and the address of the router used to reach the destination network. Names can be used in the route table if appropriate entries are in the networks and hosts files.

5. Why is RIP typically not used in a large internetwork?

Because it creates too much broadcast traffic. It can take a long time for RIP information to propagate among all routers.

Chapter 7: The Dynamic Host Configuration Protocol

Practice Answers

▶ **To determine the network adapter card address**

Page 144

1. At a command prompt, type **ipconfig /all** and then press ENTER.

There are at least two other ways to check the physical address of your network adapter card. What are they?

Go to a command prompt and type net config server

–Or–

Click the Start button, point to Programs, point to Administration Tools, and then click Windows NT Diagnostics. Click the Network tab, and then click Transports.

▶ **To create a DHCP scope**

Page 146

2. Double-click the **Services** icon. What are the names of the DHCP services?

Microsoft DHCP Server and DHCP Client.

▶ **To verify the DHCP-assigned TCP/IP information**

Page 153

2. What IP address was assigned to the DHCP client computer by the DHCP server?

The reserved client address.

3. What is the address of the default gateway?

131.107.2.1 (as assigned by DHCP).

▶ **To renew a DHCP lease**

Page 154

2. When does the lease expire?

   The answer will vary, but it should be approximately 24 hours from the current time.

5. When does the lease expire?

   The answer will vary, but it should be approximately 24 hours from the current time.

Review Answers

Page 162

1. What are the four steps in the DHCP lease process?

   A DHCP-enabled client broadcasts a request (DHCPDISCOVER) to lease an IP address.

   All DHCP servers respond with an offer (DHCPOFFER).

   The DHCP-enabled client selects an offer (DHCPREQUEST) from the first DHCP server.

   The DHCP server responds with an acknowledgment (DHCPACK) and leases the IP address to the client.

2. At what lease expiration points do DHCP clients attempt to renew their lease?

   Initially, at 50 percent of its lease life with the DHCP server that leased the address, and then at 87.5 percent of its lease life expired with any DHCP server.

3. What must be configured on the DHCP server for a DHCP client to receive a lease?

   A DHCP server must be configured with a scope of available IP addresses and subnet mask.

4. In what situations is it necessary to have more than one DHCP server on an internetwork?

   When all routers do not support RFC 1542 (BOOTP relay agent).

5. How are DHCP servers configured to provide backup for each other?

Each server is configured with a scope for the local subnet with 75 percent of the available addresses, and a scope for the remote subnet with 25 percent of its available addresses.

6. In what situations is it necessary to reserve an IP address for a client?

When there are servers on a network that contain clients that are not WINS-enabled. Clients that are not WINS-enabled must use LMHOSTS as a method of resolving NetBIOS computer names of hosts on remote networks. If the IP address of the server changes because it not reserved, name resolution using LMHOSTS will fail.

Chapter 8: NetBIOS Over TCP/IP

Practice Answers

▶ **To configure LMHOSTS for remote computer names**

Page 182

8. In the **Path** box, type **\\Server2** and then click **OK**.

What was the response?

A list of shared resources for \\Server2 appears.

Practice Scenario

Page 183

Add the appropriate entries to the following LMHOSTS files so that hosts on both networks can communicate with each other.

LMHOSTS File for Hosts on Network A

IP address	Name
131.107.24.27	LMU
131.107.24.28	Workstation1
131.107.24.29	LMserver

LMHOSTS File for Hosts on Network B

IP address	Name
131.107.8.28	Workgroup1
131.107.8.29	Workgroup2

Review Answers

Page 184

1. What methods are used to resolve NetBIOS names?

    Local broadcast, LMHOSTS file, NetBIOS name server, such as WINS, HOSTS file, and a DNS.

2. What is the function of the LMHOSTS file?

    To resolve NetBIOS names of remote hosts.

Chapter 9: Windows Internet Name Service (WINS)

Practice Answers

► **To use WINS for name resolution**

Page 206

3. Start Windows NT Explorer and attempt to browse your other computer.

    Was browsing successful?

    Yes, browsing should be successful for local hosts.

    If you were to browse a remote host computer would you be successful?

    No, browsing would not be successful for remote hosts.

► **To open the WINS database and view IP address mappings**

Page 216

6. What NetBIOS names have been registered at the WINS server by the client?

    Any NetBIOS names registered by your WINS server, the user name, if unique, and WORKGROUP (possibly multiple times).

7. How long will it be before the names expire?

    At least 6 days.

8. Are there any mappings for remote hosts?

    No.

Review Answers

Page 222

1. What are two benefits of WINS?

    Automatic name registration and resolution of NetBIOS names.

    Provides internetwork and interdomain browsing.

    Eliminates the need for local LMHOSTS file.

2. What two methods can be used to enable WINS on a client computer?

    Manually and automatically with DHCP.

3. How many WINS servers are required in an internet of 12 subnets?

   Only one is required. It is recommended to have multiple servers for backup purposes.

4. What methods can non-WINS clients use to resolve NetBIOS names?

   NetBIOS name cache, broadcasts, local LMHOSTS file, central LMHOSTS file(s), local HOSTS file, DNS, and a WINS proxy agent.

5. When should you use a WINS proxy agent?

   When subnets include non-WINS clients. The WINS proxy agent forwards broadcasts for name registration and name resolution to the WINS server.

6. After a default installation of WINS, how often is the WINS database backed up?

   Never, you have to set the backup directory first before it will start backing up automatically every 24 hours.

7. What types of names are stored in the WINS database?

   NetBIOS unique and group names.

8. How would WINS replication be configured in an environment with a slow WAN link with limited bandwidth?

   Configure the replication to occur at off-peak intervals to make best use of the link bandwidth.

9. How would WINS replication be configured in a LAN environment without network traffic problems?

   Configure the replication to occur after a few database changes to keep the servers very synchronized.

10. When does WINS use multicasting?

    To announce itself to other WINS servers and possibly auto configure as a replication partner.

Chapter 10: IP Internetwork Browsing and Domain Functions

Practice Answers

Page 238

1. Which computers require an LMHOSTS file configured to support internetwork browsing? Which computers should be configured in the LMHOSTS file?

   Computer C requires an LMHOSTS file configured with the IP address and NetBIOS name of computers G and H.

   Computer G requires an LMHOSTS file configured with the IP address and NetBIOS name of computers C and H.

   Computer H requires an LMHOSTS file configured with the IP address and NetBIOS name of computers C and G.

2. Which computers require an LMHOSTS file to support logon validation? Which computers should be configured in the LMHOSTS file?

   No computers require an LMHOSTS file because each subnet has a domain controller. If the local domain controller becomes unavailable, the following computers require an LMHOSTS file.

   Computers A and B require an LMHOSTS file configured with the IP address and NetBIOS name of computers G and H.

   Computers D, E, and F require an LMHOSTS file configured with the IP address and NetBIOS name of computers C and H.

   Computer I requires an LMHOSTS file configured with the IP address and NetBIOS name of computers C and G.

3. Which computers require an LMHOSTS file configured to support domain account synchronization? Which computers should be configured in the LMHOSTS file?

   Computer C requires an LMHOSTS file configured with the IP address and NetBIOS name of computers G and H.

   Computer G requires an LMHOSTS file configured with the IP address and NetBIOS name of computers C and H.

   Computer H requires an LMHOSTS file configured with the IP address and NetBIOS name of computers C and G.

4. If a WINS server was installed on Subnet-Y, and all computers were configured to use WINS, which computers would require an LMHOSTS file?

   None.

Review Answers

Page 240

1. Why are there problems with browsing in an IP internetwork?

   IP routers do not by default propagate domain or workgroup and host announcement packets.

2. How does a master browser on a subnet resolve the IP address of its domain master browser for a domain that spans an internetwork?

   WINS clients query for the NetBIOS name. Non-WINS clients look for entries in the LMHOSTS file with the #DOM tag for their domain.

3. How does WINS aid in the collection of domains or workgroups?

   Domain master browsers query WINS for a list of names to complete its list of domains or workgroups.

4. What is required on non-WINS domain controllers to ensure that account synchronization can be accomplished when the domain spans IP internetworks?

   Each domain controller requires LMHOSTS entries for each of the other domain controllers.

Chapter 11: Host Name Resolution

Practice Answers

▶ **To ping local host names**

Page 250

1. Type **ping Server1** (where *Server1* is the name of your computer) and then press ENTER.

   What was the response?

   Four successful "Reply from IP address" messages.

2. Type **ping Server2** (where *Server2* is your second computer) and then press ENTER.

   What was the response?

   Four successful "Reply from IP address" messages.

▶ **To attempt to ping a local computer name**

Page 250

- Type **ping computertwo** and then press ENTER.

   What was the response?

   Bad IP address computertwo.

▶ **To use HOSTS for name resolution**

Page 251

- Type **ping computertwo** and then press ENTER.

  What was the response?

  Four successful "Reply from IP address" messages.

Review Answers

Page 252

1. What is a host name?

   An alias assigned to a TCP/IP host for the purpose of simplifying access to the host.

2. What is the purpose of a host name?

   To simplify how a host is referenced. Host names are used with PING and other TCP/IP utilities.

3. What does a HOSTS file entry consist of?

   The host name or names and the corresponding IP address.

4. During resolution, what occurs first, IP address resolution or host name resolution?

   Host name resolution.

Chapter 12: Domain Name System (DNS)

Practice Answers

Scenario 1

Page 271

1. How many DNS domains will you need to configure?

   One (or zero if they have an ISP to manage the name server).

2. How many subdomains will you need to configure?

   Zero.

3. How many zones will you need to configure?

   One (or zero if they have an ISP to manage the name server).

4. How many primary name servers will you need to configure?

   One (or zero if they have an ISP to manage the name server).

5. How many secondary name servers will you need to configure?

   One (or zero if they have an ISP to manage the name server).

6. How many DNS cache-only servers will you need to configure?

   Zero.

Scenario 2

Page 274

1. How many DNS domains will you need to configure?

   One.

2. How many subdomains will you need to configure?

   Three.

3. How many zones will you need to configure?

   Four.

4. How many primary name servers will you need to configure?

   Four.

5. How many secondary name servers will you need to configure?

   Four.

6. How many DNS cache-only servers will you need to configure?

   Ten.

7. Use the following mileage chart to design a zone/branch office configuration based on the geographical proximity between each primary site and branch office. Branch offices should be in the same zone as the nearest primary site.

   Zones for each branch office (based on geographical proximity):

Portland, OR	Boston	Chicago	Atlanta
Los Angeles	Montreal	Denver	Dallas
Salt Lake City	Washington, D.C.	Kansas City	Miami
San Francisco			New Orleans

Scenario 3

Page 276

1. How many DNS domains will you need to configure?

   Zero (the domain for this company is in Geneva, Switzerland).

2. How many subdomains will you need to configure?

   11.

3. How many zones will you need to configure?

   11.

4. How many primary name servers will you need to configure?

   11.

5. How many secondary name servers will you need to configure?

11.

6. How many DNS cache-only servers will you need to be configure?

Three or more.

Review Answers

Page 278

1. Name the three components of the Domain Name System.

Domain name space, name servers, and resolvers.

2. Describe the difference between primary, secondary, and master name servers.

A primary name server has zone information in locally maintained zone files. A secondary name server downloads zone information. A master name server is the source of the downloads for a secondary name server (which could be a primary or secondary name server).

3. List three reasons to have a secondary name server.

(1) They operate as a redundant name server (you should have at least one redundant name server for each zone). (2) If you have clients in remote locations, you should have a secondary name server to avoid communicating across slow links. (3) A secondary name server reduces the load on the primary name server.

4. Describe the difference between a domain and a zone.

A domain is a branch of the DNS name space. A zone is a portion of a domain that exists as a separate file on the disk storing resource records.

5. Describe the difference between recursive and iterative queries.

In a recursive query, the client instructs the DNS server to respond with either the requested information or an error that the information was not found. In an iterative query, the DNS server responds with the best answer it has, typically a referral to another name server that can help resolve the request.

6. List the files required for a Windows NT DNS implementation.

Database file, cache file, and reverse lookup file.

7. Describe the purpose of the boot file.

The boot file is used in the BIND implementation to start up and configure the DNS server.

Chapter 13: Implementing DNS

Practice Answers

▶ **To view the default DNS server installation**

Page 287

9. Double-click each of the reverse lookup zones. What type of records does each of them contain?

NS records and SOA records.

▶ **To add a zone to a server**

Page 291

6. Click each of the resource records. What type of records does each of them contain?

NS records and SOA records.

▶ **To configure a reverse lookup zone for the primary DNS server**

Page 293

1. Determine the reverse lookup zone name for your primary DNS server by using one of these three methods:

- For class A addresses, use your first octet and append to it **.in-addr.arpa** (for example: A class A IP address of 29.122.15.88 would have a reverse lookup zone name of **29.in-addr.arpa**).

- For class B addresses, use your first two octets in reverse order and append to them **.in-addr.arpa** (for example: A class B IP address of 129.122.15.88 would have a reverse lookup zone name of **122.129.in-addr.arpa**).

- For class C addresses, use your first three octets in reverse order and append to them **.in-addr.arpa** (for example: A class C IP address of 229.122.15.88 would have a reverse lookup zone name of **15.122.129.in-addr.arpa**).

What is your reverse lookup zone name?

107.131.in-addr.arpa

Review Answers

Page 301

1. What is the purpose of entering a host name and domain name in the DNS configuration dialog box of the TCP/IP protocol *before* installing the Microsoft DNS Server service?

The DNS Server uses the host name and domain name to create default SOA, A, and NS records.

2. What is the function of the NSLOOKUP utility?

NSLOOKUP acts as a command line or interactive resolver that is used to troubleshoot DNS servers.

3. Describe the WINS lookup process.

   A Microsoft DNS Server gets a DNS query that fails DNS resolution. The host name is converted to a NetBIOS name and sent to a configured WINS server for resolution. The results are forwarded back to the original client.

4. Describe a situation where WINS lookup is useful.

   When non-Microsoft TCP/IP clients need resolution to a WINS-registering, DHCP resource such as Internet Information Server.

Chapter 14: Connectivity in Heterogeneous Environments

Practice Answers

▶ **To start an FTP session**

Page 313

What TCP port does FTP use on the server side?

TCP port 21.

Review Answers

Page 323

1. List the requirements for a computer running Windows NT to connect to a foreign host.

   TCP/IP transport and appropriate TCP/IP utilities and services.

2. List the requirements for a computer running Windows NT to connect to and interoperate with an RFC-compliant NetBIOS-based host, such as LAN Manager for UNIX.

   Common transport protocol (TCP/IP or NetBEUI) SMB server.

   Common scope ID.

3. List two differences between accessing resources on a TCP/IP-based host using Windows NT commands versus TCP/IP utilities.

   Windows NT: Use NetBIOS names. Use standard commands.

   TCP/IP utilities: Use commands specific to utilities. IP address or host name can be used.

4. Which TCP/IP utilities are used to copy files?

   FTP, TFTP, and RCP.

5. Which TCP/IP utilities enable you to run commands on a foreign host?

Telnet, RSH, and REXEC.

6. What functions does the TCP/IP network printing support provide?

Support for a network interface printer using TCP/IP.

Access to printers attached to a UNIX host.

Chapter 15: Implementing the Microsoft SNMP Services

Practice Answers

▶ **To view the new Performance Monitor objects**

Page 342

4. List the TCP/IP-related objects.

ICMP, IP, TCP, UDP, and Network Interface.

▶ **To monitor IP datagrams with Performance Monitor**

Page 343

12. Return to Performance Monitor, and view the activity that resulted from the ping.

What activity was recorded as a result of using ping?

ICMP messages and IP datagrams.

How many messages per second were recorded for ICMP?

2 (1.997)

How many IP datagrams were sent per second?

1 (0.999)

Why were there twice as many ICMP messages as there were IP datagrams sent?

Each IP datagram sent results in 2 ICMP messages—one echo request and one echo reply.

▶ **To view SNMP data**

Page 344

3. Use Snmputil.exe to determine SNMP objects related to DHCP. Type the following command on one line and then press ENTER:

snmputil getnext 131.107.2._host_id_
public .1.3.6.1.4.1.311.1.3.2.1.1.1

How many IP addresses have been leased?

There should be one address leased.

4. Use Snmputil.exe on the WINS object .1.3.6.1.4.1.311.1.2.1.17. Type:

snmputil getnext 131.107.2.*host_id*
public .1.3.6.1.4.1.311.1.2.1.17

How many successful queries have been processed by the WINS server?

The answers will vary.

5. Use Snmputil.exe on the WINS object **.1.3.6.1.4.1.311.1.2.1.18**. Type:

snmputil getnext 131.107.2.*host_id*
public .1.3.6.1.4.1.311.1.2.1.18

How many unsuccessful queries have been processed by the WINS server?

The answers will vary.

7. Use Snmputil.exe on the LAN Manager Object .1.3.6.1.4.1.77.1.1.2. Type:

snmputil getnext 131.107.2.*host_id* **public .1.3.6.1.4.1.77.1.1.2**

What is the version of Windows NT Server running on the computer?

Version 4.0; the first string returned a 4, and the second a 0.

Review Answers

Page 346

1. What are the four SNMP operations?

   get, get-next, set, and trap.

2. Which SNMP operations are initiated by a management system? Which SNMP operations are initiated by an agent?

   Management systems initiate get, get-next, and set operations.

   Agents initiate trap operations.

3. Which MIBs are supported by Windows NT 4.0?

   Internet MIB II, LAN Manager MIB II, Microsoft DHCP MIB, and Microsoft WINS MIB.

4. Which host name resolution methods does the SNMP employ?

   A HOSTS file, DNS, NetBIOS name server, broadcast, or the LMHOSTS file.

5. What is the purpose of a community name?

   To provide primitive security and context checking for agents that send traps and for management systems that receive traps.

Chapter 16: Troubleshooting Microsoft TCP/IP

Review Answers

Page 353

1. What are three Windows NT utilities useful in diagnosing TCP/IP-related problems?

   PING, NBTSTAT, ARP, and NETSTAT.

2. Which TCP/IP utility is used to verify communications from the Network Interface layer up to the Internet layer?

   PING.

3. What are the two procedures for troubleshooting an IP network?

   PING successfully and then establish a session.

Index

A

addresses *See* Address Resolution Protocol (ARP); IP
  addresses
Address Resolution Protocol (ARP)
    ARP cache 32–33, 38, 39
    capturing packets 34–37
    defined 7, 26, 29
    and frames 35–37
    and IP addresses 30–32
    overview 29
    packet structure 34
    as troubleshooting tool 348
agents *See* relay agents; SNMP agent
ANDing 72–73
Application layer 27, 351
ArcNet 27
ARP *See* Address Resolution Protocol (ARP)
ARPANET 2, 254, 255
ARPCacheLife parameter 33
ATECs xxiii
Authorized Technical Education Centers (ATECs) xxiii

B

backing up databases
    DHCP 159
    WINS 219
backup browser, defined 226
binary notation, converting IP addresses to decimal notation
  57–58, 59
B-node 176, 177, 179 *See also* LMHOSTS file
boot file, DNS 267
BOOTP protocol
    vs. DHCP 130
    and Windows NT 131
browse list
    collection process 227
    defined 226
    distribution process 228
    servicing requests 228–29
browsing *See also* Computer Browser; master browser
    internetwork 230–34
    web browsers 305, 314

C

cache
    ARP cache 32–33, 38, 39
    and DNS name servers 260, 263
    NetBIOS name cache 171, 172
Cache.dns file 266
Canonical Name (CNAME) record 265
capturing
    ARP packets 34–37
    network traffic 20–21
certification xxi–xxiii
Class A IP addresses 61
Class B IP addresses 62
Class C IP addresses 62
Class D IP addresses 62
Class E IP addresses 63
classes, IP addresses 60–63
client reservations
    adding 151–52
    defined 150
    when to use 150
CNAME record 265
communities, SNMP 333–34
compacting databases
    DHCP 160–61
    WINS 220
Computer Browser
    collection process 227
    distribution process 228
    and IP internetworks 230–34
    and LMHOSTS file 232–40
    overview 226–29
    servicing client requests 228–29
    types of browsers 226
    and WINS 231–32
copying files 6, 305, 309
course *See* training course

D

DARPA 2
database, DHCP
    backing up and restoring 159
    compacting 160–61
    list of files 160
database, DNS 264–65

database, WINS
    backing up and restoring 219–20
    compacting 220
    configuring server 216–18
    list of files 220
    maintaining 214–21
    replicating between servers 208–13
    viewing contents 215–16
datagrams *See* User Datagram Protocol (UDP)
data transfer utilities
    defined 6
    FTP (File Transfer Protocol) 6, 305, 309–13
    RCP (Remote Copy Protocol) 6, 305, 309
    TFTP (Trivial File Transfer Protocol) 6, 305, 310
    web browsers 305, 314
dead gateways 113
decimal notation, converting IP addresses to 57–58, 59
default gateway
    defined 11
    and dynamic IP routing 121–22
    example 11
    and Microsoft TCP/IP installation 13
    and remote IP addresses 31–32
    removing address 119
    restoring address 120
    and routing 113
    and static IP routers 116
Defense Advanced Research Projects Agency (DARPA) 2
DHCP (Dynamic Host Configuration Protocol)
    configuring for WINS 203–7
    configuring scope 145–50
    enabling relay agents 155–58
    how it works 132–36
    implementing 140–54
    installing servers 143–45, 153
    lease process 132–36
    managing database 159–61
    vs. manual configuration of TCP/IP 12–13, 131
    and MIB 330
    multiple servers 152
    overview 130–39
    system requirements 142–43
Dhcp.mdb file 160
Dhcpmib.dll file 330
Dhcp.tmp file 160
diagnostics utilities *See also* troubleshooting
    Address Resolution Protocol (ARP) 29–39
    defined 7
    FINGER utility 7
    HOSTNAME utility 7, 243
    IPCONFIG utility 7, 15, 16–17, 138–39, 349
    NBTSTAT utility 7, 178, 349
    NETSTAT utility 7, 348
    NSLOOKUP utility 7, 283–85, 349

diagnostics utilities See also troubleshooting *(continued)*
    Packet InterNet Groper (PING) utility 7, 15, 16–17, 348, 350
    ROUTE utility 7, 349
    TRACERT utility 7, 126–27, 349
DNS Manager
    adding domains and zones 288–89
    configuring DNS server 286–88
    enabling WINS Lookup 298
DNS servers *See* Domain Name System (DNS); Microsoft DNS Server
domain master browser defined 226
domain name space 257–59
Domain Name System (DNS)
    background 254–55
    configuration files 264–68
    configuring DNS 269–77
    how it works 255–56
    implementing Microsoft DNS Server 282–300
    for large networks 275–77
    for medium-size networks 272–75
    Microsoft DNS Server 282–300
    name resolution 261–63
    and NetBIOS names 172, 176
    registering DNS servers 270
    role of domains 257–58
    role of host names 258
    role of name servers 256, 259–60
    role of resolvers 256
    role of zones of authority 258–59
    for small networks 271–72
    and UNIX 245–46
    and Windows NT 245–46, 247, 264–68
domains
    defined 257
    root-level 257
    second-level 258
    top-level 257, 258
dotted decimal notation 57
downloading *See* data transfer utilities
Dynamic Host Configuration Protocol *See* DHCP (Dynamic Host Configuration Protocol)
dynamic IP routing
    implementing Windows NT router 126–27
    integrating with static IP routing 124–25
    overview 121–22
    and RIP 122–24
    vs. static IP routing 114

E

Ethernet 27
Event log 349

F

Fiber Distributed Data Interface (FDDI) 27
fields, header 42, 44–45, 50
File Transfer Protocol *See* FTP (File Transfer Protocol)
FINGER utility 7
four-layer model 26–27
frames
    capturing and viewing data 21, 34–37
    defined 26
    and Network Interface Layer 26, 27
    and Network Monitor 21, 34–37
FTP (File Transfer Protocol)
    defined 6, 305, 309
    installing 311–12
    list of common commands 310
    starting session 313
    syntax 309
    using to transfer files 312–13

G

gateways *See also* routers
    dead 113
    default (*see* default gateway)
    defined 112
    and remote IP addresses 31–32
    and static routing table entries 117

H

handshakes, three-way 48
hardware, course requirements xvi
hardware addresses *See* Address Resolution Protocol (ARP)
header fields 42, 44–45, 50
H-node 176
hops 113, 122
Host (A) record 265
host ID
    assigning IP addresses 66, 67, 69–70
    defined 56
    vs. network ID 56–57
    and subnetting 83, 96–102
host names
    overview 243
    relationship to domains 258
    resolving 243–48
HOSTNAME utility 7, 243
hosts *See also* host ID; host names
    monitoring using SNMP 326–29
    remote 304–8
HOSTS file
    adding entries 251
    defined 10, 244, 251

HOSTS file *(continued)*
    example 249
    and NetBIOS names 172, 175
    resolving host names 244–45, 246, 249–51
HTTP (Hypertext Transfer Protocol) 314

I

IAB (Internet Architecture Board) 3
IANA (Internet Assigned Numbers Authority) 3
ICMP (Internet Control Message Protocol) 26, 40–41
IETF (Internet Engineering Task Force) 3
IGMP (Internet Group Management Protocol) 26, 41
installing
    DHCP servers 143–45, 153
    FTP service 311–12
    Internet Explorer xviii
    Microsoft DNS Server 282–83
    Microsoft Network Monitor 18–19
    Microsoft TCP/IP 12–14
    SNMP service 336–37
    Windows NT Service Pack xviii–xix
    WINS service 198
Internet, TCP/IP history 2
Internet Architecture Board (IAB) 3
Internet Assigned Numbers Authority (IANA) 3
Internet Control Message Protocol (ICMP) 26, 40–41
Internet Engineering Task Force (IETF) 3
Internet Explorer, installing xviii
Internet Group Management Protocol (IGMP) 26, 41
Internet layer 26, 350–51
Internet MIB II 330
Internet Protocol (IP) *See also* IP addresses; IP routing
    defined 26, 42
    list of header fields 42, 44–45
    overview 42–43
    packet structure 44–45
    and routers 43
    versions of 75–76
Internet protocols *See* Address Resolution Protocol (ARP);
    Internet Control Message Protocol (ICMP); Internet Group
    Management Protocol (IGMP); Internet Protocol (IP)
Internet Research Task Force (IRTF) 3
Internet service providers (ISPs) 269
Internet Society (ISOC) 3
inverse queries 262–63
IP *See* Internet Protocol (IP); IP addresses
IP addresses
    and Address Resolution Protocol (ARP) 30
    assigning, overview 64
    assigning host IDs 66, 67, 69–70
    assigning network IDs 64–65, 67, 68–69
    binary vs. decimal notation 57–58
    classes 60–63

IP addresses *(continued)*
    client reservations 150–52
    defined 10, 56
    and DHCP 130–39
    example 10
    IPv6 75–76
    leasing 133–37
    local vs. remote 31–32, 43, 72–73
    and Microsoft TCP/IP installation 13, 14
    network ID vs. host ID 56–57
    overview 56–57
    resolving 30–32
    and subnet masks 71–74
IPCONFIG utility
    and lease activities 139
    testing TCP/IP configuration 15, 16–17, 138
    as troubleshooting tool 7, 349
IP routing *See also* Routing Information Protocol (RIP)
    implementing Windows NT router 126–27
    overview 112–14
    static vs. dynamic 114, 124–25
IPv4 75
IPv6 75–76
IRTF (Internet Research Task Force) 3
ISOC (Internet Society) 3
ISPs (Internet service providers) 269
iterative queries 261–62

J

Jet.log file 160
Jetpack utility 160

L

LAN Manager MIB II 330
LANs, and TCP/IP 27
layers
    Application layer 27, 351
    Internet layer 26, 350–51
    Network Interface layer 26, 350–51
    Transport layer 27
leases
    acknowledging 135–36
    and client reservations 150, 151–52
    offering 133–34
    releasing 139
    renewing 136–37, 154, 189, 192
    requesting 133
    selecting offers 134
    updating 139
    use of IPCONFIG utility 139
Line Printer Daemon (LPD) 7, 305, 316, 317
Line Printer Queue (LPQ) utility 7, 305, 316, 318, 322

Line Printer Remote (LPR) utility 7, 305, 316, 317–18, 322
LMHOSTS file
    and browsing 232–40
    defined 10, 179, 244
    list of predefined keywords 180
    and NetBIOS names 172, 175, 177, 178, 179–83
    resolving host names 244, 246, 248
    troubleshooting NetBIOS name resolution problems 181
local area networks, and TCP/IP 27
lookup
    enabling WINS lookup 298–300
    NSLOOKUP utility 7, 283–85, 349
    reverse 266, 292–95, 298
LPDSVC *See* TCP/IP Print Server
LPD utility 7, 305, 316, 317
LPQ utility 7, 305, 316, 318, 322
LPR utility 7, 305, 316, 317–18, 322

M

Management Information Bases (MIBs)
    defined 330
    hierarchical name tree 331–32
    list of MIBs 330–31
masking *See* subnet masks
master browser
    collection process 227
    defined 226
    distribution process 228
    LMHOSTS file on 233–34
    servicing requests 228–29
MCP (Microsoft Certified Professional) program xxi–xxiii
Metropolitan Area Network (MAN) 27
MIB *See* Management Information Bases (MIBs)
Microsoft Certified Professional (MCP) program xxi–xxiii
Microsoft DNS Server
    adding domains 289–90
    adding resource records 291–92
    adding zones 288–89, 290–91
    administering 286–95
    configuring manually 288
    configuring reverse lookup 292–95
    configuring server properties 286–88
    configuring zone properties 290
    installing 282–83
    integrating with WINS 296–300
    troubleshooting with NSLOOKUP utility 7, 283–85, 349
    viewing default installation 287–88
Microsoft Network Monitor
    analyzing network traffic 20–21
    capturing and viewing data 21, 34–37
    defined 18, 349
    installing 18–19
Microsoft Online Institute xxiii

Microsoft Roadmap xxii
Microsoft SNMP service *See* SNMP (Simple Network
    Management Protocol)
Microsoft TCP/IP *See also* TCP/IP protocol suite;
    Windows NT
    configuration parameters 10–11
    installing 12–14
    lists of utilities 6–7, 305
    overview 2–3
    resolving host names 244
    testing configuration 15–17
M-node 176
multicasting 62, 63, 213
multihomed computers 114, 200
multimedia presentations 25, 49

N

name resolution files, defined 10 *See also* Domain Name
    System (DNS); HOSTS file; LMHOSTS file
name server (NS) record 265
name servers *See also* Domain Name System (DNS); WINS
    (Windows Internet Name Service)
    database file record 265
    defined 256
    secondary 259–60
    types of roles 259–60
NBFP 167
NBTSTAT utility 7, 178, 349
NCP (Network Control Protocol) 2
NDIS (Network Device Interface Specification) 27
NetBEUI 27, 167
NetBIOS *See also* NetBIOS names
    defined 27, 166
    and internetwork browsing 230–34
    overview 166–67
    troubleshooting communications 351
NetBIOS names
    discovery 169
    duplicate names 191
    list of common names 168
    and LMHOSTS file 172, 175, 177, 178, 179–83
    overview 167–68
    refreshing registration 189, 192
    registration 169, 189, 190–91
    releasing 169, 189, 193
    renewing lease 189, 192
    resolving 171–78
    segmenting with scopes 169–70
    and WINS 187–207
NetBIOS Name Server (NBNS) 171, 174, 176, 246–47
NetBT 167, 177
NETSTAT utility 7, 348
Network Control Protocol (NCP) 2

network device interface specification (NDIS) 27
network ID
    assigning IP addresses 64–65, 67, 68–69
    vs. host ID 56–57
    and Routing Information Protocol 122–24
    and static routing table entries 117
Network Interface layer 26, 350–51
Network Monitor
    analyzing network traffic 20–21
    capturing and viewing data 21, 34–37
    defined 18, 349
    installing 18–19
network protocols, viewing list 11 *See also* TCP/IP protocol
    suite
networks *See also* Network Monitor
    capturing network traffic 18–21
    and DNS configuration 269–77
    four-layer TCP/IP model 26–27
    heterogeneous environments 304–6
    IP addresses 56–59
    routing between 112–14
    subnetting 82–84
NETWORKS file, defined 10
nodes *See* B-node; H-node; M-node; P-node
NSLOOKUP utility 7, 283–85, 349

O

objects *See* Management Information Bases (MIBs)
Online Institute xxiii
Open Shortest Path First (OSPF) protocol 114

P

Packet InterNet Groper (PING) utility 7, 15, 16–17, 348, 350
packets
    ARP structure 34
    ICMP structure 40
    IGMP structure 41
    and Internet Protocol 42–43
    IP structure 44–45
    routing 112–14
    TCP structure 50
    UDP structure 52
packet-switched networks 27
Performance Monitor 349
PING (Packet InterNet Groper) utility
    defined 7, 348
    testing TCP/IP configuration 15, 16–17
    as troubleshooting tool 348, 350
P-node 176
Pointer (PTR) record 266
Point-to-Point Protocol (PPP) 28

ports
    port numbers 46, 47
    TCP ports 46, 47
    UDP ports 51
PPP (Point-to-Point Protocol) 28
print gateways 319
printing utilities
    Line Printer Daemon (LPD) 7, 305, 316, 317
    Line Printer Queue (LPQ) utility 7, 305, 316, 318, 322
    Line Printer Remote (LPR) utility 7, 305, 316, 317–18, 322
    overview 7, 316
Print Manager 316, 317, 318, 319, 320–22
PROTOCOL file, defined 10
protocols *See also* data transfer utilities; diagnostics utilities; TCP/IP protocol suite
    Dynamic Host Configuration Protocol (DHCP) 130–39
    Internet Control Message Protocol (ICMP) 26, 40–41
    Internet Group Management Protocol (IGMP) 26, 41
    layers in TCP/IP suite 25–28
    Open Shortest Path First (OSPF) protocol 114
    port numbers 46, 47
    Routing Information Protocol (RIP) 114, 122–24
    viewing list 11
pull partners 208, 209, 210–13
push partners 208, 209, 210–13

Q

queries, name resolution 261–63

R

RAS (Remote Access Server) 27
RCP (Remote Copy Protocol) utility 6, 305, 309
recursive queries 261
Registry Editor 349
relay agents
    configuring 155, 156–57
    defined 155
    disabling 157
Remote Access Server (RAS) 27
Remote Copy Protocol (RCP) utility 6, 305, 309
Remote Execution (REXEC) utility 6, 305, 307
remote hosts 304–8
Remote Shell (RSH) utility 6, 305, 307
Request for Comments (RFC) 4–5
reserving IP addresses 150–52
resolvers, defined 256
restoring
    default gateway address 120
    DHCP database 159
    WINS database 219–20

reverse lookup
    configuring for Microsoft DNS Server 292–95
    file overview 266
    and WINS 298
REXEC utility 6, 305, 307
RFCs 4–5
RIP (Routing Information Protocol)
    and dynamic IP routing 114, 122–24
    troubleshooting 123–24
    when to use 123
Roadmap xxii
routers *See also* Routing Information Protocol (RIP)
    configuring 116
    defined 112
    and Internet Protocol 43
    static 115–20
    static vs. dynamic 114
ROUTE utility 7, 349
routing *See* IP routing
Routing Information Protocol (RIP)
    and dynamic IP routing 114, 122–24
    troubleshooting 123–24
    when to use 123
routing tables
    adding static entries 118, 120
    building 117–20
    default entries 117
    defined 112
    and Routing Information Protocol 123–25
    and static routers 116
    viewing entries 117, 118, 119
RSH (Remote Shell) utility 6, 305, 307

S

scope ID, and NetBIOS names 169–70
scopes, subnet 141–42, 145, 146–47, 148, 149–50
Serial Line Internet Protocol (SLIP) 28
serial lines 27, 28
Service Pack, Windows NT xviii–xix
SERVICES file, defined 10
setup, course xvii–xix
Simple Network Management Protocol (SNMP) *See* SNMP (Simple Network Management Protocol)
sliding windows 49
SLIP (Serial Line Internet Protocol) 28
slow convergence problem, defined 124
SMB servers 304
SNMP agent
    configuring services 339–40
    defined 328
SNMP (Simple Network Management Protocol)
    configuring agent services 339–40
    configuring security 338–39

SNMP (Simple Network Management Protocol) *(continued)*
    defined 326, 349
    defining communities 333–34
    how it works 334–36
    identifying service errors 341–43
    installing service 336–37
    and MIBs 330–32
    overview 326–29
    SNMPUTIL utility 344–45
    viewing data 344–45
SNMPUTIL utility 344–45
sockets, overview 47 *See also* Windows Sockets
software, course requirements xvi
standards 3–5
Start of Authority (SOA) record 264–65
static IP routing
    configuring routers 116
    vs. dynamic IP routing 114
    integrating dynamic IP routing with 124–25
    overview 115
subnet masks *See also* subnets
    and ANDing 72–73
    default 71–72
    defined 11
    defining for subnetting 83, 85–92
    determining requirements 84
    example 11
    and IP addresses 71–74
    and Microsoft TCP/IP installation 13
    overview 71
    and static routing table entries 117
subnets *See also* supernetting
    benefits 83
    creating scope 141–42, 145, 146–47, 148, 149–50
    defining host ID 83, 96–102
    defining subnet ID 83, 93–95
    defining subnet mask 83, 85–92
    vs. supernetting 103–5
subnetting, defined 82
subnetworking *See* subnets
supernetting 103–5
Systek Corporation 166
System.mdb file 160

T

tables *See* routing tables
TCP *See* Transmission Control Protocol (TCP)
TCP/IP Print Server 317, 319–20
TCP/IP protocol suite *See also* Internet Protocol (IP);
   Transmission Control Protocol (TCP)
    configuring manually 131
    configuring using DHCP 131
    and heterogeneous environments 304–6

TCP/IP protocol suite *See also* Internet Protocol (IP);
   Transmission Control Protocol (TCP) *(continued)*
    history 2
    LAN and WAN support 27
    layers of 25–28
    lists of utilities 6–7, 305
    naming schemes 242
    overview 2–5
    resolving host names 243–48
    RFCs 4–5
    SNMP 326–29
    standards process 3–5
    testing configuration 15–17
    troubleshooting 248–52
    Windows NT vs. UNIX naming schemes 242
Telnet 6, 305, 307–8
TFTP (Trivial File Transfer Protocol) 6, 305, 310
Time To Live (TTL) 263, 299
Token Ring 27
TRACERT utility 7, 126–27, 349
training course *See also* Microsoft Certified Professional
   (MCP) program
    hardware requirements xvi
    multimedia presentations 25, 49
    setup xvii–xix
    software requirements xvi
Transmission Control Protocol (TCP)
    and default gateway 113
    defined 27, 46
    and IP routing 113
    list of header fields 50
    overview 46
    packet structure 50
    and ports 46
    sliding windows 49
    three-way handshake 48
Transport layer, defined 27
transport protocols *See* Transmission Control Protocol (TCP);
   User Datagram Protocol (UDP)
troubleshooting *See also* diagnostics utilities
    TCP/IP problems 348–52
    using Network Monitor 18–21, 349
TTL (Time To Live) 263, 299

U

UDP *See* User Datagram Protocol (UDP)
UNIX
    resolving host names 245–46
    TCP/IP naming schemes 242
User Datagram Protocol (UDP)
    defined 27, 51
    overview 51
    packet structure 52

User Datagram Protocol (UDP) *(continued)*
    and ports 51
    and SNMP service 329
utilities, lists of 6–7, 305 *See also* data transfer utilities;
  diagnostics utilities; printing utilities

W

WANs, and TCP/IP 13, 27
web browsers 305, 314
windows, sliding 49
Windows Internet Name Service *See* WINS (Windows
  Internet Name Service)
Windows NT
    Computer Browser service 226–34
    connecting to server from remote host 305
    diagnostic tools (*see* diagnostics utilities)
    and DNS servers 245–46, 247, 264–68
    implementing routers 126–27
    installing Microsoft TCP/IP 10–14
    installing Service Pack xviii–xix
    lists of utilities 6–7, 305
    LMHOSTS file 172, 175, 177, 178, 179–83, 230, 235–
      40, 244
    Microsoft DNS Server 282–300
    Microsoft TCP/IP overview 2–3
    name resolution 10, 243–48
    and NetBIOS names 175–78
    as print gateway 319–22
    and SLIP 28
    and static vs. dynamic routing 114
    TCP/IP naming schemes 242
    troubleshooting TCP/IP problems 348–52
Windows Sockets 3, 27, 47, 329
WINS Manager
    configuring server 216–18
    defined 214
    starting 214
    viewing database contents 215–16
WINS MIB 331
WINS (Windows Internet Name Service)
    configuring client and server 197, 198, 299–300
    configuring DHCP server 203–7
    configuring proxy agents 201–3
    configuring servers as push or pull partners 209
    configuring static IP addresses 198–200
    data record 296–97
    enabling lookup 298–300
    implementing 196–207
    installing server service 198
    integrating Microsoft DNS Server with 296–300
    and internetwork browsing 231–32
    maintaining database 214–21
    name resolution 189–95, 206

WINS (Windows Internet Name Service) *(continued)*
    and non-WINS clients 198–200
    overview 187–88
    relationship to NetBIOS 187–88
    replicating database between servers 208–13
    system requirements 196–200
World Wide Web
    browser as TCP/IP utility 305, 314
    Microsoft Online Institute xxiii

Z

Zone.dns file 264
zones of authority 258–59